# A GRIM ALMANAC OF

# SOUTH WALES

## NICOLA SLY

# A Grim Almanac of
# South Wales

NICOLA SLY

The
History
Press

# ALSO BY THE AUTHOR

First published 2011

The History Press
The Mill, Brimscombe Port
Stroud, Gloucestershire, GL5 2QG
www.thehistorypress.co.uk

© Nicola Sly, 2011

British Library Cataloguing in Publication Data.
A catalogue record for this book is available from the British
Library.

ISBN 978 0 7524 6000 0

Typesetting and origination by The History Press
Printed in Malta.

# CONTENTS

# INTRODUCTION & ACKNOWLEDGEMENTS

This collection of the dark deeds and grim history of South Wales is drawn entirely from the contemporary newspapers listed in the bibliography at the rear of the book. Much as today, not all events were reported accurately and there were frequent variations between publications, particularly with the spellings of Welsh place names, which often proved incomprehensible to English newspaper reporters.

When I started researching this book, it quickly became apparent that it would almost be possible to find a mining disaster for every day of the year. One newspaper lists fifty-six colliery explosions between 1845 and 1896, involving the loss of hundreds of lives. Mining in South Wales has a grim history of its own and it has proved impossible to feature every tragedy.

As always, there are a number of people to be thanked for their assistance. My husband Richard gave constructive criticism and kept me supplied with bottomless cups of tea. I would also like to thank Matilda Richards, my editor at The History Press, for her help and encouragement in bringing the book to print. Every effort has been made to clear copyright; however my apologies to anyone I might have inadvertently missed. I can assure you it was not deliberate but an oversight on my part.

With the greatest love and respect, I would like to dedicate this book to the memory of two very special people – my beloved father, Arthur John Higginson, who died while the book was being written, and my wonderful mother-in-law, Mabel Emily Sly (*née* Mills), who was born and bred in South Wales.

*Nicola Sly, 2011*

# JANUARY

*Senghenydd Colliery. (Author's collection)*

**1 JANUARY**    **1888** Mary Ann Phillips of Cardiff called out a doctor to her husband, but by the time he arrived seventy-eight-year-old William was dead. William was heavily bruised, which, Mrs Phillips explained, was due to a fall downstairs the day before. Believing that William had been dead for some time, Dr Buist refused to issue a death certificate and, when neighbours revealed that they had heard Mary Ann hitting William, she was arrested.

Mary Ann had a history of violence and had served two months in gaol for beating William with a broom. On the morning of his death, neighbours heard blows and shouts of 'Murder' and one woman actually saw Mary Ann through a window, striking William with her hand, as he was on his hands and knees scrubbing the floor.

An inquest jury returned a verdict of wilful murder against Mary Ann Phillips and she was tried at the Glamorganshire Assizes, where she was found guilty and sentenced to death. Her sentence was later commuted to life imprisonment.

**2 JANUARY**    **1899** John and Honora Kelly appeared before magistrates in Neath, charged with neglecting their children.

The case was brought by NSPCC Inspector Mr R.H. Pearce, who visited the defendants' house on 17 December 1898, after complaints from neighbours. Pearce found two children in 'a pitiable state', sleeping in a filthy bedroom with no glass in the window and only a few sacks as bedclothes. In spite of Pearce's warnings, their living conditions didn't improve, even though the Kellys had plenty of money to spend on drink.

When Dr Thomas testified to the extent of the neglect of the two children by their parents, magistrates sentenced John and Honora to three months' imprisonment with hard labour, sending the children to the Workhouse.

**3 JANUARY**    **1869** Thirteen-year-old Elizabeth Mercer of Ystradfodwg refused to go to Sunday school and her mother eventually persuaded her to reveal that, on 27 December, her teacher offered her a shilling to go into the woods and give him a kiss. Francis Ferris then raped her, the rushing water of a nearby stream drowning out Elizabeth's desperate cries for help.

Fearful that she would be blamed, Elizabeth kept her ordeal a secret. The Mercers took her to a surgeon, who confirmed that she was no longer a virgin, but, as she had left it over a week before reporting the rape, he could find no indications that she had put up a struggle against whoever she had been intimate with. Thus, when Ferris was tried for felonious assault at the Swansea Assizes in March 1869, in spite of Elizabeth's detailed evidence against him, the jury found him not guilty and he was discharged.

**4 JANUARY**    **1857** Solicitor John Morgan of Merthyr Tydfil returned home at 11 p.m. The living room fire was almost out and Morgan rang for his housekeeper, Gwenllian Lewis, to attend to it. When she didn't respond, he went to the kitchen, finding her unconscious on the floor, her husband John cradling her head.

'How is this, John?' Morgan asked.

'I don't know indeed,' replied Lewis, explaining that he had been out and, on his return, was unable to get his wife to let him in. Eventually, he climbed over

TOWN HALL, MERTHYR TYDFIL.

*Merthyr Tydfil
Town Hall.
(Author's collection)*

a wall and broke down the door into Morgan's office, claiming to have found Gwenllian lying injured at the foot of the eleven steps leading down to the kitchen.

When Gwenllian died, a post-mortem examination showed a fractured skull and the doctor believed she had been thrown violently downstairs. Nothing was missing from the house, suggesting John Lewis as the prime suspect, since it was reasoned that anyone breaking in would have robbery as a motive and would have ransacked the premises.

Thirty-one-year-old Lewis was charged with wilful murder and admitted quarrelling with his wife and treating her with great brutality. The previous day, Morgan gave Gwenllian a sovereign to do some shopping and she received a half-sovereign change, which her husband took from her. However, Lewis insisted that, although his conduct most probably caused his wife's death, her injuries were the result of a fall downstairs that was either accidental or a deliberate suicide attempt.

At Lewis's trial on 27 February, the jury were unable to reach agreement. A new jury at the following Assizes found Lewis guilty and, still protesting his innocence, he was hanged by William Calcraft at Cardiff on 25 July.

**1894** Nine-year-old Frederick Taylor saw eight-year-old John Elias Waldron fall   5 JANUARY
through the ice at a disused quarry in Cadoxton. Frederick ran to two 'big boys',
Fred Grey and Thomas Hopkins, and told them about Waldron. Grey and Hopkins

found John's plight extremely funny and, although Frederick begged them to help, they dismissed him, saying, 'Never mind, leave him alone.' Frederick raced home and told his parents what he had seen but they too did nothing.

Meanwhile, John's parents searched high and low for their son but it wasn't until 7 January that they learned where he was last seen. Mr Waldron broke the ice and dragged the quarry with a grappling iron, recovering his son's body that afternoon.

When the police questioned Mr and Mrs Taylor, they admitted that Frederick had told them about John's accident and that they had done nothing. The police found another little boy, who also fell through the ice on the same day and had appealed to Grey and Hopkins for help. Again, the two boys left him to his fate, although fortunately he managed to scramble out of the water.

At the inquest on John's death, coroner Mr E. Bernard Reece described the conduct of Grey, Hopkins and the Taylors as '...most heartless, incomprehensible and extraordinary.' His jury agreed, returning a verdict of 'accidental death' and adding that if Grey and Hopkins had intervened, John's life might have been saved.

**6 JANUARY** **1875** An elderly man called at Chepstow police station, wanting a ticket for a night's lodgings. He was filthy, diseased and crawling with vermin, and the duty inspector sent him to the Workhouse. However, the man never got there.

He was seen drinking at several pubs in Chepstow the next day, after which nothing was seen or heard of him until the following morning, when a sick man was reported in a plantation about a mile from the town. PC Ferris found him almost naked, shivering and covered with weeping sores and flea bites. The man was carried to the Workhouse, where the nurses had never seen anybody in such a disgusting state. After a bath and delousing, he was placed in the infectious ward, where he died that evening.

He was sixty-six-year-old Henry Tuplin from Caldicott and, after speaking to his relatives, the police discovered that, five years earlier, Tuplin chose to live as a tramp, sleeping in barns and outbuildings. He was a relatively wealthy man, owning a cottage and garden worth £200, for which he received a quarterly rent of nearly £8 and, until recently, he also worked as a farm labourer.

Tuplin was so disreputable that his relatives disowned him. They last saw him about a month before his death, when he collected a half-year's rent from his tenant, which was squandered on drink within days.

Coroner Mr P.E. King held an inquest at the Chepstow Workhouse, at which the jury determined that Tuplin's demise was due to '...want of cleanliness, exposure to weather and want of proper nourishment.'

**7 JANUARY** **1929** Fifty-nine-year-old Henry Davies made his final appearance at Carmarthen Police Court, charged with murdering his wife, Mary.

On 19 December, fifty-eight-year-old Mary was found head-down in a water butt behind the couple's house in Abergwili. She had not died from drowning. There were bruises and fingernail marks on her face and forearms, her mouth was full of blood clots and she had two loose teeth, one broken tooth and numerous small cuts on the inside of her lips. Both knees were scraped and dirty, all injuries that, in the opinion of Dr Telford Martin, occurred before death.

Martin believed that Mary died after a violent attack proved too great a shock for her weak heart.

*Guildhall Square, Carmarthen, 1950s. (Author's collection)*

The police treated the death as suspicious and Davies emerged as their prime suspect. Witnesses spoke of hearing shouts of 'Help' and 'Murder' from the direction of the Davies' house and Davies was seen at around the time of his wife's death with blood on the back of his hand, along with what looked like human teeth marks. On discovering Mary's body, he made no attempt to remove it from the water butt, shouting to his neighbours that his wife had drowned and leaving them to attempt resuscitation. Furthermore, Davies had recently taken out insurance on his wife's life.

Davies's statements at the inquest were so contradictory that the jury returned a verdict of wilful murder against him. Magistrates at the Police Court concurred and he was committed for trial at the Carmarthen Assizes, where he was found guilty of the lesser offence of manslaughter and sentenced to fifteen years' penal servitude.

**1857** An inquest was held at Cardiff on the death of forty-four-year-old Catherine Murphy.

**8 JANUARY**

The Bute Docks in Cardiff were plagued by coal thieves. The coal was loaded into vessels using large chutes, each of which had a heavy counterweight on the end, and, as Catherine helped herself, the weight fell onto her head.

Bystanders struggled for fifteen minutes to extricate her, finding her skull smashed like an eggshell when they finally succeeded. There was normally a heavy wooden board nailed into the base of each coal truck, designed to prevent the weights from crushing people. However, Catherine had removed the board to make it easier to get at the coal.

The inquest jury returned a verdict of 'accidental death.'

9 JANUARY    **1867** Farm labourer Richard Clanfield was an inoffensive, taciturn man, who lived near Chepstow with his wife Ann and children, Eliza, Emily and James. His eldest son, John, had left home and another child, three-year-old Hannah, died two months earlier and was buried at the expense of the parish.

The Clanfields' neighbours believed that Hannah had met with foul play and, when fourteen-year-old Eliza suddenly died, the gossip started afresh and nobody in the village would supply Ann with a coffin. The rumours reached the ears of the police and, when PC Hardy visited the family on 9 January, he found '...a scene of wretchedness and misery.' There was just a rotting feather mattress upstairs and the children slept on a pile of chaff in the kitchen, covered by sacks. The only furniture downstairs was a table and two broken chairs and the earth-floored cottage was cold, damp and stinking.

Eliza's body was emaciated and filthy, her head covered in scabs. Coroner Mr W.H. Brewer ordered a post-mortem examination, which recorded that Eliza, who was 4ft 8in tall, weighed just 45lbs – less than half the normal weight for a girl of her height. Richard Clanfield earned good money and, in an effort to get his wife to feed the children properly, usually left his wages at the village shop. However, while Ann ate well, she gave the children only dry bread and potatoes.

When the inquest jury returned a verdict of 'wilful murder' against Ann Clanfield, on the grounds that she caused Eliza's death by 'starvation, exposure to cold and wilful neglect,' the coroner ordered the two youngest children to be removed to the Workhouse. Ann was tried at Monmouth Assizes on 31 March, where she was found guilty of manslaughter and sentenced to seven years' penal servitude.

10 JANUARY    **1863** The master of the barque *Jane* appeared before magistrates at Cardiff, charged with assault and cruelty to one of his crew. Allen Letcher's fingers became frostbitten on the voyage from Newfoundland to Cardiff and Captain Robert Taylor ordered the ship's carpenter to chop them off. When the carpenter did, Taylor demanded that he cut the fingers a second time, since he had left some longer than others. Furthermore, the Captain insisted that Letcher took his turn at the ship's pumps and tied his arms to the pump to prevent his damaged hands from slipping off.

Surgeon Thomas Pratt testified that, in the absence of immediate medical attention, Taylor had correctly treated the frostbitten fingers, first ordering them to be regularly poulticed with bread and turnips, then ordering their removal when it became obvious that they were rotting away. Letcher himself made no complaints, telling the Bench that his duties had been limited to acting as lookout.

The magistrates agreed that Taylor adopted very proper means to ensure Letcher's wellbeing, showing every care and attention. He was discharged without penalty.

11 JANUARY    **1900** Shortly after the arrival of the 7.20 p.m. train at Whitland Station, a young man was found slumped on the platform. Unable to rouse him, railway staff sent for Dr J.T. Cresswick Williams, who pronounced him drunk. He was sent to The Yelverton Arms Hotel, where he died later that night.

*Market Street, Whitland. (Author's collection)*

A label in his jacket identified its maker as 'W.G. Roach, tailor, Pembroke', and, since the man's ticket showed that he was travelling to Pembroke, police circulated his description in that area. He was quickly identified as Sydney J. Wrench, who accompanied his mother to Swansea on the 10.20 a.m. train and was returning to Pembroke when found at Whitland.

The jury at the subsequent inquest heard from Wrench's fellow passengers, who stated that he disembarked several times, believing that he was on the wrong train. One passenger noticed him foaming at the mouth.

Wrench had consumed a large quantity of alcohol on an empty stomach and in the doctor's opinion the sole cause of his death was excessive drinking. The jury returned a verdict of 'death from paralysis of respiratory centres, possibly caused by excessive doses of alcohol.'

**12 JANUARY**

**1901** As miners left Rhos Las Pit at Vochriw to attend the funeral of one of their colleagues, nine coal trams – heavy, wheeled carts used for transporting coal – broke free from a chain of twelve and careered backwards, ploughing into the men as they hurried towards the exit.

James H. Jones of Dowlais was killed instantly, while Thomas Lewis was so badly injured that he died as he was being carried home. Three horses were also killed and a further four men were injured, two of them seriously. The inquest on Jones and Lewis recorded verdicts of accidental death.

**13 JANUARY**

**1887** As fifty-year-old Margaret Scott of Swansea heated a bucket of coal tar on an open fire it boiled over, showering Margaret and her three-year-old granddaughter with boiling tar and setting the room on fire.

Passer-by John Henry Rees tried to enter the house but was beaten back by the flames. Eventually, he managed to open a window and Margaret and her granddaughter, Margaret Hammett, were pulled clear.

Sadly, Rees's efforts were in vain since little Margaret died from her burns the following day. Her grandmother lingered in Swansea Infirmary for several days before succumbing to her own burns.

14 JANUARY    **1852** Abel (or Abraham) Ovans was furious when his partner, Eliza Dore, gave birth on 1 December 1851. He refused to touch the infant and told people he wished she were dead.

On 14 January, the couple were evicted for non-payment of rent. They spent one night at a beer house then took new lodgings in Charles Street, Newport, but when they arrived there, they had no baby with them. The next morning, a naked baby girl was found in a pond. The inquest recorded a verdict of 'found drowned' and a reward of 5s was offered for information leading to her identification.

It had not gone unnoticed that Eliza's baby was missing and, when asked, she gave conflicting accounts of her daughter's whereabouts. Eventually, someone suggested to the police that the child had met with foul play.

When questioned, Ovans denied that Eliza had ever given birth, while Eliza insisted that the baby was with its grandmother, near Bristol. Superintendent English asked her if Ovans knew, to which Eliza replied that Ovans handed the baby over to her mother, who called when Eliza was out.

When the couple were arrested, Eliza changed her story, now saying that Ovans took the baby from her as they walked to their new lodgings, saying he wouldn't live with her if she kept it and refusing to maintain it. He disappeared for ten minutes and returned with the child's clothes wrapped in her shawl, telling Eliza that he had 'done away with it' and threatening to beat her if she told anyone.

The couple appeared at Monmouth Assizes on 24 March, where both were found guilty of wilful murder and sentenced to death, although the jury recommended mercy for Eliza. Awaiting her execution, Eliza changed her story again, saying that Ovans was not her daughter's biological father and that she had stripped the infant and thrown her into the pond. Even so, Eliza received a respite and, on 25 November, was transported to Van Dieman's Land for life. Ovans was hanged by William Calcraft at Monmouth on 16 April.

**1900**  Twelve-year-old William John Rees appeared before magistrates at Neath.    **15 JANUARY**
   A few nights earlier, Evan Davies met the child on the streets at half-past eleven at night. Cold and hungry, William told Davies that he was too afraid to go home because his parents beat him.
   Davies took the boy to his own home, where he gave him a hot meal and a warm bed for the night but, when William left the next morning, so did a watch, worth 25s. It was later found at William's parents' house, and returned to its rightful owner.
   Magistrates were afraid that the boy would become a habitual criminal if not checked. He was fined 1s plus costs and the police were ordered to give him six strokes of the birch.

**1871**  John Pearce appeared before magistrates in Newport charged with    **16 JANUARY**
assaulting his wife. The couple had been married for twenty-three years and had seven children, but Pearce divided his time between his wife and his mistress, Mrs Jenkins, spending three or four days a week living with each. Pearce had recently asked his wife if he might bring Mrs Jenkins to live in their house and was furious when she refused. The catalyst for the beating with which Pearce was now charged was his wife spending £2 on clothes for their children, to replace those that he destroyed in his temper.
   Pearce denied everything, but two witnesses supported Mrs Pearce's accusations. A neighbour stated that she hit Pearce with a broom handle to stop him attacking his wife, adding that if she hadn't intervened, she believed that Mrs Pearce would have been choked to death. In addition, a senior police officer testified that Mr Jenkins had complained to him about his wife's affair with Pearce.
   Pearce was only prepared to admit that he once went to a public house with Mrs Jenkins, and was astonished when the magistrates sentenced him to two months' imprisonment with hard labour and bound him over to keep the peace for twelve months.

**1891**  After a day in Newport, lock-keeper William Whittaker and his wife    **17 JANUARY**
headed home to Alteryn. They spent an hour at The Rising Sun Inn then continued walking along the canal bank.
   William stopped to empty his bladder and Sarah Whittaker walked on ahead. When he arrived home William was surprised that Sarah wasn't there waiting for him. He knocked up his neighbours and asked them to help him search, and, at midnight, they discovered Sarah's body in the canal, beneath the Crindau Bridge.
   At an inquest held by coroner Mr E.H. Davies, the jury were told that Sarah had drowned. She was not drunk, nor were there marks of violence on her body

or any signs of natural illness. William insisted that he was walking just a few yards behind her and heard no splashing or cries for help.

With no explanation for forty-nine-year-old Sarah's death, the jury returned an open verdict of 'found drowned.'

*Above: Alteryn. (Author's collection)*

*Right: Lock-keeper's cottage, Alteryn Canal. (Author's collection)*

18 JANUARY **1900** Seventy-year-old Patrick O'Connor appeared before magistrates in Cardiff charged with 'living on the earnings of infamy.'

When police visited his house in Millicent Street, they heard complaints from several girls there about O'Connor's refusal to work and his reliance on their earnings. The main complainants were O'Connor's own daughters, Mary and Lizzie, who were forced to prostitute themselves to support their father, who spent his time drinking and fighting.

'Why don't you lock him up, as you do others?' pleaded Mary. The magistrates were only too pleased to oblige and sentenced O'Connor to three months' imprisonment with hard labour.

**1892** After the chimney at Fernhill Colliery at Treherbert was wrecked by a **19 JANUARY** heavy storm, steeplejacks were called in to repair it and as Patrick O'Neill was working on the renovation, he suddenly slipped and fell 80ft to his death. The fall shattered his skull like an eggshell, severely damaging his brain.

Twenty-one-year-old Patrick from Hereford had been a steeplejack for just three weeks and had received no training, nor was he wearing any safety equipment. In spite of this, an inquest jury ruled his death accidental and attributed no blame to his employers for his demise.

**1883** In New Oxford Street, Swansea, Robert Williams woke in the early hours **20 JANUARY** of the morning to find his general store on fire.

Robert, his wife and their two youngest children slept in one bedroom above the shop, the two middle boys in a second and the two oldest in a third. Robert and his wife each picked up a child and, while his wife and baby escaped through the door, Robert smashed the window in the oldest boys' bedroom and climbed out. Having seen his wife and four of the children to safety and ensured that help was on its way, Robert went back for twelve-year-old Robert Charles and fourteen-year-old Ellis. Sadly, although their father and others made heroic efforts to rescue them, both boys perished.

Passers-by Francis Lawrence and Thomas Collins dashed up the burning staircase but were unable to locate the boys in the thick, suffocating smoke. The police arrived with a ladder and made repeated attempts to reach the boys. Ellis was eventually rescued barely alive, while young Robert was found under his bed when the fire was extinguished.

At an inquest held by coroner Edward Strick, Robert recalled checking the premises before retiring to bed, extinguishing the lamps and making sure the fires were safe. The shop stocked flammable items, such as varnish and oil, which fed the flames and, in the opinion of several witnesses, inadequate water pressure contributed to the two fatalities. It took almost thirty minutes before a proper jet of water could be directed at the flames.

The jury returned verdicts of accidental death on Robert and Ellis, asking that the efforts made by Lawrence, Collins and the policemen should be formally commended.

**1897** Several people saw a woman walking alongside the canal in Newport, **21 JANUARY** carrying a baby. Then, nothing more was seen of her until a bargeman noticed her body floating in the canal. When the body was recovered and the police were informed that she was last seen with an infant, they dragged the canal with grappling hooks, retrieving the body of a baby girl.

A handkerchief in the woman's pocket identified her as Emily Louise Chambers. Emily had borne five children, one of whom died the week before baby Eva's birth. A second child was recuperating from an operation and a third convalescing after a severe attack of scarlet fever. A fourth was poorly with the same illness and was confined in a hospital for infectious diseases. Emily herself had been suffering from a sore throat and was convinced that she and Eva had diphtheria. Having been up all night with six-week-old Eva, thirty-three-year-old Emily reminded her servant to prepare for a visit from the doctor at lunchtime then slipped out of the house.

An inquest was opened by coroner Mr Lyndon Moore. At first it was not clear whether Emily deliberately threw herself into the canal or whether she fell in by accident, perhaps blown off the path by a gust of wind. Then servant Annie Lewarne found a note addressed to Emily's husband: 'Dear Charlie – my grief seems more than I can bear. I have prayed and prayed for help but it does not come and it is going from worse to worse. The baby is ill and I am choking. With all my love to dear children and you. May God bless you.'

The note seemed to indicate that Emily had committed suicide. Although she was depressed because of her children's illnesses and tired due to caring for a new baby, nobody suspected that she was desperate enough to kill herself, not even Dr Garrod Thomas, who had visited the Chambers' home to treat the children once or twice a day for the past month.

The jury returned an open verdict of 'found drowned' on both deaths, extending their sympathy to Charles Chambers, who was devastated at the latest tragedy to befall his family.

**22 JANUARY**    **1889** The construction of the Rhondda and Swansea Bay Railway was nearing completion and one of the last jobs was to finish the tunnel beneath the mountains at Abergwynfi. As labourers removed some supporting timbers to build a brick arch at the tunnel's mouth, there was a sudden fall of earth and rock, burying the gang beneath tons of debris.

Initial reports gave the death toll as seven but fortunately some labourers had just gone for breakfast when the fall occurred. Only four were buried, two of whom escaped alive and immediately began digging for their colleagues.

It was several hours before the body of George Smitherham was recovered and it was later determined that he had suffocated, whereas George Lever was crushed by the weight of soil and rocks.

The contractor had an excellent safety record and had taken every possible precaution to avoid accidents. Verdicts of accidental death were later recorded on both victims.

**23 JANUARY**    **1893** A new shaft at the colliery at Aberdare Junction had reached a depth of 268 yards. Great care was taken to check for loose or dangerous material and, as the sinkers descended deeper, the shaft was walled. However, on 23 January, a large triangular stone fell from the side, hitting several men at the pit bottom.

Seven were killed and, at the inquest on their deaths, it was revealed that the bottom 19 yards of the shaft had not been walled. Coroner Mr Reece charged his jury with deciding whether there was negligence or criminal responsibility on the part of those whose duty it was to examine the shaft and take the necessary precautions against accidents. The jury found the deaths to be purely accidental and attached no blame to anyone.

**1893** As four men worked on a platform, constructing a new furnace stove **24 JANUARY** at the Dowlais Works, Cardiff, a bracket supporting the scaffold planks broke. James Johnson grabbed another bracket and William Perkins clung desperately to planks above him, but Frederick Thomas and Anthony Appleby fell almost 60ft to the ground. Thomas died instantly and Appleby, who landed on top of him, was rushed to Cardiff Infirmary with injuries to his head and back.

An inquest held by coroner Mr E.B. Reece heard that the contractors had an excellent safety record. However, an inspection of the scaffold showed that the horizontal arms of the supporting brackets had been lengthened and these extensions failed under the combined weight of the men.

The jury found that 'the deceased lost his life through the collapse of a scaffold caused by the insufficient strength of the bracket to bear weight.' Shortly after the conclusion of the inquest on Thomas, Appleby died without regaining consciousness.

**1877** Information reached the police that fifty-seven-year-old Isaac Alger **25 JANUARY** was keeping a brothel in Swansea, and, after watching the premises all night, officers decided that they had sufficient evidence to charge him. PCs Payne and Gill entered Alger's house and were confronted by Alger, who pointed a pistol at Payne's head and pulled the trigger. Fortunately, the gun misfired and Alger was taken to the police station and charged with attempted murder.

'Only the attempt, mind,' Alger cautioned.

He appeared at the Cardiff Assizes charged with 'having unlawfully attempted to discharge a loaded pistol at Stephen Payne, with intent to murder him.' His defence counsel challenged the legality of the charge, since the officers entered Alger's house without a warrant and were therefore trespassing, giving Alger every right to resist their entry.

Presiding judge Mr Justice Mellor consulted Mr Justice Lush and they decided that, since Payne and Gill were in uniform, the charge against Alger was legitimate. Even so, the jury found him guilty of the lesser offence of 'attempting to do grievous bodily harm' and recommended leniency, since he had a long and distinguished Army service. Alger was sentenced to eighteen months' imprisonment with hard labour.

**1883** During the night of 26/27 January, the steamer *Agnes Jack* was wrecked **26 JANUARY** in Port Eynon Bay. The disaster was discovered by a farm labourer, who heard shouts for help as he walked to work early on 27 January, and at daybreak, two masts were visible above the water, with a number of men clinging to them.

A gale force wind and mountainous seas prevented the launch of boats and although attempts were made to fire lines, all fell short of their target. Horrified spectators could only watch as those clinging to the masts fell into the sea or

tried unsuccessfully to swim ashore, until the ship finally sank, taking with it all on board.

The entire crew drowned, along with Llanelli pilot Phillip Beynon. Four of the seventeen victims were buried in Port Eynon churchyard.

**27 JANUARY** **1884** An explosion of gas occurred at the Naval Steam Colliery, Penygraig.

Blasting holes were prepared on Saturdays and fired on Sundays and, had the explosion occurred on any other day, the fatalities would doubtlessly have been even greater, since the colliery employed between 350 and 400 men during the working week. On this occasion, six firemen and five ostlers, who had gone to tend to the sixty-five horses kept below ground, lost their lives. The horses also perished.

Fireman Daniel James should have been at work but overslept by fifteen minutes – he was hurriedly dressing at home when he heard the explosion.

**28 JANUARY** **1907** After his wife left, David Evans of Pontypool engaged housekeeper Rhoda Willis (aka Leslie James), who began work on 28 January.

Rhoda persuaded her employer that they could make money by posing as a married couple and adopting babies for payment. Initially reluctant, Evans eventually consented and Rhoda placed an advertisement in the evening newspaper.

She received several replies and, on 10 April, collected the illegitimate child of Emily Stroud from Abertillery. Rhoda kept the baby until 7 May, when she agreed to take a second. Telling Evans that she had arranged for Emily's baby to be adopted, she dumped it on the steps of the Salvation Army Home in Cardiff. It was found suffering from exposure and died on 15 May.

Rhoda collected another infant on 8 May, although she was later to return it, after the child's mother pined for her baby. On 5 June, Rhoda collected the illegitimate daughter of a woman named Maud Treasure, along with some baby clothes and £6 in gold.

By then, Rhoda had moved into lodgings and, according to her landlady Hannah Wilson, she went out and got drunk. On 6 June, Hannah heard a crash from Rhoda's room and found her lying on the floor, having fallen out of bed. As Hannah helped Rhoda, she spotted the body of a newborn baby girl.

The police were called and, when a post-mortem examination revealed that the infant had suffocated, Rhoda was charged with wilful murder. At the Swansea Assizes, Rhoda claimed that the baby was ill when she collected it from Maud Treasure's sister and died from natural causes during the journey to Cardiff. However, when a handwriting expert showed that Rhoda had written the note left with the baby abandoned at the Salvation Army Home, the jury realised what a callous and calculating woman she was and found her guilty.

She was executed at Cardiff by Henry Pierrepoint on 14 August, her forty-fourth birthday.

**1899** A penniless sailor was picked up in Bute Street, Cardiff, suffering from *delirium tremens*. He was taken to the asylum at Bridgend and newspapers later reported that he was making a satisfactory recovery. **29 JANUARY**

Five months earlier, the sailor inherited a legacy of £800 from his father and resolved to spend the entire amount on alcohol. He assured doctors at the asylum that he only ever drank beer and never touched wine or spirits, but his story was viewed with disbelief when it was calculated that, to spend his entire inheritance in five months, he would have consumed around 12,000 gallons of beer.

**1607** On a bright, sunny day, a devastating flood affected the Bristol Channel, killing an estimated 2,000 people. The Welsh coast from Laugharne to Chepstow was particularly badly affected, with survivors describing 'huge and mighty hills of water' advancing at great speed and sweeping away everything before them, flooding an estimated 200 square miles of land and killing thousands of farm and wild animals. Those people that survived retreated to the roof tops or climbed trees and church steeples, many remaining in their precarious positions for days until the floods retreated. Originally thought to be a warning from God to the people of England, more recent research has speculated that the flood may have been caused by either a storm surge or a tsunami. **30 JANUARY**

**1910** An inquest was held in Cardiff on the death of sixty-three-year-old retired commercial traveller, Isaac Morgan. **31 JANUARY**

Morgan went to visit a sick friend on 29 January. His family weren't unduly worried when he didn't return, assuming that he was sitting up with his friend, but when they went outside the next morning, they found Morgan lying dead in the back yard.

The inquest concluded that he had slipped and fallen over on the icy yard, banging his head and knocking himself out. In the bitterly cold weather, he froze to death within feet of his own back door.

The inquest jury returned a verdict of 'accidental death.'

# FEBRUARY

*Newport, 1905. (Author's collection)*

**1903** During a gale on 31 January, the Waterford steamship *Christina* beached as she tried to enter harbour at Port Talbot. It was decided to try and refloat her on 1 February and the Mumbles lifeboat was asked to attend.

When the lifeboat arrived, the tide was still not quite high enough, so coxswain Tom Rogers decided to enter the river Aberavon to wait until it was. As the lifeboat manoeuvred, she was struck broadside by a wave and capsized.

Most of the crew were thrown out of the boat but it righted itself and four scrambled back on board. The lifeboat then drifted towards the breakwater and they were able to get ashore. One of the crew was a strong swimmer and managed to assist three men to safety, but although the harbourmaster and a group of French sailors did their best to rescue the remaining crew members, Tom Rogers, Daniel Claypitt, George Michael, James Gammon, Robert Smith and David John Morgan lost their lives.

The crew of the *Christina* were never in any danger, since the ship was beached in such a way that they could have walked ashore. However, since it was feared that they would insist on staying on board while the ship was refloated, the lifeboat was summoned as a precautionary measure.

**1881** Shoemaker Evan Thomas of Kidwelly sent his eleven-year-old son, John, to deliver some shoes. He was paid a half-sovereign but never arrived home with the money.

People living on his route were quizzed and Mrs Hughes told searchers that John had played with David and Benjamin Mazey, and had gone into the Mazey's home. Mrs Hughes distinctly heard David saying that his mother was out.

John's mother spoke to Mrs Mazey, who insisted that she watched John walking towards Trimsaran. Her house was searched and no trace was found of the missing boy. However, Mrs Hughes was adamant that John went inside and, the next day, the police found his body in a ditch at the bottom of the Mazeys' garden, covered by grass and earth. His skull was smashed and his jaw broken in several places, while his brain lay in a neighbour's garden.

Thirteen-year-old David and eleven-year-old Benjamin said that John fell off a swing in their garden, injuring his head. When doctors determined that John's injuries could not have been caused by falling off a swing, the boys said that John fell from an outhouse roof.

John was given food when he delivered the shoes and his stomach contents suggested that he died no later than six o'clock on 2 February. The area was searched on 3 February and it then rained overnight. Since John was not found during the first search and his clothes were relatively dry, it was deduced that his body was dumped on 4 February. The police made further enquiries and learned that the Mazey boys had changed a half-sovereign on 3 February and, when spots of blood were found on their clothes, along with human hair attached to the nails in David's boots, both were charged with John's wilful murder and their mother, Jane, with being an accessory after the fact.

At the Swansea Assizes in May, doctors were positive that John's head injuries could not have resulted from a fall but, given the extent of the damage to his skull, thought it improbable that such young boys would have possessed sufficient strength to inflict them. Mr Justice Cave told the jury that the boys should be given the benefit of any doubt and all three Mazeys were acquitted. Nobody else was ever charged with John's murder.

**3 FEBRUARY**    **1883** Coroner Dr John Hughes held an inquest at Carmarthen on the death of fourteen-week-old Emily Ann Evans.

Emily was a fractious baby and her mother, Elizabeth, habitually gave her doses of 'cordial' to quieten her. Having run out of her usual mixture, Elizabeth borrowed some from neighbour, Jane Thomas.

She gave Emily four drops and the baby was asleep within minutes but soon afterwards, Emily went very pale and, when her mother tried to wake her, Emily's eyes rolled back in her head and she remained unresponsive.

Elizabeth sent for a doctor and, recognising that Emily was suffering from narcotic poisoning, Dr P.W. Hughes gave her an emetic to induce her to vomit. Sadly, it was ineffective and Emily died.

The bottle of cordial borrowed from Jane Thomas contained half a drachm of laudanum in one fluid ounce of treacle and water. Druggist Mr J.P. Richards told the inquest that four drops was a lethal dose for a child of Emily's age, even though Jane claimed to have given her own baby fifteen drops before passing the mixture to Elizabeth.

The jury returned a verdict of 'death by misadventure' and the coroner warned Elizabeth to be more careful about what she gave her children in future, telling Jane Thomas that it was a wonder he wasn't holding an inquest on her baby too.

**4 FEBRUARY**    **1869** Michael Toomey died from inflammation of the brain, arising from a wound on his forehead. On 17 January, forty-year-old Bridget Allens and her husband were drinking in The Windsor Hotel at Penarth and started an argument with Toomey over a handkerchief. The dispute became so intense that the landlord asked all three to leave and, outside, several witnesses saw Bridget pick up a large stone and hit Toomey on his forehead. He dropped to the ground unconscious, blood pouring from his head.

When Toomey died, Bridget was charged with wilful murder, appearing at the Glamorganshire Assizes in March 1869.

Toomey and Bridget were very drunk at the time of the assault. Thus, although Dr Payne was certain that death resulted from an injury to the forehead, he couldn't rule out the possibility that Toomey had just drunkenly fallen face-down onto a stone. Although witnesses saw Bridget hit Toomey, when the judge summed up, he steered the jury towards drunkenness as the ultimate cause of death. They accordingly found Bridget Allens not guilty and she was discharged with a caution.

**1831** Colliers William Morgan, Rees Evan and Nicholas John, who worked underground at the Aberdare Iron Works, were crushed by a fall of rock. John's spine was shattered, although he was alive and fully conscious when rescued. He was able to explain that the three men had opened an air vent and were resting and smoking their pipes when the unexpected fall occurred. Morgan and Evan were dead when rescuers reached them and John died shortly afterwards. Between them, they left two widows and fourteen children.  **5 FEBRUARY**

**1871** In less than twenty-four hours, four serious accidents occurred in Troed-y-rhiw. The first occurred near the Duffryn Furnace, when the driver and fireman of a train belonging to the Plymouth Iron Company were thrown off the engine. Thomas Davis was the more severely injured, sustaining a compound fracture of his leg. The second tragedy occurred on the Taff Valley Railway near Mountain Ash, when a platelayer was killed by a train. Nobody knew anything about the accident until the train arrived at Aberdare Junction, bearing the man's leg on the front. The third catastrophe occurred near Gethin Pit, where a labourer was run over and killed by a train, while the fourth happened to John Rees at the refinery of the Duffryn Works. As he was cooling red hot iron with water, it exploded and it is believed that he later died from his injuries.  **6 FEBRUARY**

**1831** A pilot boat was swamped in the bay at the mouth of the river Neath and sank instantly, with the loss of all four crew. The bodies of David Williams, John Eddow and William Emmanuel were recovered the next day, while that of the captain, David Evans, remained undiscovered for some time. Emmanuel was about to marry, whereas his shipmates were already married with children. Mrs Evans was heavily pregnant at the time of her husband's death and Mrs Eddow had very recently given birth to the couple's first child.  **7 FEBRUARY**

**1889** The ferry between Pen and Bentlass was packed with people attending Pembroke Market. On 8 February, a strong wind was blowing, causing water to wash over the sides of the boat and it was thought that one of the female passengers stood up to prevent her clothes from getting wet. Her actions capsized the ferry.  **8 FEBRUARY**

The capsize occurred in the Pembroke Gut River, about a mile below Pembroke, a lonely stretch of water almost half a mile wide, which was rarely frequented by other vessels. Hence there was no ready assistance for the ferry and all nine of its occupants drowned. At the subsequent inquest, the jury recorded verdicts of 'accidental death' on the victims, adding a rider that restrictions should be placed on ferry boats to limit the number of passengers that they were permitted to carry.

**9 FEBRUARY** **1871** It was fourteen-year-old Margaret Todd's job to collect sawdust from the saw sheds for the Abernant Brick and Tile Works, where it was used in the brick-making process.

On 9 February, Margaret and another girl approached sawyer John James and asked if there was any sawdust in his saw pit. James, who was sharpening his saw at the time, told them that there wasn't but said that they could pick up any sawdust that was lying around. Since the saw was running, James cautioned the girls against going into the pit, then went to another part of the saw mill.

Minutes later, Margaret's companion ran screaming to James that Margaret was being killed. James rushed back, to see Margaret's dead body being violently spun around by the shaft that turned the saw.

An inquest was held later that day, at which the jury questioned the safety of allowing girls to collect sawdust while the saws were in motion. It was explained that Margaret went into the pit against the orders of the man in charge and that it would cause great expense and inconvenience to the company to keep stopping the saws every time sawdust was needed. Satisfied by the explanation, the jury returned a verdict of 'accidental death.'

**10 FEBRUARY** **1907** A fire in Newport claimed the lives of four people. The blaze originated in a shop owned by George Probert and was first noticed by tram driver Ernest Pike, who broke open the shop door but was unable to enter the premises due to the fierceness of the flames.

*High Street, Newport, c. 1920. (Author's collection)*

Pike succeeded in rousing the eleven people who lived above the shop, and Mr and Mrs Probert escaped through the rear of the building, along with their two sons and three of their seven lodgers.

Four lodgers failed to grasp the serious danger to their lives. All were later seen at a window at the front of the premises and a ladder was fetched to try and save them. However, flames billowing from the shop prevented rescuers from reaching them and, although they were urged to jump, they were too afraid, even though they were only 14ft above ground level. The bodies of Henry Albert Johnson, David John Pomeroy, his wife Margaret and their eleven-month-old son were recovered once the fire was extinguished.

**1875** The body of labourer Edward Davies was found at a lime kiln in Swansea. **11 FEBRUARY** Davies had been working away from home for about nine weeks and when he got back, on 10 February, his wife was out at work. Davies decided to pass the time waiting for her return at the pub.

It was supposed that, having had several drinks, he became sleepy and lay down at the side of the kiln for a snooze and, at some time during the night of 10/11 February, his clothes caught fire. The body was dreadfully charred when found and one leg had been burned completely off.

At a subsequent inquest, the jury returned a verdict of 'accidental death.'

**1900** Cardiff coroner Mr E.B. Reece held consecutive inquests at the Town Hall **12 FEBRUARY** on two children, who died in unrelated accidents with paraffin lamps.

Seven-year-old Ethel Mabel Davies was badly burned when a lighted lamp set fire to her clothing. In a panic, she ran out into the street, where the flames were beaten out by passers-by. She died from shock in hospital the following day.

A lamp was kept burning overnight in the bedroom of seven-month-old Hubert Forth, who was found dead by his mother when she went to wake him on 11 February. Doctors determined that he had died from convulsions, caused by inhaling fumes from the lamp.

**1921** Thomas Thomas managed the Star Supply Shop in Garnant. A conscien- **13 FEBRUARY** tious man, he regularly worked late balancing the shop's books.

On 13 February, assistants Millie Richards and Phoebe Jones worked until after 9 p.m., leaving their boss poring over the accounts. Phoebe, who lived next door, went to a concert and, when she returned at 11.25 p.m., the shop lights were still burning. She glanced through the window and saw her boss's white shop coat and apron hanging on the banisters, as they were when she left work.

At 9 a.m. the next morning – a Sunday – Phoebe was woken by her landlord Morgan Jeffreys, who also owned the shop. Jeffreys told Phoebe that the shop's basement door was open and suggested that she check that everything was all right.

The shop had been robbed of around £130 and Thomas Thomas lay dead in the basement. He had been hit over the head with a broom and also stabbed in the stomach and throat. Thomas's trousers and waistcoat were undone, so that the stab wounds went directly into his flesh, rather than penetrating his clothing, and his body was cold, suggesting that death had occurred between 10 p.m. and midnight.

Since Millie was positive that she bolted and barred the basement door before leaving the shop, it seemed probable that the murderer was already in the basement. There was no sign of a struggle, indicating either that Thomas knew his killer or was taken by surprise. The degree of violence used suggested that the murderer wanted to make absolutely sure that his victim would not survive to identify him, yet a local man would know that Thomas banked the shop takings on Fridays and Tuesdays and might have waited until there was more cash on the premises to rob the shop.

Several people passed the shop during the night and, apart from the fact that the lights were on, saw nothing untoward. The one exception was housewife Diana Bowen, who heard a scream and thud at about 10.15 p.m., but didn't investigate further or report what she heard.

The jury at Thomas's inquest returned a verdict of 'wilful murder by person or persons unknown' and the murder remains unsolved.

14 FEBRUARY  **1900** As the recent heavy snow gave way to rain, farmer John Chilton spotted some cloth sticking out of a rapidly melting snow drift at Brynmawr. A closer look revealed a woman's body buried in the snow.

She was quickly identified as thirty-three-year-old Kate Cronin, who was last seen two days earlier, very drunk and staggering from one side of the road to the other.

An inquest was later held by coroner Mr R.H.A. Davies at the police station, Brynmawr, at which the jury returned a verdict of 'death from exposure in the snow while under the influence of drink.'

15 FEBRUARY  **1867** Sarah Jacob of Llanfihangel-ar-Arth told her mother that she had stomach pains and had coughed up some bloody froth. She quickly fell into a coma, punctuated by a series of convulsive fits.

She remained comatose for almost a month before recovering consciousness, when she began taking regular meals of rice or oatmeal and milk. However, these meals were almost immediately regurgitated and, by October 1867, her daily intake of food had dwindled to a teaspoonful of pureed apple. On 10 October, Sarah stopped eating altogether, apart from an occasional sip of water, and, when she died on 17 December 1869, Hannah and Evan Jacob claimed that their daughter had eaten or drunk nothing for two years, two months and one week.

Reverend Evan Jones was highly sceptical, insisting that survival without sustenance was impossible and accusing her parents of fraud. The Jacobs were adamant that 'the Big Doctor' (God) was providing for Sarah and miraculously keeping her alive.

People flocked from far and wide to see 'The Welsh Fasting Girl' and those admitted to her bedroom were expected to leave gifts of money. As Sarah developed celebrity status, some of the money was used to dress her in fancy clothes and trinkets. By February 1869, even Evans appeared convinced that Sarah was thriving on little more than fresh air and wrote to the newspapers suggesting that she should be fully investigated. A parish meeting was convened and a group of volunteers agreed to watch Sarah for a fortnight, to establish whether or not she was given food.

Although the watchers were convinced that Sarah was given nothing more than a few drops of water to moisten her lips, a couple admitted to dozing off or being drunk during their watch and they were not permitted to approach Sarah's bed, although her parents and younger sister did so frequently.

In an effort to settle the matter once and for all, Dr Fowler of London arranged for four nurses from Guy's Hospital to watch Sarah constantly, searching anyone who approached her. Fowler believed that Sarah's 'illness' was simply a hysterical condition and he instructed the nurses not to deny her food but to ensure that nobody was feeding her surreptitiously.

As soon as the nurses arrived, Sarah's physical condition deteriorated. Her bowels and bladder ceased to function and she appeared to be dying. Her parents were urged to abandon 'this cruel experiment' but insisted that Sarah wouldn't eat, whether the nurses were there or not.

When Sarah died, her parents were charged with manslaughter. Both were found guilty at the Carmarthen

Assizes and, in passing sentence, the judge accused them of sacrificing Sarah's life to maintain a fraudulent deception. Evan was sentenced to twelve months' imprisonment and his wife to six, both with hard labour.

**1862**  As the SS *Great Eastern* was guided into dry dock at Neyland for repairs, a rope to the tug *Blenheim* caught in one of the ship's screw propellers.  **16 FEBRUARY**

Thirteen of the *Blenheim*'s crew realised what was about to happen and threw themselves overboard, but four remained on the tug as she was sucked towards the giant propeller and disappeared under water. Fortunately, before it was smashed to pieces, the tug briefly resurfaced and wedged between the propeller and the ship for long enough to rescue the four men.

Meanwhile, those who had jumped overboard were rapidly washed out to sea by the tide. A sailor jumped off the deck of the *Eastern* and seized one man by the hair, holding him above water until both were rescued. Eleven of the thirteen were saved but two drowned, even though there was a ferry in the immediate vicinity. To the disgust of those watching, ferryman James Vaulk ignored the plight of the drowning men and made no effort to save them.

**1829**  William Jones was seen skulking in a garden in Brecknock, stealing garments left drying on a hedge. As soon as he realised he had been spotted, Jones fled, but was caught by Sergeant Morgan of the Royal Welsh Fusiliers, who  **17 FEBRUARY**

escorted him to the borough gaol. The gaoler placed him in a cell at the top of the building, having first removed all of Jones's clothes to prevent him from escaping.

A little later, a factory worker was startled by the sudden appearance of a naked man. Standing on his bunk, Jones tunnelled through the ceiling of his cell and onto the gaol roof. From there, he descended to the roof ridge of an adjoining house and walked along the ridges of nine more, before entering a house in Castle Street through an open window in the attic. He went downstairs to a first-floor bedroom, tied the quilt to the bedpost and lowered himself out of the window into the street, crossing the back yards of the neighbouring houses until he reached the factory.

Unfortunately for Jones, his nakedness placed him at a disadvantage and he was quickly taken to the more secure county gaol. The following morning, magistrates committed him for trial at the next quarter sessions, where he was found guilty of larceny and sentenced to three months' imprisonment.

**18 FEBRUARY** **1870** Twelve-year-old George Londen died in Cardiff Infirmary, following an accident three days earlier.

Londen was employed to carry tools on the Llanishen railway line. On 15 February, engine driver George Forbes stopped his train to shunt some wagons and, when it started again, the sudden jerk caused Londen to fall onto the tracks, where he was run over by four trucks and the engine. Londen's arm and leg were crushed and, when he got to hospital, a decision was made to amputate them but, although Londen survived the operation, he died soon afterwards.

At an inquest held at the Infirmary by coroner Mr Rees, the jury determined that he had died as a result of his injuries, rather than the surgery.

**19 FEBRUARY** **1864** Evan and Mary Williams went to bed at their home in Hirwain and, early the next morning, their neighbours were awakened by their young daughter screaming hysterically 'Mother and Father are dead!' Evan hung from a hook in the kitchen ceiling, his body stiff and cold. Upstairs, Mary lay in bed, a woollen muffler pulled tight around her throat.

An inquest later heard that, although Evan and Mary were happily married, Evan had lost his job and was depressed. It was surmised that he had strangled his wife then cut a section of clothes line, with which he hanged himself. The jury returned verdicts of wilful murder and suicide during a bout of temporary insanity.

**20 FEBRUARY** **1900** Sixty-three-year-old haulier Henry Blatchford went to work for Cardiff milkman Mr Sweetman, but didn't return home as expected.

His family alerted the police, who found Blatchford shot in the head and buried in Sweetman's garden. He was practically naked and his clothes had been burned and buried.

Thomas Henry Sweetman, the milkman's son, made a statement implicating a neighbour, John Henry Thompson. Both men had spent time in asylums and Thomas, who was a hunchback, had twice been confined as a lunatic.

Thompson denied all knowledge of the murder, but eighteen-year-old Thomas was arrested and charged. It was thought that Thomas was jealous of Henry, since he was permitted to collect money from customers, which Mr

Sweetman didn't trust his son to do. However, the truth behind the seemingly motiveless murder was never revealed since, by the time the case came for trial in March, Sweetman was judged unfit to plead and ordered to be detained until Her Majesty's Pleasure be known.

**1941** During the Second World War, Swansea was the target of a prolonged **21 FEBRUARY** Luftwaffe assault that became known as the 'three-night-blitz', during which approximately 1,250 high-explosive devices and 56,000 incendiary bombs were dropped on the city. Over almost fourteen hours of air raids on the nights of 19, 20 and 21 February, it is estimated that between 230 and 270 people were killed, nearly 400 injured and at least 8,000 left homeless.

The first night's bombing almost obliterated Swansea city centre, as nearly 900 high-explosive bombs were deployed, the damage worsened by direct hits on gas and water mains. On the following night, stick bombs claimed the lives of nearly fifty residents of Teilo Crescent.

**1847** A coastguard spotted some wreckage on the shore at Mumbles. He alerted **22 FEBRUARY** his superior officer, who sent men to protect it, while trying to establish where it had come from.

It was the remains of the ship *Brechin Castle*, which was sailing from Adelaide to Swansea carrying copper ore, mail and a few passengers. Within fifteen miles of her destination, she struck a rock close to the Mumbles Head lighthouse and although there was sufficient time to launch the ship's lifeboats, they were, in the words of the contemporary newspapers, 'dashed to atoms.'

The entire crew of fifteen lost their lives in the disaster, as did ten passengers. The ship and her cargo, estimated to be worth more than £20,000, were said to be fully insured.

*Mumbles Head lighthouse and Battery. (Author's collection)*

**23 FEBRUARY** 1871 A cat belonging to Jane Davies of Merthyr Tydfil presented her with a baby's foot! Jane contacted the police, who soon found the rest of the baby sewn into a woman's petticoat and stuffed under the turf at the river bank, near Jane's home.

Although the body had been eaten by wild animals and most of the internal organs were missing, surgeons found no marks of violence. They estimated that the child was three or four weeks old, noting that it was well nourished and had pap in its mouth but they were unable to determine a cause of death.

Police enquiries focused on domestic servant Hannah Evans, who arrived in Merthyr on 7 February to visit her sister. Although Hannah gave birth in Cardiff on 7 January, she had no baby with her.

Asked about her youngest child, Hannah pointed to a little boy. She denied having recently been pregnant but eventually made a statement in order to protect her mother and sister, in which she related travelling from Cardiff on the train with her baby and finding the child dead in her arms when she arrived at Merthyr. In desperation, she sewed the child's body into her petticoat and hid it.

Hannah was charged with concealing the birth of her child, appearing at the Glamorganshire Spring Assizes. Although witnesses testified that the baby was ill on the day before Hannah left Cardiff, Mr Justice Mellor was sceptical. When the jury found Hannah guilty, Mellor told her, 'This is not a common case of concealment. There are circumstances of grave suspicion surrounding the case. I shall not act upon those suspicions but still I must distinguish between it and an ordinary case of concealment.' Telling Hannah, 'You might have stood there under a graver charge if further evidence had been given,' he sentenced her to twelve months' imprisonment with hard labour.

**24 FEBRUARY** 1910 The two-day trial of William Butler, aka Thomas Clements, for murder concluded at the Monmouth Assizes.

His victims were Charles and Mary Thomas of Bassaleg. Eighty-year-old Charles spent many years working as a woodman for Lord Tredegar and was rumoured to have a substantial nest egg, hence when the couple were found battered to death in their bed on the morning of 12 November 1909, it was supposed that robbery was the motive.

The killer gained access to the cottage by breaking a window, apparently protecting his or her hand with an item of child's clothing, which was left at the scene of the crime. The garment belonged to neighbour Mrs West's child and the victims' front door key was found on a windowsill at her cottage.

Mrs West suggested that the police should interview Butler, who had lodged with her for a year but had been

*Tank Cottage, Bassaleg – scene of a double murder in 1909. (Author's collection)*

TANK COTTAGE. BASSALEG. MON.
SCENE OF DOUBLE MURDER.

asked to leave, having become too affectionate towards her fifteen-year-old daughter. When Mrs West refused to allow Butler to marry the girl, he became abusive and she summoned him to appear before magistrates.

Butler was furious, waving the summons in Mrs West's face and promising her that she would rue the day she issued it and that he would ruin her in less than a week. Just days later, Mr and Mrs Thomas were bludgeoned to death with a hammer and efforts were made to implicate Mrs West.

The police traced Butler, finding that he had been spending money freely since the murders. Although the killer failed to find the couple's life savings of £150, about £3 was stolen, including five florins, and Butler had paid a debt with five florins. Butler claimed to have been asleep in bed throughout the night of 11/12 November but William Williams came forward to testify that Butler visited him at home in Cardiff between 9 p.m. and 9.30 p.m., presumably in an attempt to establish an alibi. However, the most conclusive evidence against Butler was the presence of blood spots on his clothes.

Found guilty, sixty-two-year-old Butler was hanged by Henry Pierrepoint at Usk on 24 March.

**1905** On a train journey on the Taff Vale Railway, Edward Samuel May dropped his umbrella. As he bent to retrieve it, a sudden jerk caused him to fall against the carriage door, which flew open, spilling him onto the track. **25 FEBRUARY**

A train travelling in the opposite direction ran over his feet and May claimed compensation from the railway. The case was heard at the Swansea Assizes in August but the jury failed to reach agreement, hence the highly unusual case was forwarded to the next Assizes in December, where it was heard in the Civil Court by Mr Justice Lawrence.

May was found between Porth and Pontypridd, with his legs almost severed. (They were later amputated at the hips.) Yet May, who weighed 15st 6lb, had supposedly fallen from a train moving at twenty-eight miles per hour but had no other injuries apart from a scratch on his nose, and had no tears or soiling to his clothes. The injuries to his legs were straight and parallel, as if he had simply laid them across the track and allowed a train to run over them.

No doors were open when the train reached Pontypridd and, using an actual train door in court, engineers demonstrated the impossibility of closing it improperly, adding that, while the train was in motion, the wind speed would prevent an open door being closed.

*Mr Justice Lawrence.*
*(Author's collection)*

All the doors were checked by guard James Dudson before the train left Porth. Dudson paid particular attention to the second-class compartments, in which May claimed to have travelled, since they were often besieged by third-class passengers, and the guard told the court that there were only two male passengers travelling second-class that night, neither of which was May. Furthermore, May had sent off coupons for insurance policies from three different magazines, allowing him to claim in the event of an accident.

The trial jury concluded that May had deliberately placed his legs under a train in order to claim the insurance. Had he succeeded, he would have received £500 for the loss of both legs.

**26 FEBRUARY** **1906** A crowd of almost 500 people gathered outside a cottage in Senghenydd, hoping to witness a ghostly phenomenon.

The occupant – a miner – was plagued by strange, disembodied rapping sounds that followed him wherever he went. Although he and his family moved house, the knocking occurred at each new property and the local vicar and police were determined to solve the mystery.

With the miner alone in an upstairs room, distinct raps were heard on the cottage walls. Although the room was in darkness, the policemen switched on their lamps as soon as they heard the bangs and saw nothing untoward. The miner moved to another room and, this time, the knocking appeared to come from inside an empty cupboard, far beyond his reach. In a third room, the noises were heard again, this time in full light. Now they apparently emanated from beneath the very chair on which the miner was sitting.

The vicar requested all present to join him in a prayer for peace, after which the unnamed miner asked for police protection, fearful that the mob outside might harm him if they believed that he was haunted.

**27 FEBRUARY** **1860** As *City of Paris* sailed towards Waterford, she met with *Nimrod*, whose captain asked the captain of the *Paris* how much he would charge for a tow to Milford Haven. *Paris* quoted £1,000 but *Nimrod* was only prepared to offer £100.

Although *Paris* suggested leaving the remuneration to be settled by the ships' owners, *Nimrod* refused all offers of help and, since the weather was moderate at the time and there was no apparent danger to life or property, *Paris* sailed on.

Nothing more was seen of *Nimrod* until seven o'clock the next morning, when she fired her guns in distress, having been driven into rocks at St David's Head by heavy seas. Although the sea was too rough to enable ropes to be thrown to the ship, she was close enough to shore for people on the cliffs to hear the plaintive cries of those on board and to see them falling to their knees and praying for survival.

When *Nimrod* finally split into three and sank, all fifty of her crew and passengers drowned, including several women and children.

**28 FEBRUARY** **1947** An inquest was held at Haverfordwest on the deaths of three soldiers, who died at the Anti-Aircraft School of Artillery on 11 February.

The inquest heard from Captain J.T. Palmer REME who stated that during a practice firing of the 3.7 inch gun, the back half of the breech ring blew off as a

HIGH STREET, HAVERFORDWEST.

*High Street,
Haverfordwest,
1950s. (Author's
collection)*

shell was fired, killing the three men and wounding seven others. He added that the gun was in good order and had been inspected only the previous day.

The coroner reasoned that this was a tragedy that could neither have been foreseen nor prevented and the inquest jury recorded a verdict of 'death due to multiple injuries caused by a gun explosion during firing practice.'

**1888** Coroner Mr Edwards held an inquest at Newport on the death of fifty-seven-year-old Caroline Mundy.  **29 FEBRUARY**

Caroline visited the Infirmary on 24 February complaining of a troublesome cough. Surgeon Mr W. Bassett prescribed cough medicine and dispenser John Jordan made up the mixture, but neither Bassett nor Jordan realised that Caroline and her husband were illiterate. Although the medicine was clearly labelled 'take one tablespoonful with water every four hours', nobody explained this to Caroline, who drank it at will. By that evening, she had taken at least four times the recommended dose, without water, and was complaining of stomach ache. Her husband sent for a doctor but, by the time he arrived, she had died.

Thus, the question for the inquest jury was whether the medicine had caused or hastened Mrs Mundy's death and, if so, were the surgeon and dispenser negligent.

Mr Jordan said that he made up the medicine from memory and accidentally omitted the paregoric – a preparation of opium. Mr Bassett, who conducted a post-mortem, stated that Mrs Mundy's heart was weak and fatty and that she died from heart disease, adding that, without paregoric, the medicine was completely harmless.

The coroner, who obviously found Jordan's insistence that the one dangerous component had been left out of the medicine highly suspicious, suggested that, since Bassett had an interest, an independent medical gentleman should be asked to examine Mrs Mundy's body. However, the jury didn't feel this necessary, recording a verdict of death from heart disease. The coroner recommended that future patients should be given verbal instructions on how to take their medicine.

# MARCH

*Shire Hall, Monmouth. (Author's collection)*

**1892** Nurse Mary Ann Grainger appeared at Cardiff Police Court charged under the Public Health Act with failing to disinfect her clothes.

In December 1891, Mrs Grainger was nursing a patient with scarlet fever and, when her landlady's son fell ill with the disease, the Cardiff medical officer suspected that Mrs Grainger might have brought it to the house. He prohibited her from working until her clothing had been thoroughly disinfected, in spite of which, she attended a confinement on 3 January. The new mother, Mrs Taylor, died four days later from complications arising from scarlet fever.

Mrs Grainger's defence counsel maintained that his client had no idea that she was in contravention of the Act and, in Mrs Taylor's case, she was summoned urgently in the middle of the night and dressed hurriedly. Having been deserted by her husband five years earlier, Mrs Grainger needed to work to support herself and therefore threw herself on the mercy of the court, since she would find it almost impossible to obtain employment if convicted.

Since Mrs Grainger had been told several times to disinfect her clothes, she could hardly plead ignorance as a defence for what the magistrates described as '...scattering death broadcast.' Saying that the offence was one of the utmost gravity, they fined her the maximum penalty of £5, plus costs.

**1886** Twenty-eight-year-old David Roberts was executed at Swansea by James Berry, for the murder of David Thomas on 23 October 1885.

In November 1885, Berry officiated at an execution at Norwich where the condemned man's head was pulled clean off his shoulders. Since then, Berry had experimented with shorter and shorter drops and, for Roberts – who weighed 13 stone – he planned to use a rope just 3ft 7in long.

Reporters were horrified to see Roberts's body heaving convulsively on the end of the rope for three minutes, before they were asked to leave the execution chamber. Berry and the prison officials refused to explain why the reporters were so precipitously dismissed and insisted that Roberts died instantly, but the reporters were equally insistent that he twitched and struggled to draw breath for several minutes.

In 1888, a Home Office Memorandum prohibited all drops of less than 5ft.

**1927** Having spent a week waiting for favourable weather conditions, John Godfrey Parry Thomas took his high-speed car, 'Babs', onto Pendine Sands. Fifteen minutes later, he became the first ever driver to die in pursuit of the land-speed record.

Thomas was driving against the advice of his doctor, having barely recovered from a severe bout of influenza. Nevertheless, he appeared confident, if a little nervous and preoccupied. He was killed on his third run, during which his speed was clocked at 179.5 miles per hour.

Onlookers watched as the car swerved, skidded, somersaulted and then burst into flames. Although mechanics and a doctor reached the car in under a minute, forty-two-year-old Thomas was dead and, in order to extricate his body from the burning wreckage, the crew were forced to break his legs. A post-mortem examination showed that he died instantly, scalped from the nape of his neck to his forehead, his skull almost severed from the base. It was established

*Pendine. (Author's collection)*

that a driving chain had broken or become disengaged, either hitting Thomas on the head or wrapping around his neck.

'Babs' was buried in the sand dunes on Pendine Sands but was excavated and restored in 1969.

4 MARCH **1895** An inquest was held on the death of twenty-three-year-old Mark Morris, who died in Swansea Prison from erysipelas – a bacterial infection arising from wounds apparently inflicted by the police.

On 15 February, magistrates sentenced Morris to one month's imprisonment, having found him guilty of trying to prevent the arrest of an old man, who was involved in a scuffle outside a pub. At the inquest, Mark's mother recalled being told by neighbours that the police were killing her son. She rushed to the scene to find blood streaming from Mark's head and her daughter with her arms around her brother's neck, begging the police not to kill him. Several more witnesses spoke of the excessive force used against Morris by the police, even though he was not resisting them.

The inquest resulted in a verdict of manslaughter against three officers – William Evans, George Perkins and Thomas Thomas. The three appeared at the Glamorganshire Assizes, where they were found guilty and each sentenced to three months' imprisonment with hard labour.

5 MARCH **1868** Captain Gwyn Lewis, John Newall-Moore and Andrew Macintosh-Bell appeared at the Glamorgan Assizes.

The case against them stemmed from a letter written to a local newspaper, in which George James May of Neath wrote: '...a gentleman was in the habit of watching ladies bathing on the Briton Ferry sands with a powerful opera glass.' Lewis was harbour master at Briton Ferry and jumped to the conclusion that he was the subject of May's letter and that such an insult deserved a public horse whipping.

Lewis appeared at a cricket match, waiting until May took the wicket before marching across the field of play, with Newall-Moore and Macintosh-Bell behind him. He asked May to confirm his identity then struck him twice on the head with the butt of a whip.

May snatched up a stump with which to defend himself but was quickly disarmed and a scuffle ensued, during which Lewis hit May on the head, knocking him unconscious. May was stretchered off the pitch, so badly injured that he had to spend the night with his head covered with ice to reduce the swelling.

Lewis, Newall-Moore and Macintosh-Bell appeared before magistrates in Swansea charged with unlawful assault and beating, with intent to kill and murder. The Bench heard that Macintosh-Bell took a swordstick to the cricket match and, although he did not draw it, he struck a bystander with the cane. May's solicitor also pointed out that the men had kicked and beaten his client while he was on the ground and that Newall-Moore had shouted, 'Kill the ******* out of the way!'

The defence insisted that there was no intent to kill but a case of common assault, which May brought on himself by publicly and falsely maligning Lewis. The magistrates agreed that there was no intent, so the charge at the Assizes was the lesser one of unlawful wounding. All three defendants were acquitted.

**1914** Edgar Lewis George Bindon appeared at the Cardiff Assizes charged with murdering twenty-year-old Maud Mullholland.     6 MARCH

Bindon and Maud were neighbours but when they started courting, Maud's parents were appalled, feeling that Bindon was not good enough for their daughter. At their insistence, Maud broke off the relationship and began courting Bernard Campion.

Bindon was furious and, on 4 November 1913, he appeared at Maud's house brandishing a loaded revolver and demanding to see her. Maud's father managed to disarm him and Maud angrily told Bindon she wanted nothing more to do with him. The following day, the spurned sweetheart bought another revolver.

On 9 November, Maud and Bernard went for a walk and Maud left Bernard at his tram, before walking home alone. On Cowbridge Road, Bindon suddenly appeared out of the darkness and shot her several times. There were several witnesses and Bindon made no effort to escape, saying, 'It is alright. I have had my revenge and will die with a good heart.'

There was little doubt about his guilt, yet his trial jury deliberated for more than an hour before returning a guilty verdict. It later emerged that, while they were unanimous in believing that Bindon was guilty, they were unsure about whether or not to recommend mercy. The three jurors who wanted a strong recommendation for mercy won the debate but their victory proved meaningless, since nineteen-year-old Bindon was hanged by John Ellis at Cardiff Prison on 25 March 1914.

**1827** When livestock owned by Llanfoist farmer William Watkins began to sicken and die, he and his servant Thomas Jenkins went in search of Mary Nicholas, along with village blacksmith, Henry Evans, and shoemaker John Prosser.     7 MARCH

Believing that she had bewitched the animals, the men seized ninety-year-old Mary and dragged her almost a mile to Watkins's farm, attracting a crowd of around seventy spectators. When they reached the farm, Mary was made to kneel behind a young horse and bless it.

Since the only way to remove a witch's power was to spill her blood, one man drew a thorn across Mary's arm. Next, she was stripped to the waist and intimately searched for the extra nipple that witches possess to allow the devil to suckle. Not finding it, the men cut off a hank of her hair, since a witch's hair would not burn. In doing so, they found a wart on her head, which they decided was the missing nipple. They then discussed ducking her to see if she would float but fortunately the crowd dissuaded them, pointing out the possible consequences of plunging such an old woman into cold water.

Mary was eventually rescued by her daughter and her four tormentors charged with assault and inciting a riot. They appeared at the Monmouth Assizes in April, where they were found not guilty of rioting but guilty of assault. The judge commented that it was such an unusual case that he needed time to consider an appropriate punishment and deferred sentencing the culprits, eventually deciding on various terms of imprisonment for all four.

**8 MARCH** **1886** As the steam tug *Rifleman* waited to reverse into West Bute Dock at Cardiff, there was a sudden explosion. Large portions of the tug were blown skywards, along with the unfortunate crew members, and, when the vast cloud of steam cleared, what remained of the hull could be seen sinking.

There were plenty of boats on hand to attempt to rescue the crew, some of whom had actually been blown onto dry land. George Phillips and George Arthur Clare were found alive, although badly injured, and the bodies of James Henry Pill (or Pell), John Lovell and Thomas Owens were recovered soon afterwards, while mate William Henry Gerrish was missing presumed dead. All four were married and between them left nineteen fatherless children.

Clare and Phillips were rushed to the *Hamadryad* Hospital Ship, where Clare died within moments of arrival and Phillips early the following morning. Yet perhaps the unluckiest victim was Charles Hunt, who was working on board the ship *Clothilde*, several hundred yards from the explosion, and was struck by the remains of the *Rifleman's* boiler and practically decapitated.

A later inquest into the deaths of the victims identified a possible defect with one of the ship's boiler's safety valves, into which it appeared that a pin had been deliberately screwed to prevent the sudden escape of steam.

**9 MARCH** **1891** The blizzards and strong gales affecting much of the United Kingdom were especially severe in South Wales. At Cwmavon, the chimney of The Rolling Mill Inn blew down, crashing through the roof of a neighbouring house and killing thirteen-year-old Thomas John Griffiths and his six-year-old brother, David William, as they slept.

Fifteen-foot deep snowdrifts brought trains to a halt and at Cwmtillery, colliers John Lewis and Alfred Price were found buried in the snow. Lewis was dead and Price was suffering from exposure and hypothermia and is believed to have died soon afterwards. A similar fate befell a woman in the Rhondda Valley.

**10 MARCH** **1888** Sailor David Davies was tried at Cardiff for the murder of his wife, Mary Jane. That he had killed her by cutting her throat was not disputed and the jury were asked to rule on his mental state at the time.

Davies and his wife had no home of their own. While he was at sea, Mary lived with her mother in Swansea and her husband joined her whenever he had shore leave. Davies and his mother-in-law didn't see eye to eye and sometimes Davies stayed at his brother-in-law's house without his wife, seeming depressed and complaining of living on 'uncomfortable terms' with his wife's mother.

On 7 February, Mrs Walters heard a shout of 'Murder' from the bedroom shared by Davies and his wife and found her daughter with her throat cut from ear to ear. Mary bled to death before medical assistance arrived and her husband went straight to the police station and handed himself in.

At the trial, Dr Pringle, the superintendent of the County Lunatic Asylum at Bridgend, gave his opinion that Davies was of unsound mind. Davies had a sister who was 'hopelessly insane', another described as 'an imbecile' and a third who suffered from temporary fits of insanity. Having heard that, the jury found him guilty but insane and he was ordered to be confined during Her Majesty's Pleasure. He was sent to Broadmoor Criminal Lunatic Asylum.

**1886** Twenty-month-old Susan Lily Evans died at Cardiff.     11 MARCH

In November 1885, Susan, her mother and her three siblings were forced into the Workhouse, where they remained for twenty-two days. Benjamin Evans swore that he did whatever he could to provide for his family but was hampered by his wife's addiction to drink. Mrs Evans told a different story, accusing her husband of neglecting her and their children for the past two years, forcing them to sleep on bare boards and refusing them money for food, even when he had it in his pocket.

Under duress, Evans agreed to support his family and moved them to rooms in Helen Street. Landlady Kate Bennett observed that Mrs Evans had only one dress, which was almost transparent with wear. Evans had no furniture and would only allow a fire to be lit when he was at home and, although he paid his rent regularly, he provided no food for his family other than bread with a scraping of butter. At all times, he ensured that there was plenty of cheese and bacon in the house, which he alone was allowed to eat. He refused to buy milk for Susan and forced his eight-year-old child to beg for food on the streets. When neighbours took pity on Susan and bought beef extract for her, Evans ate it himself.

Kate eventually tired of Benjamin's neglect of his family and, on 1 March, called in a doctor to examine Susan. The surgeon could find no evidence of illness but considered Susan to be very underweight and ordered her mother to feed her a quart of milk a day. Mrs Evans was unable to persuade Benjamin to pay for the milk and, when Susan died on 10 March, she weighed just 8lbs 6ozs.

Evans was charged with causing Susan's death by negligence, appearing at the South Wales Assizes in Swansea. Found guilty, he appealed for clemency, for the sake of his wife and children. Remarking that he had shown very little paternal affection and could easily have deprived himself of some of his cheese and bacon to provide milk for his baby, the judge sentenced him to ten months' imprisonment.

**1950** A flight was due to land at RAF Llandow at around 3 p.m., carrying   12 MARCH seventy-eight rugby fans returning from a match in Ireland, which ended in victory and the Triple Crown for the Welsh team.

*The Law Courts, Cardiff. (Author's collection)*

Police Constable John Davies saw the Avro Tudor V plane approaching the airfield at an unusually low altitude. The pilot increased the engine speed to gain height but the plane stalled and nosedived to the ground, just missing a farmhouse and only yards from Sigginston village.

Davies telephoned for assistance before cycling to the site of the crash, to be met by a scene of devastation. Many of the plane's seats had broken free from their mountings and were piled at the front of the aircraft, their occupants still strapped in, while bodies and personal effects were strewn around the field.

Although eight people were brought out alive from the wreckage, only three survived, all of whom were sitting at the rear of the plane. Two men walked from the crash virtually unscathed – brothers-in-law, who sat in the mid-section on the journey out to Dublin. On the return journey, they were late boarding the aircraft, having gone to buy flowers for their wives.

Many of the victims' relatives witnessed the crash as they arrived to collect passengers. One seventy-five-year-old widow lost all three of her sons – all of whom were married with children – and four children were orphaned by the crash. The final death toll was eighty crew and passengers, making it the worst ever air crash to that date in terms of fatalities.

The cause of the crash was never satisfactorily explained although several theories were advanced at the enquiry held at the Law Courts, Cardiff. One was human error, although the pilot was experienced. Alternatively, the plane may have been improperly loaded, with too much weight at the front, causing a shift in the centre of gravity and making it unstable. A third suggestion was that the pilot's seat broke free from its mountings as the plane climbed and accelerated.

At the inquest, Dr Robert Miller testified that forty-five of the victims had died from shock. The jury returned verdicts of 'accidental death', although the plane's owners were found guilty of contravening the aircraft's Certificate of Airworthiness and fined £50, with £100 costs.

13 MARCH **1889** Zulu Thomas Allen was tried at the Glamorganshire Assizes for the wilful murder of Frederick Kent.

At 5 a.m. on 19 February, the landlady of The Gloucester Arms, Swansea, was awakened by the sound of a match striking and saw a 'coloured' man in her bedroom. Mrs Kent woke her husband and, as he grappled with the intruder, she reached for the pistol that her husband kept under his pillow and fired, hitting the intruder's right thigh. He immediately fell to his hands and knees and crawled under the bed.

He then seized a mirror and flung it at the Kents, before blowing out the candle that lit the room and making his escape. When Mrs Kent relit the candle, she found her husband bleeding from his throat and chest and he died from his injuries later that morning.

All the police needed to do was to find a man with a bullet wound and within an hour of Frederick Kent's death they apprehended twenty-six-year-old Allen, who had a bullet from Kent's gun lodged in his thigh.

Allen explained that he was taken to the pub by a prostitute, who told him to go upstairs and wait under the bed until she arrived. However, the jury didn't believe him and he was found guilty and hanged at Cardiff Prison on 10 April.

**1884** William Anthony was driving his train across a temporary bridge over the **14 MARCH** River Avon on the Rhondda and Swansea Bay Railway and was halfway across when the bridge collapsed.

The engine and seven wagons fell into the river, with Anthony and his stoker, Patrick Hopkin, whose skull was fractured in the accident. Hopkin was pulled from the river dead and at the inquest Anthony stated that, in his opinion, the collapse was caused by the train jarring or jerking, rather than by excess weight or speed.

An inquiry showed the bridge to be in good order and made from high quality materials. However it spanned almost 70ft, without any props in the middle and, in the opinion of the inquest jury, was simply not up to bearing the weight of the train and fully loaded wagons. They fell short of finding anybody criminally negligent, returning a verdict of 'accidental death'.

**1912** William Edward Williams succumbed to meningitis, resulting from a **15 MARCH** lacerated eyeball. Williams was the referee at a football fixture at Wattstown, where twenty-three-year-old plumber and amateur footballer Edwin George Hundsford played on the losing side. Taking exception to a remark made by Williams, Hundsford sought him out after the final whistle and punched him, and, when Williams died, Hundsford was charged with his manslaughter.

Having pleaded guilty at the Swansea Assizes, Hundsford was sentenced to just one month's imprisonment with hard labour. Williams's mother later unsuccessfully sued the South Wales Football Association for compensation.

**1945** Twenty-nine-year-old Lily Grossley died in Bridgend Hospital. **16 MARCH**

The area around Bridgend had been in uproar since 10 March, when seventy Germans escaped from Island Farm Prisoner of War Camp. Mrs Grossley's husband told police that on 12 March, he and Lily were walking at Porthcawl when some Germans tried to steal her handbag. Grossley, a Canadian soldier, drew his service revolver to defend her and the Germans fled. Firing after them, Grossley claimed to have accidentally shot Lily.

New Promenade, Porthcawl.

*New Promenade, Porthcawl. (Author's collection)*

Lily backed his statement but the police soon realised that the Grossleys were not being entirely truthful. Although the couple had a two-year-old son, police found that they had never married and that Lily's real name was Lily Griffiths. Grossley, who was absent without leave from his unit, already had a wife in Canada.

When the police confronted the couple with their deception, both changed their statements, now saying that Grossley tried to shoot himself, accidentally shooting Lily as she struggled to disarm him. According to Lily, he suffered from phosphorous burns on his back and was taking strong medication for pain. He had been drinking on the night of the shooting and, despondent about the prospect of his imminent return to Canada, decided to commit suicide.

When Lily died, Howard Grossley was charged with wilful murder, appearing at the Swansea Assizes in July. Shortly before her death, Lily herself had stated that the shooting was an accident and Grosslcy's defence counsel insisted that, at very worst, Grossley could only be charged with manslaughter. However the prosecution stressed that the angle of the gunshot wound suggested that the gun was deliberately aimed at Lily. This argument proved more convincing to the jury, who found Grossley guilty.

Thirty-seven-year-old Howard Joseph Grossley was executed at Cardiff on 5 September 1945.

**17 MARCH    1920** The trial of Thomas 'Tom' Caler for wilful murder concluded at Cardiff.

On 14 December 1919, Alice Ali of Christiana Street, Cardiff noticed that her neighbour's front door was ajar. Knowing that Ahmed Ibrahim was away on business, Alice called out to his wife, Gladys May, who should have been at home with eight-month-old Aysha Emily and two-year-old May. When there was no response, Alice went inside, finding Gladys and Aysha with their throats cut.

Alice raced to the police station, returning with Inspector Adams, who found May alive and well in a bedroom. Post-mortem examinations on the two victims indicated that someone had raped Gladys after her death.

The house had been ransacked but the only thing missing was a gramophone with a horn. A few broken pieces of the horn had been left behind, as had a suitcase, which had no connection to the Ibrahim family. Inside were an empty razor case and some letters addressed to Tom Caler.

Caler, who came from Zanzibar, was a fireman aboard SS *Fountains Abbey*, which was docked at Cardiff. Nightwatchman Pridu Rahn told the police that Caler returned to ship at about 2 a.m., carrying a gramophone and a parcel. When Rahn approached Caler, he threw the parcel into the water.

Caler claimed to have been on board his ship from 10 p.m. onwards. However, one of his shipmates confirmed Rahn's story, saying that Caler was ashore from 3 p.m. on 13 December until 2 a.m. on 14 December and was carrying a gramophone and some broken records when he returned.

When the police located a witness who had seen Caler near Christiana Street at around 8 p.m. on 13 December, Caler was charged with two counts of wilful murder. 'I don't know nothing about it. I never kill. I was boozed last night. After the public-house closed, I went to Maria Street and smoked an Indian hookah,' protested Caler.

Although no relationship between Gladys and Caler was ever established, the evidence against him was so strong that the jury found him guilty, even with no apparent motive for the killings. Regardless of whether Caler and Gladys were intimately involved or complete strangers, he was hanged by John Ellis at Cardiff Prison on 14 April 1920.

**1891** The Honourable Stephen Coleridge saw two little boys, aged about five, **18 MARCH** begging in the streets of Cardiff. They were ragged, cold and hungry and one was barefoot, with badly bleeding feet.

Coleridge called a policeman and the boys were taken to the police station and then to the Workhouse, while their parents were traced.

Frederick Radford had been out of work for two weeks and claimed that the money his son earned begging was the family's only income. Radford, his wife and their seven children had just one bed in their filthy house, on which the whole family slept.

When the police visited John Collins in his equally squalid home, he pulled a handful of silver coins out of his pocket and assured them that his boy had no need to go out begging. Yet although Collins earned around £2 a week, the only food in the house was a crust of dried bread.

Both fathers appeared at Cardiff Police Court charged with sending their children out to beg. Each was fined £5, or one month's imprisonment with hard labour, while the boys were sent to a Children's Home.

**1869** Quack doctor and herbalist John Howells appeared at the Glamorganshire **19 MARCH** Assizes charged with feloniously killing and slaying Sarah John at Merthyr Tydfil.

Sarah gave birth to a baby, who then died, leaving her breasts engorged with milk. She developed painful abscesses, which were treated by surgeons Mr Ward and Mr Probert.

When the abscesses didn't heal, Sarah consulted Howells, who recommended healing plasters. Almost as soon as the plasters were applied, Sarah began

*General view of Cardiff. (Author's collection)*

vomiting and complaining of a burning sensation in her breasts. Her husband called Mr Ward, who removed the plasters and treated Sarah until she was better.

Although she stopped vomiting, the abscesses were as bad as ever, the pain driving Sarah almost out of her mind. She went back to Howells, who once again gave her plasters to apply to her breasts. Sarah was seized with sickness and diarrhoea and this time Ward was unable to save her. She died four days after her appointment with Howells.

Ward sent the plasters to Professor Alfred Swaine Taylor at Guy's Hospital, who found them to contain a mixture of white, brown and yellow arsenic. Since applying such large quantities of arsenic to open wounds would result in its absorption into the body, Sarah's death was deemed due to arsenic poisoning.

Unfortunately, the prosecution failed to prove that Sarah had obtained the plasters from Howells and, without such proof, there was nothing to implicate him in her murder, since Sarah could have obtained the lethal plasters from anybody. The presiding judge instructed the jury to acquit Howells, who walked from court a free man.

20 MARCH **1874** The Usk Petty Sessions dealt with charges relating to thefts of bedding and clothing from Monmouth county gaol.

On 14 February, prison wardress Diana Bateman boarded the Monmouth train carrying a bundle, which she no longer had on her return to Usk later that day. As items had been reported missing from the prison, the Usk police contacted their Monmouth colleagues and Sergeant McEvoy visited pawnbroker William Henry Price to ask if Diana had ever pledged any items. Price insisted that she hadn't.

McEvoy questioned Diana's married daughter, Diana Chard, who surrendered three pawn tickets from Price's shop. Once again, Price denied dealing with

Diana Bateman and was promptly arrested for receiving stolen property, as was Diana's husband, Thomas Bateman. They too appeared at the Petty Sessions, along with another wardress, who pawned some blankets on Diana's behalf. (Diana Chard would also have been summoned but gave birth only the previous day.) Finally, John and Louisa Ward and John and Mary Mason, were charged with receiving stolen goods on 12 March. On that day, Diana stole three blankets, twelve pairs of stockings and three sheets, which she later gave to the Wards, who shared the spoils with their neighbours, the Masons.

Magistrates dismissed the charge against Thomas Bateman, who worked away from home and had no idea of his wife's activities, even though he was wearing a pair of stolen stockings when apprehended. The Masons, John Ward and the other wardress were also discharged but Price and Louisa Ward were committed for trial at the Quarter Sessions, which were due to open on 24 March. (Both were acquitted.)

Diana Bateman was sentenced to six months' imprisonment with hard labour for each offence. However, since she named those who received the stolen property, her sentences were concurrent, meaning she would only actually spend six months in prison.

**1903** Twenty-one-year-old Thomas Lewis appeared at the Cardiff Assizes charged with murdering his sweetheart, Ethel Adlam, at Ystrad.

On 27 December 1902, Lewis, Ethel and her mother were visiting his father, when a drunken quarrel flared up. Lewis stormed out of the house with Ethel. When they didn't return, Ethel's mother went to look for them, finding her daughter's hat on the bank of the Rhondda river.

Lewis was found sleeping off his intoxication beneath a henhouse in his father's garden. Asked about Ethel, he said that she went home hours earlier,

21 MARCH

*Lower Ystrad, 1967. (Author's collection)*

LOWER YSTRAD

*Mr Justice
Phillimore.
(Author's collection)*

but later, with Ethel still missing, he said she got into a temper with him and threw herself into the river. Ethel drowned in the Rhondda, in water less than a foot deep. If she committed suicide, she tore off most of her clothes and scratched her face before doing so.

When Lewis was charged with her wilful murder, he changed his story again, explaining that Ethel tried to drown herself and fainted. The scratches and disarrangement of her clothing occurred as he struggled to rescue her.

At Lewis's trial, the prosecution suggested that he had either drowned Ethel by holding her underwater or had attempted to rape her, forcing her into the river to escape him.

Mr Justice Phillimore instructed the jury to consider several scenarios. If Ethel committed suicide, could Lewis have saved her? Even if he could, he was not bound to do so and was therefore not guilty of her murder. If Ethel was escaping a felony, falling into the water and drowning, then Lewis would be guilty of manslaughter. If, in the course of this felony, Ethel was rendered unconscious or in any way unable to save herself from drowning, this was murder, as was the case if Lewis deliberately placed her in the water or physically prevented her from getting out.

To Phillimore's obvious surprise, the jury found Lewis guilty only of manslaughter, adding a recommendation for mercy. His hands tied by the verdict, Phillimore sentenced Lewis to fifteen years' penal servitude.

**22 MARCH** **1859** During heavy gales, a French lugger and a Dutch brig beached on Cefn Sidan Sands. Between tides, the two boats attracted a great number of fascinated visitors from the area, among them three young boys from Pembrey.

Brothers Evan and David Davies, aged fourteen and twelve, and nine-year-old Henry Morgan, went to see the wrecks and were about to head for home via Kidwelly Quay when they realised that they were cut off by the tide. In full view of helpless spectators on the shore, the boys ran backwards and forwards, waving their arms and screaming desperately for help, until the sea rose and they finally vanished beneath the water.

**23 MARCH** **1831** As the steam packet *Frolic* travelled from Haverfordwest to Bristol, she hit rough weather at Ness Sands. Precisely what happened next is not known but the ship was wrecked, with the loss of all crew and passengers.

Nobody knew exactly how many people were on board *Frolic* but it was estimated that between seventy and eighty lost their lives and, over the next few days, several bodies were washed ashore.

The captain, a Lieutenant in the Royal Navy, was lashed to the ship's rigging so it was assumed that the ship hadn't sunk immediately. Captain Jenkins left a pregnant widow and eight children – a ninth had died only a few days earlier. The ship's steward also left a pregnant widow and four small children.

Most of the passengers came from Milford Haven, Tenby and Haverfordwest and included eighteen sailors, on their way to join South Sea whalers, three runaway apprentices and army officers Colonel Gordon, General McCleod and Major Boyd, who was travelling with his wife and three servants.

**1870** Coroner Mr William Vaughan James held an inquest on the death of stationmaster William Henry Williams. The waiting room at Tenby Station was a small wooden building, at the end of which was a ticket and telegraph office. As Williams sat at his desk on 23 March, the window was suddenly shattered by an enormous stone, which struck Williams on the head, killing him instantly.

The stone, which weighed 14lbs, came from the limestone quarry about 200 yards from the station. Workmen blasting a large rock drilled a hole, which they filled with gunpowder and detonated. The explosion sent chunks of rock flying in all directions, the largest of which crashed through the station window, neatly slicing off a portion of the stationmaster's skull before shattering the waiting room door.

The inquest jury heard allegations that the quarrymen had been negligent in failing to adequately protect the blast site and five labourers were charged with feloniously killing Williams.

In the event, only foreman Edward Manuel stood trial for manslaughter at the Pembrokeshire Assizes. However, since the judge felt that it was impossible for anyone to have foreseen that the stone would be projected towards the station, or that it would travel so far, he ordered the jury to acquit Manuel.

**24 MARCH**

**1900** Mrs Bowen of Pontygwaith wondered aloud what had happened to her lodger of nine years, Rees Davies, whose bed had not been slept in and who had not appeared for breakfast. Suddenly, Mrs Bowen's ten-year-old son piped up: 'He has fallen down Enoch's quarry and been killed.' The boy told his mother that he had dreamed that a fatal accident had befallen fifty-year-old Rees, who was now lying at the bottom of the quarry.

**25 MARCH**

*Pontygwaith, 1919.*
*(Author's collection)*

Rees was indeed dead, exactly as the child's dream had foretold. He occasionally visited friends at Penygraig and the inquest supposed that he had missed his way home in the dark and accidentally turned off the path too soon. A verdict of 'accidental death' was recorded.

**26 MARCH**   **1859**  Twenty-six-year-old cripple Matthew Francis appeared at the Monmouthshire Assizes, charged with the wilful murder of his wife, Sarah, at Newport on 12 March. Francis wanted only to join his wife in heaven but his wish was thwarted, at least temporarily, since two key witnesses were ill and prosecution counsel Mr McMahon asked for a postponement until the summer Assizes. Hence it was not until 4 August that Francis finally got his day in court and reluctantly pleaded not guilty.

The court heard that Francis and Sarah argued constantly throughout their marriage and had both behaved violently towards each other. Sarah summoned Francis for beating her but the case was dismissed when she refused to appear against him. Eventually Sarah left, but Francis was bereft without her and tried numerous times to persuade her to return home. On 12 March, after she told him that she would never come back, he cut her throat.

Francis never denied killing his wife. He suffered a violent epileptic fit in court and begged doctors who rushed to attend him, 'Let me go to her.' However it was left to the jury to decide his fate. When they found him guilty and Mr Justice Willes pronounced the death sentence, Francis responded, 'It is a just sentence. I deserve it. I am willing to die.'

He finally got his wish on 23 August, when he was executed at Monmouth Prison by William Calcraft. Even so, it took him more than five minutes to expire.

**27 MARCH**   **1874**  Mother and son Caroline and Jonathan Flower appeared at the Monmouth Assizes charged with the manslaughter of Jonathan's wife, Maria, at Trynant.

Maria had been partially paralysed by illness for almost eight years and, around Christmas 1873, she became totally bedridden. Jonathan worked long hours, although he spent most of his wages on drink and his wife's daily care was left to seventy-four-year-old Caroline, assisted by John and Maria's fifteen-year-old daughter.

Forty-five-year-old Maria was kept in the most terrible conditions imaginable. Although there were comfortable beds upstairs, she slept downstairs on a mattress balanced on heaps of stones. Unable to move, Maria lay in her own urine and excrement, until 'Granny' Flower decided that she should be bedded on straw like an animal. Even then, Granny didn't bother with clean straw but used soiled bedding from the hen house.

Maria was starved, beaten and abused until eventually, concerned neighbours intervened, dragging Jonathan's own bed downstairs and providing nourishing food for Maria. Sadly, their intervention was too late and, when Maria died, surgeon Mr Hale found her emaciated and covered with bruises and bedsores. He gave the cause of death as exhaustion, accelerated by ill-treatment and, at an inquest held at Crumlin by coroner Mr W.H. Brewer, the jury returned a verdict of manslaughter against Jonathan and Caroline.

At their trial, the presiding judge Lord Coleridge summed up the case in such a way that the jury could do little else but find both prisoners guilty. Coleridge sentenced each to twenty years' penal servitude, remarking as he did so that he was afraid to trust himself to voice his opinion on their conduct.

**1900** At daybreak, train brakeman Cornelius Tutsall spotted a body on the rails **28 MARCH** close to the viaduct near Pontypridd. He reported his observation to the police, who found the mangled remains of a man, whose pockets contained 12s, a penknife, keys, a watch and chain and a train ticket.

The police put what remained of him in a sack and took him to the Workhouse infirmary, but were turned away on the grounds that the mortuary there was only intended for inmates of that institution.

Police Sergeant Rees and PC Phillips carried the remains to the mortuary at Treforest, but were told that there was no room for the body. The two policemen had to lay the body on the grass, while the sexton accompanied PC Phillips to the home of the clerk to the burial board. Eventually permission was gained for the dead man to be placed in the cemetery mortuary and the police set about identifying him.

They soon heard of a man missing from Clydach Vale. After appearing at the police court on 26 March and being fined 10s for committing a nuisance, thirty-two-year-old David Hughes went to Cardiff with a friend to watch a rugby match. Somehow he and his friend got separated and Hughes never arrived home.

Mrs Hughes identified the watch and chain in the dead man's pockets but could offer no suggestions as to how her husband came to be on the railway line. The police found out nothing more about Hughes, other than that he was last seen at Cardiff, and a verdict of accidental death was eventually recorded at the inquest on his mysterious demise.

**1859** Henry and Ellen Jayne appeared at the Monmouthshire Assizes charged **29 MARCH** with the manslaughter of Ann White.

On 15 March, Henry and Ellen of Llangattock left home to hawk the tins that Henry had fashioned. They had only been married for a few months but had six children between them, who they left in the care of the eldest, who was eleven years old. They neglected to leave any food, with the exception of the remains of a small loaf of bread.

The Jaynes went on a pub crawl and didn't return for several days, while their children grew hungrier and hungrier, and were forced to beg food from the neighbours.

On the morning of 19 March, two-year-old Ann White – Ellen Jayne's illegitimate daughter – was found dead in bed by her older brother. Informed of her death, the coroner ordered a post-mortem examination and surgeon Mr J. Brewer determined that Ann died from diseased lungs, which showed signs of tuberculosis. Her liver was double the normal size and there was no food whatsoever in her shrunken stomach and bowels. Brewer was certain that lack of sustenance hastened Ann's death but she was so ill that he doubted whether she would have been capable of eating, had food been available to her.

At the Jaynes' trial, presiding judge Mr Baron Channell told the jury that, on Brewer's evidence, want of food could hardly be cited as the cause of death and suggested that the prisoners should be discharged. After a few minutes' deliberation, the jury agreed, pronouncing the Jaynes 'not guilty.'

**30 MARCH**　**1861** Twenty-five-year-old Thomas Carroll appeared at the Monmouthshire Assizes charged with the manslaughter of Bryan Fary.

Fary was a travelling Irish tinker and, in November 1860, he was living at Pontypool, since his granddaughter was about to be married to Carroll. A pre-nuptial celebration took place in the local pub, during which large quantities of beer, cider, port wine and whisky were consumed, and, perhaps inevitably, a fight broke out.

The fight ended when Carroll dashed out of the pub, returning with a long stick, which was as thick as a man's wrist. Swearing and cursing, he threatened to do serious damage to a number of people present and, as he swung the stick round, it connected with the side of Fary's head. Fary, who was in his eighties, fell to the floor unconscious, blood pouring from his mouth, nose and ears.

He died a few days later, when a post-mortem examination showed that the cause of death was severe lung disease, although the surgeon stated that the injuries to Fary's head had doubtless accelerated his end.

The key issues for the jury were whether or not the blow had directly caused – or even hastened – Fary's death and whether it was intentional or accidental. The jury decided that the blow was intentional, finding Carroll guilty of manslaughter and he was sentenced to nine months' imprisonment with hard labour.

**31 MARCH**　**1909** William Joseph Foy appeared at the Cardiff Assizes charged with murdering prostitute Mary Ann 'Sloppy' Rees.

Her death occurred on the night of 23/24 December 1908 at a disused coke oven in Ynysfach. Sloppy and Foy walked there from Merthyr Tydfil, with John Bassett and Mary Ann Graney, but, when they arrived, Sloppy was obviously annoyed and flounced off alone. Foy went after her, returning fifteen minutes later and laughingly explaining that she wouldn't be returning as he had thrown her down the shaft of a blast furnace.

Bassett and Mary Ann Graney persuaded him to give himself up and escorted him back to Merthyr, where he met two policemen patrolling on the High Street. 'I want you to lock me up,' he told the surprised officers, explaining that he had thrown Sloppy down a hole at the old works because she threatened to inform the authorities that he was living off her immoral earnings.

By the time his case came to court, Foy had changed his story, claiming that Sloppy's death was an accident. He stated that, having caught up with her, he tried to persuade her to come back to their friends, grabbing her arm and trying to pull her with him. Sloppy struggled, accidentally falling backwards down the 30ft-deep shaft.

Yet nothing about Foy's cavalier behaviour at the time of her death supported his claim that she died accidentally. Her friends heard no screams and Foy laughed when he told them of Sloppy's fate, making no mention of any accident. The jury found him guilty as charged and he was sentenced to death.

An appeal failed and Foy went to the gallows at Swansea Prison on 8 May 1909. He appeared before executioner Henry Pierrepoint smoking and wearing a jaunty sprig of fern in his buttonhole and, such was Pierrepoint's dexterity that he managed to place the hood over Foy's head and hang him without even breaking the condemned man's last cigarette.

# APRIL

*Pontypridd, 1906. (Author's collection)*

**1 APRIL** **1942** Cardiff coroner Gerald Tudor held an inquest on three privates from the Welsh Regiment, who drowned in the River Taff while taking part in training manoeuvres.

On 22 March, the men were ordered to cross the Taff, while dressed in full battle order, and Corporal Aneurin Williams told the inquest that he stepped into a hole in the river bed and found himself up to his neck in water. Although he looked for his men, they had disappeared from view in the deep pool.

The coroner recorded three verdicts of 'death by misadventure', adding that William Duff, John Menkavitch and Joseph Robinson died for their country, even though they hadn't lost their lives on a foreign field of battle.

**2 APRIL** **1930** Workmen started painting the Clarence Road Bridge in Cardiff on 23 February 1930, and the staging on which they worked was dismantled and re-erected several times as the men progressed over the bridge. It was thoroughly tested at every stage but, on 2 April, it gave way, sending Leonard Buley and cousins Sidney and George Robb into the River Taff.

Those working further along the bridge, heard a crash and saw that a section of staging had collapsed. They threw planks and ropes to their colleagues in the water and Buley managed to grab a piece of wood but couldn't hold on. George Robb swam towards Buley and supported him but the muddy river was flowing very fast and the three were rapidly carried downstream. Their bodies were pulled from the river three-quarters of an hour later and, in spite of prolonged attempts at artificial respiration, all three drowned.

At the inquest, foreman Alexander Gordon Robb, who was Sidney's brother, could only theorise that all three must have put their weight on one plank. The inquest jury returned verdicts of 'accidentally drowned', finding no evidence of any negligence in the construction of the staging. George Robb was the only one of the three who could swim and it was thought that he could easily have saved himself, had he not tried to help his workmates.

**3 APRIL** **1861** Many local and national newspapers printed an account of the grim death of John Rees at Mountain Ash.

Rees, a labourer in a lime works, accidentally fell through the crust on top of the burning lime. His desperate screams brought his workmates rushing to assist him but they were unable to extricate him and had to watch and listen as he slowly roasted to death in the kiln.

At the subsequent inquest, the jury returned a verdict of accidental death on Rees, who was in his thirties and described as a 'steady, well-conducted man.'

**4 APRIL** **1808** Nineteen-year-old William Williams was executed at Cardiff, having been found guilty of the murder of twelve-year-old David William (or Williams) at Llantrissant.

David told a playmate that William was guilty of a shocking crime and, when this gossip filtered back to William, he waited in a field to catch David alone. Having taken issue with the boy, William knocked him down and kicked him several times in the head and stomach. He then deliberately bent David's body backwards until the child's spine snapped, before cutting a stake from a nearby hedgerow and, having carefully sharpened it with his knife, stabbing David several times in the neck and belly. He later returned to the body under cover of darkness and concealed it in a ditch.

Although William fled the area, he was unable to stop talking about David's murder. He confessed his guilt prior to his execution.

**1900** Charles Spencer tendered a half-sovereign to pay for his bus fare at Roath    5 APRIL but conductor Thomas Jenkins had no change. The two argued about how Spencer should pay his fare and, when the bus stopped at the terminus, they began scuffling. Suddenly, sixteen-year-old Jenkins fell to the ground dead.

There were numerous witnesses, who attended the inquest held by coroner Mr E.B. Reece on 6 April, by which time Spencer had already been charged with causing Jenkins's death.

The witnesses had all seen and heard completely different things. Some had seen Spencer punch Jenkins, others swore that Spencer did not touch him, merely raising his arms in self-defence when Jenkins rushed at him '…in the most excitable manner.' Some saw Jenkins fall backwards, some saw him pitch forwards onto his face. Some testified that Jenkins had challenged Spencer to a fight, others believed that Spencer had threatened to 'knock the impudence' out of Jenkins when his journey ended.

The inquest hinged on the evidence of Dr Robinson, who conducted a post-mortem examination on Jenkins. Robinson found no external marks of violence but noted slight bruising on the top of the frontal lobe of the brain, along with a fractured second vertebra. Both injuries would have resulted in instantaneous death and both might have been caused by either a blow or a fall.

With no consensus of opinion and no clear direction from the doctor, the inquest jury gave Spencer the benefit of the doubt and returned a verdict of 'death by misadventure.'

**1886** Bostock and Wombwell's Menagerie was in town, stabling some of their    6 APRIL animals behind The White Lion Inn, Aberdare. A group of boys sneaked to the stables and began to feed the large female elephant, Madame Jumbo. Sixty-five-year-old David Watkins was an amused spectator, as the enormous animal delicately transferred the illicit treats to her mouth with her trunk, but, before long, one of the boys decided that it would be fun to give the elephant stones instead of biscuits.

This drove Madame Jumbo berserk and she dashed at her tormentors, who scattered, climbing a nearby wall to safety. Watkins was far less agile and Madame Jumbo knocked him over with one sweep of her trunk and gored him with her tusks.

The commotion alerted her keeper but, when he tried to rescue Watkins, Madame Jumbo turned on him, forcing him to run for his life. By the time the keeper had sought help, Watkins was fatally injured.

At the inquest, the jury returned a verdict of 'accidental death', placing no blame on the owners of the menagerie for the tragedy.

**1871** A number of Swansea people went on an excursion to Briton Ferry. In the    7 APRIL evening, almost 800 flocked to catch the last train home and, as it pulled into the station, the crowd surged forward impatiently. Thirteen-year-old Isabella

Hill and her twenty-three-year-old sister Mary Jane were caught in the crush and fell between the carriages and the edge of the platform.

Isabella's right arm was ripped almost completely off and she died instantly. Her sister sustained a fractured leg and most of the flesh was torn from her side. As she was pulled from beneath the train, she asked for Isabella then said that some men pushed them, before fainting. She was reported to have died the following day but the newspapers later corrected themselves to write that she was recovering in Swansea Hospital. However, although she initially rallied, she died on 15 April.

Coroner Mr Cuthbertson opened the inquest on Isabella's death at the Jersey Marine Hotel and although the jury concluded that she had been accidentally pushed under the train, they blamed the accident on the Great Western Railway for not having enough staff on duty to deal with the crowds and for providing inadequate lighting on the platform and in the railway carriages.

Some contemporary newspapers report that a young boy also fell at the same time but escaped with slight bruising.

**8 APRIL** **1890** William Evans was a promising young constable who was soon to be married. However, he seemed to annoy his sergeant at Cowbridge police station who, rightly or wrongly, twice reported him for neglect of duty. On 8 April, Sergeant William Martin chastised Evans for being absent from duty that afternoon and, as usual, Evans seemed to sulk at the reprimand.

At around midnight, Evans came across Martin engaged in an argument with Mark Roberts, who had a longstanding grudge against Martin.

Martin accused Roberts of being drunk and ordered Evans to lock him up. Evans took Roberts's side, telling Martin, 'You don't know your duty, threatening to lock up a man for no offence. You are not fit to be a sergeant. I know my duty better than you and am a better man.'

Infuriated, Martin swung at Evans, knocking him to the ground. The two scuffled and, when they were eventually separated by the landlord of a nearby pub, it was immediately apparent that the sergeant was badly injured. His left eye had been completely gouged out and dangled on his cheek and there were fingernail scratches around both eyes.

Evans handed himself in to his colleagues, claiming that the injury was an accident. Nevertheless, he was committed for trial at the Assizes charged with 'feloniously wounding and causing grievous bodily harm to one William Martin with intent to maim, disfigure and disable him.'

Although several witnesses testified that Martin was drunk at the time of his injury and Martin himself admitted to having drunk brandy in two hotels prior to the scuffle, the crucial factor for the judge seemed to be that Evans had shown '...not one fragment of regret' for the terrible injury to Martin, whether deliberate or accidental. Thus, when the jury found Evans guilty, Lord Chief Justice Coleridge penalised him heavily, sentencing him to fifteen years' penal servitude. He described Evans as a disgrace to his uniform, adding that this was the most ferocious crime, short of murder, over which he had ever presided.

**9 APRIL** **1870** At 2.40 a.m. Mr Manning, a guest at the Glamorgan Hotel, Cardiff, was awakened by shouts of 'Fire!' Manning's bedroom was already full of dense, choking smoke but he groped his way downstairs to the hotel's backyard. His cries were heard by two police constables, who hurried to fetch the fire engine.

Within minutes, the entire building was ablaze. Although there was no sign of the fire engine, two firemen managed to get in through the back door, bringing out landlord Mr Stacey and his seven-year-old grandson, Frederick. Both were alive, although Frederick expired soon afterwards and Stacey three days later.

When the fire was finally extinguished, the charred bodies of Stacey's thirty-year-old daughter, Sarah, and her four-year-old son, Sidney, were recovered, along with that of hotel guest Arthur Giles.

It proved impossible to establish the cause of the fire, although the police and fire brigade came under heavy criticism for their response. The steam fire engine had to be pushed and dragged and took more than thirty minutes to reach the fire. Then a platform had to be constructed to get the fire engine onto the Canal Wharf. Firemen drew water from the canal to tackle the fire but it was some time before there was enough steam pressure to propel the water higher than the first-floor window and a nearby purpose-built fire hydrant was overlooked. Worse still, neither the police nor the fire brigade thought to bring the fire escape. 'There are grave and serious omissions,' reported *The Western Mail*, adding that the fire brigade operated on 'a system of disorganisation' and demanding that the truth be told, however unpalatable it may be.

**1897** A band struck up outside a seaman's boarding house in Cardiff and twenty-one-year-old Filippo Pace paused to listen to the music. Suddenly, a complete stranger rushed out of the boarding house and stabbed him.  **10 APRIL**

Pace bled to death within minutes and his assailant, Giuseppe Ferragie, was charged with his wilful murder. Once in custody, Ferragie elected to remain mute and, by the time of his trial at the Swansea Assizes in July, he had not spoken a single word.

The court heard that Ferragie was a Maltese sailor, who had previously served in the Navy and was present at the bombardment of Alexandria. He was so affected by the experience that he was invalided out of the service as mad and detained in a lunatic asylum.

Mr Justice Ridley told the jury that they must decide whether Ferragie was mute by malice or by visitation of God. The jury plumped for the latter and Ferragie was found unfit to plead and ordered to be confined during Her Majesty's Pleasure.

**1885** The servants of Rachel and Thomas Thomas of Laugharne heard screams in the early hours of the morning. They took little notice, being accustomed to frequent violent rows between their master and mistress, but were surprised to find that Mrs Thomas was not up and about at her usual time the next morning. After half an hour passed with no sign of her, one of the servants knocked at the bedroom door and asked if Mrs Thomas was there.  **11 APRIL**

'Yes, she is here,' replied Thomas, offering no further explanation for his wife's tardiness.

Soon afterwards, one of the male servants noticed blood dripping through the kitchen ceiling, which was directly below the Thomas's bedroom. He ran

*Broadmoor Criminal Lunatic Asylum, 1906. (Author's collection)*

to a neighbouring farm and asked the servant there for help but the two men were unable to get into the bedroom. They went to the police station at St Clears and were accompanied back to the farm by Inspector William Williams and PC Bowen. The policemen lifted the bedroom door off its hinges, finding Rachel Thomas dead on her bed, with multiple stab wounds and her throat cut. Even as the police entered the room, Thomas plunged a knife into his own throat, inflicting seven wounds before he could be disarmed. Yet none was serious and Thomas lived to be tried for his wife's wilful murder.

Originally brought to the Assizes in the same month as the murder, the proceedings were postponed to allow investigations to be made into his mental health. Thomas was a heavy drinker but suddenly stopped drinking about six weeks before his wife's death. Neighbours and relatives revealed that he had been behaving very strangely of late and was subject to delusions – he had even attempted suicide.

When the case came to trial on 18 July 1885, Thomas was judged unfit to plead and was sent to Broadmoor Criminal Lunatic Asylum during Her Majesty's Pleasure.

12 APRIL 1863 Having eaten food prepared by his wife, Lydia, Dan Williams began vomiting, as did their daughter but, while Mary Williams quickly recovered, Dan grew worse. He complained of crippling pain and burning sensations in his stomach, numbness in his limbs, a dry mouth and throat, a swollen tongue and eventually the skin on his body began to peel off.

Dan's illness continued until his wife left him in late April. Every time he ate anything she served, he suffered violent attacks of vomiting, sometimes even throwing up blood. Lydia often added powders to his food, which she said were medicines to ease his symptoms.

When Lydia left the marital home in Llanunda, Mary took over the cooking and Dan's vomiting ceased as suddenly as it had started. However, by that time he was severely debilitated and, on 20 April, he made a deposition before JP Moses Griffiths, describing his symptoms and stating that he had seen his wife adding powders to his food and drink.

Dan died on 28 April and samples of his intestines, along with two packets of powder found in the house, were sent to analytical chemist William Herapath for testing.

Herapath found no trace of any poison in the intestines, a fact that didn't surprise him as Dan had experienced several days of purging and vomiting after what was believed to have been his last ingestion of poison. The mysterious powders proved to be oxalic acid and a mixture of oatmeal and white arsenic. There were twenty-seven grains of arsenic in the packet and Herapath knew that three grains was a fatal dose, although he had never known a case where the interval between ingestion of a fatal dose of poison and death was so long.

Lydia Williams was arrested and committed for trial at the Pembrokeshire Assizes, charged with wilful murder. Having heard Dan's deposition, the medical evidence and the testimony of a number of neighbours, who stated that Lydia had asked them for something to kill mice, the jury deliberated for thirty minutes before returning their verdict and astonishingly finding Lydia Williams guilty of the intent, but not of the murder. Even so, she was sentenced to penal servitude for life.

**1884** Instead of attending church at Llanmaes, fifteen-year-old servant Mary Saunders went to the service at Llantwit Major, in order to see her sweetheart.

The next morning, Mary complained of a headache and pains in her side and, when her conditioned worsened, it was decided to send her home to her parents at Lisworney, where her mother found a 'gathering' (abscess) at the top of her daughter's thigh. Elizabeth Saunders poulticed the swelling and, when there was no improvement, sent for surgeon Dr Edwards from Cowbridge. However,

13 APRIL

*Llantwit Major.*
*(Author's collection)*

Edwards was away from home and didn't arrive for almost thirty-six hours, by which time Mary was near death.

After her death, Edwards reported to the police that she had died from the effects of being violently raped, probably by several men. Coroner Mr E.B. Reece was notified and requested a post-mortem examination. Dr Evan Thomas Davies found no indications of violence against Mary and gave the cause of death as blood poisoning from the abscess on her thigh. She died a virgin.

There were nine witnesses set to appear at the inquest but, having heard the medical evidence, Reece deemed it unnecessary to call them. Having returned a verdict of death from natural causes, many of the jurors expressed surprised that Dr Edwards was not called, since he had assured many of them that Mary had died from violence. The police confirmed that Edwards had been asked to assist at the post-mortem but had refused because of squeamishness.

**14 APRIL** **1936** An inquest was held at Pembroke Dock on the death of sixty-five-year-old William Hitchings.

Hitchings had a pathological fear of dogs, which began in 1915 when two German Shepherds jumped up at him. The inquest heard that, on 11 April, William was seen running through Pembroke with an excited dog barking at his heels and, such was his terror and his eagerness to escape that he accidentally ran into the sea.

Although the cause of his death was officially drowning, a post-mortem examination showed that his heart was in such poor condition that, in all probability, he only had a fortnight to live.

*Pembroke Dock.*
*(Author's collection)*

**15 APRIL** **1842** Labourer Valentine Hughes returned to his home near Raglan for lunch slightly earlier than expected, to find his meal not yet ready. Unperturbed, he asked his wife Maria to prepare him some bread and cheese and, while she did so, he played with their twenty-two-month-old daughter, Eliza. When Valentine left to return to work, Eliza toddled to the door after him and lifted her arms to be picked up. Maria told him to kiss her goodbye.

Little did Valentine know that it was to be his last goodbye as, that afternoon, Maria drowned Eliza in a pan of water before disembowelling her. She was later judged insane.

**1925** Seventy-four-year-old Frederick Vaughan and his seventy-two-year-old wife, Sarah Ann, were found dead at their Newport home.

Their maid, Temperance Clark, took the couple early morning tea but at midday the Vaughans were still sleeping and Temperance couldn't rouse them. She was about to telephone for assistance, when the couple's doctor arrived for a pre-arranged appointment.

The doctor found the bedroom oppressively hot, a thermometer registering 115 degrees Fahrenheit. The Vaughans abhorred draughts and kept their bedroom door and windows tightly shut at all times. Unfortunately the chimney was blocked by a jackdaw's nest and thus the gas fire in the bedroom was improperly ventilated. As it burned through the night, all the oxygen in the tightly sealed room was used up and the couple were asphyxiated in their sleep.

Doctors ruled the cause of both deaths as 'accidental asphyxia by inhaling carbon monoxide fumes' and the inquest jury returned verdicts of 'death by misadventure'.

**1899** When the men at the Maritime Colliery, Pontypridd, returned to the surface at the end of their shift, one of the cages was out of action, due to a problem with the rope. The miners were directed to another shaft but, with more than 100 men waiting to ascend, there was a considerable queue.

As eight men were drawn up, the cage suddenly tilted and two were thrown out, falling 600ft to the pit bottom. Edwin Parish and Evan Evans were mangled almost beyond recognition and a third miner had a narrow escape when someone seized him as he was about to slide out of the cage.

Both Evans and Parish were in their fifties and were married with large families – Parish alone had eleven children.

**1891** Coroner E.H. Davies held an inquest at Newport Town Hall on the death of four-year-old Arthur Whiting.

Arthur was treated for a slight curvature of the spine and his father and stepmother were warned several times that the boy was too thin. Eventually an official complaint was made to the police about his condition and Inspector Brooks ordered Minnie Whiting to get a doctor for Arthur.

The Whitings ignored Brooks and Arthur – who was insured – died from starvation. He weighed only twelve and a half pounds and, at its thickest, the circumference of his thigh was only four inches.

The inquest jury returned verdicts of manslaughter against John and Minnie Whiting, in spite of John's claims that he left the childcare to the 'Missus'. They appeared at the Monmouthshire Assizes in July 1891, where the jury acquitted John but found Minnie guilty of manslaughter. She was sentenced to six months' imprisonment with hard labour.

**1880** As Mr Paine passed Gwern Colliery at Llansamlet, he heard a man shouting 'Oh dear! Oh dear!' Paine followed the cries to the colliery carpenter's shop and found sixty-nine-year-old nightwatchman Thomas Fowley being beaten by a uniformed policeman.

Paine joined Fowley in begging the constable to stop and eventually Fowley was able to struggle to his feet. 'I'll kill the old *****!' He has struck me senseless,' the policeman threatened, punching Fowley in the face and knocking him into a heap of scrap iron. Fowley stood up again but was punched a second time. This time the blow knocked him out and he died two days later without regaining consciousness.

Earlier that evening, Fowley ordered the policeman, Herbert Plumley, off the colliery grounds. An argument developed between the two men, during which Plumley alleged that Fowley hit him.

Plumley was charged with 'felonious killing and slaying', appearing at the Swansea Assizes on 7 August. It was proven that Plumley had a slight abrasion on his cheek at the time of his arrest and the prosecution counsel suggested that Fowley had struck the first blow. The judge told the jury that their verdict would depend on how much credence they gave Paine's account, reminding them that Plumley had received 'the highest character' from his superiors in the police force.

The jury obviously found Paine very credible, since they returned a guilty verdict, although they tempered it with a recommendation for mercy on account of Plumley's good character. He was sentenced to ten years' penal servitude.

20 APRIL  **1846** Gabriel Davies of Carmarthen was horrified to discover that he had signed up for the military during a drunken spree with his friends. Still half drunk, he took out his knife and began to cut off one of the fingers of his left hand and, when the knife was taken from him, he tried to bite the finger off.

*Carmarthen from the air. (Author's collection)*

When that failed, Davies determinedly walked to the yard at the rear of a public house, placed his finger on a block of wood and chopped it off with one stroke of a hatchet. His self-mutilation had the desired effect of ending his brief military career.

21 APRIL  **1842** 'Tamar' Edwards lived in Merthyr Tydfil with her son Richard, aka Dick Tamar. Dick had a reputation for violence and his wife, Margaret 'Peggy', had recently left him and returned to live with her parents at Rhydycar, taking the couple's blind son.

Dick persuaded Peggy to return and, arriving back in Merthyr on 18 April, she was surprised to find her mother-in-law absent. She was even more surprised on 21 April to find Tamar's body hidden beneath the bed. Peggy reported her gruesome discovery to the police, who immediately began a search for Dick. He was arrested five days later and charged with his mother's wilful murder by manual strangulation.

Tried at the Cardiff Assizes in July, Dick was found guilty and sentenced to death. He was hanged outside Cardiff Gaol by William Calcraft on 23 July 1842 and, before he died, made a statement implicating his wife in his mother's murder. According to Dick, when Peggy complained that Tamar was beating her, Dick hit his mother, knocking her over. Peggy then strangled her, aided by her own mother and brother.

Ironically, five years earlier, Dick Tamar was suspected of murdering a girl, whose charred body was found on an ash tip. Tamar swore that he hadn't left the house at the time of the girl's murder and the Grand Jury found 'no bill' against him. He was also tried for the murder by strangulation of prostitute Ellen Murphy in January 1840 but acquitted.

Note: Various different dates are given in the contemporary newspapers for the finding of the body, including 18, 21 and 23 April.

**22 APRIL**

**1876** Labourers building a new railway tunnel at Cymmer were blasting through the hard limestone rock with gunpowder and dynamite. Suddenly, there was an explosion that was heard twenty miles away. About 60 yards of the tunnel collapsed, burying the navvies in the rubble and early reports suggested that at least thirty had been killed.

Many men were seriously injured and some of the bodies recovered were mutilated almost beyond recognition. Eventually, thirteen deceased were identified and two more men were still in a critical condition when the inquest concluded.

A labourer was seen working with a lighted candle and another struck a match to light his pipe immediatcly before the explosion occurred. The inquest jury concluded that the thirteen men had died due to an explosion, although there was no evidence as to how it occurred. Diamond Rock Boring Company was later summoned for storing between 150 and 200lbs of dynamite in a manhole within the tunnel and fined £25 plus costs.

**23 APRIL**

**1885** Forty-eight-year-old sailor John Blackborough (or Blackborrow) appeared at the Swansea Assizes charged with the manslaughter of James Empsom on 30 March.

Blackborough returned to Penarth after three months at sea to find Empsom living with his wife. To add insult to injury, Empsom was unemployed and the money that Blackborough sent home was the couple's only means of support.

Blackborough and Empsom went to the pub to try and thrash the matter out between them and, after spending most of the day drinking, they returned to Blackborough's marital home, where Blackborough reluctantly left his wife with her lover.

Empsom followed him out onto the street shouting and cursing, eventually slamming the door in Blackborough's face. Hearing his wife screaming from within, Blackborough began to pound the door with his fists and eventually Empsom came out and punched him in the face.

The two men scuffled for a while then Empsom suddenly shouted, 'You coward, you have stabbed me,' before knocking Blackborough over again. Empsom was bleeding heavily from a wound in his left side, through which his bowels protruded, and he died the following day.

At Blackborough's trial, his defence counsel suggested that the wound was inflicted accidentally in the struggle for possession of the knife, maintaining that Blackborough was acting in self-defence. The jury found Blackborough guilty of manslaughter, although they recommended mercy on the grounds of provocation. He was sentenced to nine months' imprisonment.

**24 APRIL**   **1869** Sixty-two-year-old Mary Jones lived in a farmhouse in Nant-y-Derry, Brecon, described in the contemporary newspapers as '...a most dreary and desolate spot.' Mary's friends begged her to move somewhere less isolated but Mary had lost her husband two months earlier and was reluctant to leave the place where he died. She made a living selling poultry and ponies and was rumoured to have a substantial nest egg hidden at home.

Mary was last seen alive on 24 April by her neighbour, John Jenkins. When he passed early the next morning, there was no sign of her, although Jenkins spotted that one of the farmhouse windows was open. He mentioned this to his wife and, when Mrs Jenkins sent her daughters to check on Mary's welfare, they found a heap of smouldering rubble on Mary's kitchen floor, which was emitting the most terrible stench.

They ran for their father, who discovered Mary's charred body beneath a pile of coal, wood and straw. A post-mortem examination revealed that her skull was fractured, most probably by blows from a leg broken from a kitchen chair.

Mary's killer(s) had gained entry to her house by prising a bar from a window and using it to jemmy the door open. There was no sign that the house had been ransacked and Mary's life savings were still in a box in a tea chest in the bedroom, while a basin containing £2 sat on a dresser, close to where her body lay. As far as could be established, nothing had been stolen.

An inquest was opened by Brecon coroner Mr J. Williams and adjourned to allow the police more time to make enquiries. When the inquest concluded on 25 May, the police had fully investigated several suspects, including John Jenkins, a woodcutter named Walter Grundy, and father and son Rees and Thomas Rees. However, all had unshakeable alibis and the inquest jury eventually returned a verdict of 'wilful murder against some person or persons unknown.'

**25 APRIL**   **1899** Magistrates convened at Swansea Police Court to rule on the obscenity of six pictures, seized from the South Wales and Monmouthshire Mutoscope Company Limited. The pictures were used in penny-in-the-slot machines and featured semi-nude women, who actually moved!

They were seized by the Swansea Police following a complaint from Walter Webber, who needed three visits to the machines to make sure the images really were obscene. Prosecuting solicitor Mr Slater insisted that the pictures did more

than '...offend against the canons of good taste', believing that they '...tended to make lustful desires and corrupt the morals of those who saw them.'

*Birds' eye view of Swansea. (Author's collection)*

Having watched the pictures several times, the magistrates stated that the case revolved around the definition of the word obscene, ruling the pictures no more obscene than antics that went on at the music halls every night.

'Would you consider them decent?' persisted Slater.

The Bench pointed out that the word 'decent' didn't appear in the Obscene Publications Act 1857 and was therefore of no relevance. The police were ordered to return the images to the defendants without delay.

**1892** As she walked on the mountainside near Pontypridd, Agnes Wells was violently attacked by two men and robbed of her purse and its contents.

26 APRIL

Fortunately for Agnes, the mountain was visible from the distant police station, where an alert sergeant's attention was attracted by a flurry of movement on the hillside. He fetched his binoculars and watched the whole attack, his view of the incident so clear that he was able to identify the perpetrators.

At the Swansea Assizes, Daniel Llewellyn and James Gwynne were later found guilty of robbery with violence. Gwynne was sentenced to nine months' imprisonment with hard labour and Llewellyn, who had shown the most violence, received twelve months' imprisonment with hard labour and twenty strokes of the cat-o-nine-tails.

**1876** The death of three-year-old John Howells at Maesteg put an end to many months of suffering at the hands of his mother. John was the illegitimate son of thirty-five-year-old Hannah Wilkes who, after marrying, treated her son with appalling cruelty.

27 APRIL

The boy died from diarrhoea resulting from emaciation and, at the time of his death, weighed only 18lbs, compared to a normal weight of 30lbs for a child of his age. Neighbours had seen Hannah beating John with a leather strap, picking him up by the neck and throwing him about. He was once left outside in the snow half naked and was rarely fed.

The jury at the Glamorganshire Summer Assizes found Hannah guilty of killing her son and she was sentenced to twelve months' imprisonment with hard labour.

**28 APRIL 1847** David Hughes went to seek work in the Merthyr area, leaving his wife, Mary, and three children living with his sister, also named Mary Hughes, who kept The Carriers' Arms public house near Llanbydder.

On 28 April, Aunt Mary went out, leaving her sister-in-law playing with the children. When Aunt Mary returned, the door was locked and the key tucked just underneath it. Aunt Mary called out to her sister-in-law and, receiving no response, began to search the house. As she walked upstairs, she saw the children hanging by their necks from the roof beams. She ran for a neighbour, who helped her cut down the bodies, but all three were dead and there was no sign of their mother.

On 3 May, labourer David Owens and his friend spotted a dishevelled woman wading through the river at Llanddewybrefi, roughly ten miles from Llanbydder. When they asked her if she was Mary Hughes, she initially denied it but eventually admitted her true identity. The men asked how she could be cruel enough to murder her children, at which Mary began to sob bitterly.

She told the men that her family was impoverished and that, in the past, her father helped them out with money. Having recently argued with her father, she feared that he would no longer help and decided to kill her children rather than watch them starve.

Although Mary begged to be allowed to die, Owens took her to the nearest police station. Committed for trial on the coroner's warrant, twenty-eight-year-old Mary appeared at the Carmarthenshire Assizes on 13 July 1847 charged with three counts of wilful murder. She was acquitted by reason of insanity and ordered to be detained as a criminal lunatic.

**29 APRIL 1858** When railway labourer David Davies of Neath quarrelled with workmate William Jeffreys and the two squared up to fight, the last thing Davies expected was for Jeffreys to fall down dead at his feet. Davies swore that he hadn't laid a finger on Jeffreys and a post-mortem examination suggested that he was telling the truth, since it revealed such extensive heart disease that the slightest excitement or upset would probably have proved fatal.

By that time, an inquest jury had returned a verdict of manslaughter against Davies, who had to face trial at the next Assizes. Mr Justice Crompton directed the jury to acquit Davies, so that he could be discharged and his name cleared.

**30 APRIL 1883** George Isaac Knight of Blaen-y-Cwm spent much of the day drinking with his lodger, William Pride. Eventually Pride arrived back home alone and Knight's wife, Harriet, sent her brother to drag her husband out of the pub.

Knight was very drunk and told Harriet that he would not be going to work that night, at which Harriet asked him how they were expected to live.

Knight seemed irritated that Pride had arrived home first and began an argument, which soon became physical and spilled into the street. Neighbour Mrs Ashman intervened and pulled Pride into her own home, locking the door behind them. This angered Knight even more and he went back to his own home and picked up an eleven-inch knife. With that in one hand and a smaller knife in the other, Knight stood outside Mrs Ashman's house threatening Pride with certain death. Harriet tried to calm her husband down, telling him 'Don't be foolish, George,' but her words were far from a calming influence, as her husband suddenly swung at her, plunging the knife into her back.

As Harriet fell to the ground mortally wounded, her husband ran for the mountains, with several neighbours in pursuit. They eventually cornered him and persuaded him to return home, where he locked himself in and vowed to kill anyone who tried to enter. However, a few minutes later, he laid down his knives and surrendered.

Tried at the Glamorganshire Assizes for wilful murder, Knight was found guilty, albeit with a strong recommendation for mercy because of an absence of premeditation. Sentenced to death, his sentence was commuted to one of life imprisonment.

# MAY

*The Fountain, Merthyr Tydfil, 1924. (Author's collection)*

**1891** Twenty-one-year-old David Thomas Edmunds died at the Cardiff Infirmary, following an accident on 30 April.

The inquest, held by coroner Mr E.B. Reece, heard that David Edmunds was driving a train from Aberdare to Newport, with his son – the deceased – acting as fireman. As they neared Pontypridd Station, the signals were against Edmunds's train and, knowing that there was a train in front of him, he settled down to wait.

After forty-seven minutes, Mr Edmunds senior was still waiting patiently and climbed off the train to stretch his legs, leaving his son in the cab. There was a steep incline on the railway line between Edmunds's train and the one in front and, to his horror, Edmunds saw a brake van and several coal wagons approaching his train at speed. Edmunds shouted to his son to put the train in reverse and jump clear but he was too late.

Hophna Gibbon and Samuel Saint, who were in the brake van, were seriously injured and when Edmunds junior was extricated from the wreckage, he was found to be extensively scalded. Although Saint and Gibbon ultimately recovered, Edmunds died from his scalds.

*The Infirmary, Cardiff. (Author's collection)*

A draw bar connecting the back nine wagons and the brake van to the foremost train had sheared, causing them to roll down the incline into Edmunds's train. The inquest jury returned a verdict of 'accidental death'.

**1895** Michael Courtenay of Barry Dock took his estranged wife and her lover to Cardiff Police Court, charging both with assault.

Courtenay told magistrates that on 29 April, his wife and Edward Ryan climbed through his bedroom window using a ladder and threw his cork leg downstairs, thus ensuring that he could not run away. They then brutally kicked and beat him and stole 24s from his pocket, before making their escape.

*Barry Dock, 1910.*
*(Author's collection)*

Courtenay's son – also named Michael – slept with his father and, although he testified that his mother and Ryan had come into the bedroom, he hadn't seen his father being attacked. Since the charge against Ryan and Mrs Courtenay was for assault rather than theft, the magistrates immediately dismissed the case.

3 MAY    **1895** Haverfordwest publican John Devereux had been unwell for months, although doctors were unable to find the cause of his symptoms or suggest anything to relieve them. Devereux complained of stomach pain and a strange sensation below his heart, as if something were moving about inside him.

After a meal of beef hash, followed by a glass of gin and water, Devereux felt sick. His wife fetched a bucket and, when she went to empty it, she noticed a live wasp.

Knowing that the bucket was clean before her husband used it, Mrs Devereux strained the contents, finding more than twenty wasps in her husband's vomit. Devereux's doctor later microscopically examined the insects and confirmed that they were wasps, although their wings did not appear to have been used for flying. Although the doctor doubted that wasps could survive inside a man's body, Devereux was prepared to swear an oath that he had vomited them up and that, since doing so, his stomach pains had eased and he had no further crawling sensations.

4 MAY    **1900** Mr Williams of Llandow drew some water from his farm well. Noticing scum on the surface of the water, he tried again, this time drawing up the torso of a baby. Only the right arm was still attached – the head, legs and left arm were missing and it was obvious that a sharp instrument had been used to carve the infant into pieces.

The police dredged the well in the hope of finding more body parts and retrieved the head, part of one thigh, some intestines and an afterbirth. Dr Sheppard examined the remains and concluded that the baby had lived a separate life and estimated that it was probably around three days old when it was dismembered.

Suspicion fell on Mrs Mary Jane Perrin, a twenty-five-year-old servant at the farm, who was charged with concealment of birth. However, when she appeared before magistrates at Bridgend Police Court, the prosecution were unable to present any evidence against her and she was discharged.

**1882** Haulier Owen Sullivan was employed by the Dowlais Iron Company to ferry loads of spoil to the Gellyfaelog Tip at Merthyr Tydfil. **5 MAY**

The tip was a popular, if highly dangerous, playground for local children and, as Owen prepared to empty his cart, a little girl picking rags realised that two little boys were in the way.

'Don't tip the cart, Owen, there are children below,' she called.

'Oh, to hell with them,' Owen responded.

The tip was about 100ft high and the large stones from Sullivan's cart accelerated rapidly to the bottom, one striking four-and-a-half-year-old David John Evans and fatally injuring him. At an inquest on his death, the jury returned a verdict of 'death by misadventure' but magistrates later committed Sullivan for wilful murder.

He appeared at the Swansea Assizes on 2 August, where his defence counsel maintained that this was a case of homicide by misadventure, his client having simply misunderstood the little girl's warning. Numerous witnesses were called to testify that Sullivan was a kind and humane man and the jury gave him the benefit of the doubt, finding him not guilty.

**1839** Forty-five-year old Cardiff butcher John Davis died from rabies. **6 MAY**

For three days after the onset of his symptoms, Davies was unable to tolerate the presence of any liquid in his bedroom. Even the sound of water poured from a jug, or his lips being touched with a segment of orange, sent his body into violent spasms. Throughout his illness, Davis remained rational, fully aware of the gravity of his condition and able to discuss his symptoms clearly with his doctor.

According to the contemporary newspapers, '...extreme excitement of the brain and whole nervous system happily terminated his struggles.'

**1832** The *Palmerston* steam packet waited for a favourable tide to enter Swansea harbour. Seeing a chance to make money, three youths borrowed a boat and rowed out, offering to convey passengers to the shore. **7 MAY**

Captain Walters seemed in a hurry to proceed to Tenby and allowed the Swansea-bound passengers to board the boat with their luggage. In all, thirteen people crowded onto the little boat, which started to take on water and quickly sank.

*Palmerston* launched her own boat and managed to save ten people. However, three were lost, their bodies recovered the next morning. They included a thirteen-year-old boy from Kent, who was travelling to Wales for the benefit of his health.

At the inquest, held by coroner Charles Collins, the jury returned verdicts of 'accidental death' on all three victims but censured Captain Walters for refusing to land passengers at Swansea and for not inspecting the ferry to ensure that it was seaworthy.

**8 MAY** **1882** A rumour spread around Cardiff Docks that stevedores William Parsons and Michael Cocklin were working for below the going rate. Accordingly, they were paid a visit by three men, who proceeded to give them a thorough beating and kicking.

Dock labourers Patrick Keefe and Michael Mead were later arrested for the vicious assaults but refused to name their accomplice, who had not been apprehended by the time they appeared before magistrates at the Borough Police Court.

Magistrates found both men guilty. Keefe was sent to prison for one month for the assault on Parsons and Mead, who participated in both assaults, was sentenced to two months' imprisonment.

**9 MAY** **1876** Gwilym Jones died from an abscess on the brain and Johanna Sullivan of Merthyr Tydfil was committed for trial for his manslaughter.

Gwilym was one of a number of boys playing near Johanna's garden on 21 April, who deliberately soiled the laundry she had just hung out to dry. When Johanna remonstrated with the gang, they cheeked her and threw stones. Johanna retaliated by scooping up a brick and throwing it at the boys, hitting Gwilym on the forehead, causing him to stagger and fall down a cinder tip.

Johanna argued that she had thrown only mud and small coal at the boys and that Gwilym sustained his injury falling over, while attempting to run away. Her defence counsel contended that she had been sorely provoked but the judge instructed the jury that, no matter what the provocation, nothing could justify throwing dangerous missiles. The jury concurred, finding Johanna guilty and she fainted as the judge sentenced her to nine months' imprisonment with hard labour.

**10 MAY** **1852** Two mining disasters took place in South Wales.

At the Middle Duffryn Pit in the Aberdare Valley, an explosion of fire damp claimed sixty-five lives. Some were as young as nine years old and brothers William and Charles Marks, aged fifteen and eleven, died only five months after their father was killed in an explosion at another pit. After lengthy enquiries, it was concluded that a large discharge of gas had somehow ignited and the inquest found no neglect or culpability on the part of the mine owners.

On the same day, an explosion at the Gwendraeth Colliery near Pembrey caused the workings to flood and all but one of the twenty-eight men working underground drowned.

**11 MAY** **1874** After an evening spent drinking, Jonathan Cooke of Pontypool set out to walk home and, at four o'clock in the morning, his body was found on the railway line. He left a wife and five children.

Instead of using the footbridge, Cooke normally walked down a steep bank and across the railway track. Marks on the bank indicated that he had slipped at the top and fallen headfirst to the bottom, ending up with his head and right hand resting on the track. During the night, one or more trains struck him, knocking his brain clean out of his head.

Coroner Mr E.D. Batt held an inquest on 12 May, recording that Cooke was accidentally killed while trespassing on the railway line. His shortcut would have saved him only a few yards.

**1874**  James Henry Gibbs led a double life. He met his wife, Susan Ann, while they were both in service in Hampshire. In 1871, Gibbs took a job as butler at Llanrumney Hall, St Mellons and, soon afterwards, met Mary Jones. Even though he was engaged to Susan, Gibbs started courting Mary, who believed that she was his only girlfriend.

On 30 July 1873, Gibbs married Susan and found lodgings for her about five miles from Llanrumney. He visited frequently and the couple appeared happily married, until Susan heard rumours about Mary Jones. James wrote to her, assuring her, 'I am a married man now and what do I want with another young woman?' Mary also heard whispers that James was married but he denied it and, just before Christmas 1873, took her to meet his father, introducing her as his future wife.

On 9 May 1874, Susan went to meet James, returning to tell her landlady Mrs Mahoney that she was very frightened and was considering leaving. When Susan went to meet James again on 12 May, she told Mrs Mahoney not to wait up for her and, when she didn't return, it was assumed that she had left for good.

For the next few weeks, James wrote to Susan's relatives claiming that she was ill. He visited Mrs Mahoney and told her that Susan had gone to Reading and, on 22 May, he arranged to marry Mary.

Nobody suspected that Susan had met with foul play until 3 June, when a farmer detected an obnoxious stink arising from a ditch and found the badly decomposed body of a woman, whose remains had been ravaged by animals and insects. It was Susan Gibbs and, since her throat was more decomposed than the rest of her body, doctors surmised that it had been cut.

Although the evidence against her husband was entirely circumstantial, he was tried for wilful murder at the Monmouth Assizes on 7 August and it took the jury only twenty minutes to find him guilty. He was hanged by William Marwood at Usk on 24 August, protesting his innocence to his last breath.

**1839**  The destruction of the newly-erected toll gates at Efailwen marked the first in the series of the so-called Rebecca Riots in South Wales, which continued until 1843. The rioters frequently concealed their identities by wearing women's clothing and wigs and the name Rebecca is said to originate from a verse in the Bible: 'And they blessed Rebekah and said unto her, Thou art our sister, be thou the mother of thousands of millions, and let thy seed possess the gate of those which hate them.' (Genesis, 24:60)

The background to the riots was a period of crippling financial hardship for Welsh farmers. Their landlords were from the privileged classes and had little empathy with the tenants. Many were English and the farmers resented having to pay ever-increasing tithes to the Church of England. The last straw was the introduction of tolls on public roads, which the farmers had to pay in order to transport their crops and bring in fertiliser.

The farmers and their labourers banded together and, disguising themselves as women, destroyed the toll gates at Efailwen, repeating the act a week later when the gates were replaced.

For the next four years, the Rebeccaites struck at random throughout South Wales, destroying toll gates and the farms and crops of their landlords, burning down toll-houses and attacking Workhouses, which they saw as the ultimate degradation in the government's response to poverty.

Although South Wales had no formal constabulary, magistrates swore in special constables to deal with the rioters and, as a last resort, the militia were deployed. Not everybody supported the Rebeccaites and, concerned that they were too violent and lawless in their battle against authority, some local people informed on the leaders. Yet when an elderly toll-house keeper was shot during a riot at Hendy on 9 September 1843, the inquest jury ruled that Sarah Williams 'died from the effusion of blood into the chest, which occasioned suffocation, but from what cause is to this jury unknown.'

Several men were tried for their parts in the riots but there was usually a sympathiser who would provide an alibi for those suspected. Those who were convicted were transported, sometimes for life.

**14 MAY** **1886** Elizabeth Welsh appeared at the Glamorganshire Assizes charged with the manslaughter of Elizabeth 'Liz' Jordan.

On 29 March, Liz visited Margaret Howlett, who was also entertaining her two sisters, Mary Stokes and Elizabeth Welsh. The four women were drinking and a heated argument arose between Margaret and Elizabeth Welsh. Elizabeth picked up a quart milk jug, intending to throw it at her sister but Liz remonstrated with her, saying, 'You two are sisters. Don't go on like that, for shame.'

The jug handle was cracked and as Liz held up her arm to deflect the throw, Elizabeth Welsh was left clutching the handle, while the body of the jug shattered on Liz's arm.

Margaret staunched the bleeding with her apron then applied wet cloths. She suggested fetching a surgeon but Liz assured her that she was fine, although she consented to see a doctor when she was still bleeding forty-five minutes later. Having been treated, she insisted on going home where, on returning from his job as an engine driver on 31 March, her common-law husband found her dead.

An inquest returned a verdict of manslaughter against Elizabeth Welsh, the jury recognising that there had been no malice shown and no intent to harm. The jury at her trial concurred and she was found guilty and sentenced to seven months' imprisonment.

**15 MAY** **1892** The barque *Earl of Aberdeen* was sailing from Barry to Monte Video, when she struck the 'Hats and Barrels Rocks' off Milford

Haven and sank. There was just enough time to launch the ship's lifeboat, although it was soon swamped by rough seas, which washed away those on board.

Some of the crew scrambled into the ship's rigging and eleven were rescued by HMS *Foxhound*, but such was the speed of the sinking that many men went down with the vessel and, in total, sixteen lives were lost.

**1924** Normality was finally restored to Nelson, near Cardiff, in the early hours of the morning, following the devastation caused by eighteen-month-old Vernon Jones.

16 MAY

The previous evening, John Portolock, a neighbour of the toddler's, returned to his fruit shop in Commercial Street with a lorry load of stock. Vernon clamoured for a ride in the lorry but, as John lifted him aboard, Vernon accidentally touched the starting lever. The lorry set off with Vernon in the driver's seat, crashing into a lamp post a little further down the street and plunging the whole area into darkness. It took several hours for the power to be restored.

Fortunately, Vernon emerged from the crash completely unscathed, although Portolock's lorry was a write-off.

**1894** A prize fight was fought at Aberdare between Thomas Robert Edwards and David Rees, which the public were charged 2s each to watch.

17 MAY

In the third round, Rees failed to beat the count. Edwards claimed victory but the referee insisted that the two men fight on and, in the fourth round, Rees was knocked out. He fell backwards, hitting his head against the stone floor with a crash that resounded through the room.

Cerebral fluid was leaking from one ear and there were numerous scratches and bruises all over his face and upper body. A post-mortem examination showed

*Aberdare, 1950. (Author's collection)*

that Rees had a fractured skull, beneath which his brain was almost a pulp. In addition, his spine was fractured between his first and second vertebra.

At an inquest held by coroner Mr R.J. Rhys at Aberdare Police Court, the jury returned verdicts of manslaughter against all those connected with the fight. In total, eleven men were charged – Edwards, the six men who acted as seconds to the two combatants, two timekeepers, the referee and the fight organiser. All appeared at the Glamorganshire Assizes, where there was great argument about the legality of the fight. Eventually, the jury acquitted all eleven defendants, who were discharged without penalty.

**18 MAY** **1856** A violent gale blew as some teenagers played a game of pitch and toss in Landore Court, Cardiff. Without any warning, the chimney stack of The Queen's Hotel suddenly blew down, burying four young people in rubble.

The crash was heard at the police station and a number of policemen rushed to the site and began digging through the debris with their bare hands. Only one of the four survived – one was pulled dead from the mass of fallen masonry, a second died on the way to the Infirmary and a third died two hours later.

On 20 May, an inquest was held on the deaths of thirteen-year-old Daniel Macarty and Florence Macarty and James Twig, who were both nineteen. The jury returned verdicts of 'accidental death' on all three.

**19 MAY** **1874** Farm labourer Frederick Albert Hawkins was washing sheep in the River Usk and, for a lark, decided to take one across to the opposite bank. As he waded back, he deviated slightly from the course he had taken over the river and unexpectedly found himself in deep water. Suddenly, he stepped into a hole in the river bed and sank. Moments later, one of his hands appeared above the water, disappearing again within seconds.

*Sheep washing.*
*(Author's collection)*

SHEEP WASHING.

Hawkins was a good swimmer and also a practical joker, so his boss and fellow labourers stood patiently on the bank, waiting for him to resurface. When it dawned on them that Hawkins was in trouble, they fetched a boat and began a frantic search but, by the time he was found, Hawkins was dead and all attempts to revive him failed.

Coroner Mr E.D. Batt held an inquest at The Royal Oak Inn, Llantrissant and the jury returned a verdict of 'accidental death by drowning.'

**1884** As PC Williams patrolled in Tylorstown, he met John Evans drunkenly offering to fight all comers.                                                      20 MAY

Williams asked Evans to go home. 'Go home yourself you bastard,' replied Evans and took a swing at the policeman. By now, a hostile crowd had assembled, so Williams took Evans into Tylors Hotel and as soon as the door closed behind them, a barrage of stones was thrown by the mob outside, one of which broke a window.

After taking Evans's details, Williams released him with a caution. However, when Williams left the hotel, Evans was waiting for him and, picking up a stone, began to hit the policeman over the head.

Williams called for help and a man appealed for calm, telling the angry men, 'Now, boys, the policeman is doing nothing to you, so be quiet.' At that, a man named John Rees kicked him, before joining Evans in his attack on the policeman. Williams took refuge in a shop, which was pelted by stones and had the bottom half of its door kicked in before the crowd dispersed.

John Evans, John Rees and a third man, John Huddlestone, were later arrested for the assault on Williams, who had a wound on his left ear and contusions on his head and hip. Although Rees insisted that he was in Aberdare at the time of the offence, all three men appeared before magistrates at the Ystrad Police Court. Very few of the witnesses were prepared to give evidence but magistrates eventually sentenced Evans to three months' imprisonment with hard labour and fined Huddlestone and Rees £5 and £2 respectively, with costs.

**1886** Joseph Shurmer appeared before Mr Justice       21 MAY
Hawkins at the Swansea Assizes charged with
raping his fourteen-year-old daughter Annie
at Llangattock. Although two offences were
alleged, Shurmer was tried only for the first,
which occurred on 10 February.

Although the jury found Shurmer guilty,
Hawkins immediately referred the case to the
Court of Criminal Appeal on a legal tech-
nicality.

At the time of the rape, Annie was ill
with typhoid fever and died on 7 March
before the case could come to court.
Much of the evidence against Shurmer
came from a deathbed deposition given
by Annie to a Justice of the Peace and,
according to Shurmer's defence counsel,

*Mr Justice Hawkins
from the* London
Illustrated News.
*(Author's collection)*

the deposition wasn't legal. Although Shurmer was present at his daughter's bedside, he had not been formally notified in writing that the deposition was taking place, nor had he been specifically told that he had the right to ask questions.

The appeal was considered by Lord Chief Justice Coleridge, Mr Justice Denman and Mr Justice Day, who differed in opinion. Eventually, by a majority of two to one, the judges found for the defence and ordered the conviction quashed and expunged from Shurmer's record.

22 MAY 1882 Emma Morgan (aka Clark) was separated from her husband and worked as a prostitute in Cardiff, under the watchful eye of twenty-three-year-old Jeremiah Mahoney, who acted as her pimp.

On 22 May, Emma was entertaining a client at a brothel in Charlotte Street when Mahoney knocked at the door and asked for her. As soon as he was admitted, he walked over to Emma and punched her. Emma fell to the floor, her head hitting a bench as she fell and Mahoney gave her three swift kicks, before picking her up and throwing her down again.

Emma managed to struggle to her feet and sought refuge in another brothel but Mahoney followed her and kicked her in the back and lower stomach, inflicting severe injuries.

Before long, she developed erysipelas – a bacterial infection – which eventually caused the failure of her heart and other vital organs. When her death on 17 June was directly attributed to the injuries she received from Mahoney, he was charged with wilful murder.

His trial at the Swansea Assizes was unusual in that most of the witnesses were prostitutes or brothel keepers. Nevertheless, they were able to convince the jury that Mahoney was guilty of manslaughter and he was sentenced to twenty years' imprisonment.

23 MAY 1891 Coroner Ivor Evans held an inquest at Solva on the death of thirty-year-old Enoch Jenkins.

On 12 May, Thomas Jenkins, a relation of Enoch's, was driving cattle home from Haverfordwest Fair when a cart driven by William Thomas scattered them. Jenkins was furious and chased after the cart to get the name of the driver. A scuffle ensued, during which William Thomas picked up a stone and shied it at Thomas Jenkins. His aim was poor and the stone hit Enoch.

When Enoch arrived home, his father bathed and poulticed the minor wound on his forehead and, the next day, Enoch walked to a nearby village and back, a distance of twelve miles. On his return, he felt unwell but no doctor was called until 19 May, when Enoch's brother Amos told Dr Hugh Owen Hughes that his brother was suffering the effects of 'a little blow on the head.' By then, it was too late to save Enoch, who died on 20 May.

When Hughes conducted a post-mortem examination, he found a half-inch long wound over Enoch's right eyebrow. There was a small piece of stone firmly lodged in the bone of Enoch's skull and another under his scalp and the skull bone had been driven back into his brain, resulting in a fatal abscess.

The inquest jury returned a verdict of manslaughter against William Thomas, who was tried at the Pembrokeshire Assizes on 11 July. One of the main witnesses was Dr Hughes, who, after describing Enoch's injuries, told the court that, when he was first called, Amos told him that the stone was thrown by Thomas Jenkins. Hughes also added that, had he been consulted earlier, he could have saved Enoch and that the deceased had almost certainly worsened his condition by walking.

Although Amos denied ever having accused Thomas Jenkins, the jury were convinced by the doctor's evidence and acquitted William Thomas.

**1901** Just before five o'clock in the morning, the Aber Valley was shaken by three explosions at the Universal Colliery, Sengenhydd. If anything about such 24 MAY

disasters could ever be described as fortunate, this one occurred when the majority of the night shift had already ascended and before the day shift had reported for work. Even so, eighty-three men were entombed and, from the outset, there was little hope for their survival. Only one man was rescued alive – ostler William Harris was found nestled against the body of a dead horse. He was badly burned and unconscious, occasionally repeating the words, 'Jack, oh Jack, let us run to the cabin.'

The disaster, which left 220 children fatherless, was believed to have been caused by coal dust, although what caused it to explode was the subject of much debate. The management appeared to blame a miner lighting his pipe but there were also theories that blasting, rock falls or refilling lamps may have been responsible.

The pit was the scene of another tragedy in 1913, when 439 miners lost their lives in a devastating explosion.

*'The Melancholoy Mine disaster in Wales' as depicted in* The Sphere. *(Author's collection)*

*The funerals of victims passing the scene of the disaster, as depicted in* The Sphere. *(Author's collection)*

*A woman identifies the body of her husband, as depicted in* The Sphere. *(Author's collection)*

**25 MAY** **1878** Twenty-seven-year-old Charles H. Dovton took his fiancée, Miss Davies, and her mother on a pleasure cruise from Neyland to Lawrenny. They hired a small boat, engaging a fourteen-year-old boatman's son named Evans to help sail it.

It was evident to Evans that Dovton had no experience of sailing and was more interested in entertaining the ladies than in controlling the boat. As the party reached Pembroke Dock, Dovton lounged in the stern, reading aloud from a book, the boat yawing hither and thither, while Evans tried unsuccessfully to persuade him to pay more attention to sailing.

Suddenly, the sail gibed and the boat capsized, throwing all four occupants into the water. Evans managed to cling onto the upturned keel but the other three sank without trace.

There were several other vessels in the vicinity and Evans was rescued but, although a shawl, two hats and a book were pulled from the water, there was no sign of the bodies of Dovton and his companions.

Many witnesses were later to comment on the unskilful handling of the boat and, coupled with the account of the accident by Evans, it was concluded that the tragedy was due to Dovton's gross carelessness or ignorance.

**26 MAY** **1936** As twenty men worked underground at the Loveston Colliery, near Tenby, there was a sudden influx of water into the mine, thought to have broken through from an old working. Those furthest from the water ran for their lives, some escaping through an airshaft and others hauling themselves hand-over-hand up an iron haulage rope. Seven men were trapped by the water, including twenty-six-year-old Joseph Phillips, who ran to warn the men higher in the workings then went back to try and save his younger brother, Ernest.

The mine's pumps were lost in the flood but replacements were quickly borrowed from other pits and desperate efforts were made to pump out the workings. Sadly, the water gradually rose and all hope was lost for the seven men remaining below ground.

**1894** Isaac Fantham and David Price of Cardiff hired a dog cart to take two lady 27 MAY friends to Chepstow while, in Newport, Herbert Lancefield, Herbert Ernest Evans and Frank Adams hired a pony and trap, intending to make the same trip.

Leaving Chepstow, the two parties met and started racing. At first the contest was friendly but, as the Newport boys overtook the Cardiff party, Adams made a derogatory remark. From then on the race became increasingly bad tempered, with both vehicles vying for position and a great deal of profanity passing between their occupants.

Eventually, the Cardiff boys forged ahead, then pulled over and lay in wait. They boarded the Newport trap as it passed and a fight ensued, which left Lancefield, Evans and Adams unconscious.

The Newport boys summoned the Cardiff boys for assault and the Cardiff boys cross-summoned, alleging that they were the ones who were assaulted. They accused the Newport boys of being drunk and behaving indecently in front of the ladies, of barging their vehicle off the road and of lashing out with a horsewhip. Although the Cardiff boys admitted fighting, they told magistrates that the Newport boys attacked Price first and Fantham went to his defence.

The magistrates dismissed their cross-summons and fined Price £3 and Fantham £2. They were later heard to complain that this was exactly what they expected from Newport magistrates.

**1888** Edward Irvine appeared at Newport Police Court charged with assaulting 28 MAY his brother and sister and with cruelty to two dogs.

On returning home from the pub, Edward opened the yard gate to get to the back door. His father's two dogs should have been chained but one seized Edward by the crotch of his trousers.

Edward grabbed a broom and hit the dog. The second dog joined the first and Edward tried to break free, eventually using his knife to stab the first dog, causing it to lose an eye.

Edward's brother and sister both sustained minor knife cuts when they tried to stop him from hurting the dogs. However, neither was prepared to appear against their brother, so the charges of assault were dropped. The magistrates agreed that a man viciously attacked by a dog had every right to defend himself by whatever means and discharged Edward without penalty.

**1876** Thomas Williams and Thomas Jones were on Penrhiwllech Mountain 29 MAY hunting for foxes when Williams lifted a large stone to see what was beneath it.

The stone weighed around one and a half cwt and, having lifted it, Williams sent it tumbling down the mountainside. Only then did Jones notice a young boy standing 150 yards below them. He shouted a warning to the child, who jumped out of the path of the stone.

However, the stone unexpectedly broke apart and one piece hit the child on the head, knocking him unconscious. When twelve-year-old Llewellyn Thomas died from his injuries, Williams was charged with killing and slaying him and appeared at the Glamorganshire Summer Assizes.

His defence counsel Mr H. Allen maintained that Llewellyn's death was a tragic accident and, at very worst, homicide by misadventure. In his summing up of the case for the jury, judge Mr Baron Pollock seemed to support this view and the jury found Williams not guilty.

30 MAY    **1899** Morris Mort and William Worth were engaged to clean out a sewer on Commercial Street, Neath, but, on opening the sewer, they found it too full. Expecting the levels to fall, they decided to return to the corporation yard to collect a replacement cover for the manhole, since the existing one was broken into three pieces. They left the manhole open, stationing John Reynolds by the hole to prevent any of the local children meeting with an accident.

Reynolds was elderly and partially crippled and, although he stood within eighteen inches of the sewer entrance, several children persisted in trying to jump over the manhole, ignoring his repeated warnings that it was dangerous. Suddenly, nine-year-old Clifton Collins fell through the opening into the rushing water below.

The volume of effluent was too high for a rescue attempt and it was more than an hour before Clifton's body was recovered, having been washed almost 15 yards along the sewer. A post-mortem examination revealed that he broke his neck in the fall and died instantly.

At an inquest held by coroner Howel Cuthbertson, the jury asked why the workmen had not placed their ladder over the hole as a temporary barrier. The men had considered the idea but felt it too dangerous, thinking that the children may have tried to run along it and fallen through the rungs. It was intimated that a younger, fitter watchman might have been able to save Collins but Reynolds was adamant that no-one could have prevented the terrible tragedy.

The inquest jury eventually decided that nobody was to blame and returned a verdict of 'accidental death.'

31 MAY    **1874** John Gay was a patient on Ward 4 at Glamorganshire County Asylum, where those inmates classed as most dangerous were housed. On the night of 31 May, all of the inmates were in bed, with the exception of five who were on cleaning duties.

One of the warders sent Gay to fetch a mop from the ward lavatory and, hearing a crash, turned to see him collapsing. Another inmate, Thomas Griffiths, had dealt Gay a fearsome blow with a spade, splitting open his scalp and knocking him senseless. Although the asylum doctors were on hand to treat him, Gay died the next morning.

At the inquest, the asylum governors called for the coroner to return a verdict of wilful murder, saying that, if he could not do so, Griffiths should be taken before magistrates. The coroner explained that the law would not allow this, as Griffiths was obviously insane and it appears that the coroner's views prevailed, since there is no evidence that Griffiths faced any charges in relation to Gay's death.

# JUNE

*Swansea Town Hall. (Author's collection)*

1 JUNE  1910 Haulier Mr Doel was leading a horse across the yard at the Glamorgan Colliery when one of the coal trams that the horse was pulling accidentally came into contact with a live electric wire.

At the horse fell down dead and Doel, who was holding the metal leading chain, was unable to let go. His body jerking spasmodically, he let out a prolonged scream, eventually falling across the horse's body.

Edward Abbott ran to assist him, leaning over one of the trams in order to reach the unconscious man. Since the tram was still electrified, Abbott received a fatal shock. Doel was eventually pulled clear once the power had been turned off and survived the incident, although in the apt words of the contemporary newspapers, he '...suffered greatly from shock.'

2 JUNE  1900 Ten-year-old John Murray and thirteen-year-old Isaac Burnell appeared before magistrates at Cardiff charged with stealing three eggs, worth 1d each, from a hen house at the Canton Slaughterhouse, belonging to Mr David John.

John witnessed the boys stealing the eggs and ran after them – one egg was dropped during the chase but the remaining two were recovered and produced as evidence in court. The boys admitted their offence and magistrates decided that both should be sent to an Industrial School until they attained the age of sixteen.

3 JUNE  1831 In the early nineteenth century, Merthyr Tydfil rapidly transformed from an agricultural area to a place of great industry. The boom in the iron industry meant high wages and people flocked to capitalise on the town's new-found wealth. Yet Merthyr was ill- equipped to deal with an influx of new inhabitants, having poor quality housing and inadequate water supplies and sanitation.

The boom lasted until 1829, when a three-year depression hit the iron industry. There was no such thing as workers' rights and many labourers found themselves laid off or having their wages reduced. Things came to a head on

*General view of Merthyr, 1905. (Author's collection)*

31 May 1831, when bailiffs tried to seize property belonging to a man named Lewis Lewis, in settlement of his unpaid debts.

With the backing of his neighbours, Lewis prevented the bailiffs from taking all but one trunk, which was handed to a shopkeeper. With an army of followers, Lewis retrieved his property and set about attempting to liberate other recently seized goods.

By 3 June, there were almost 2,000 people behind Lewis and magistrates sent a request to the militia for assistance in quelling the uprising. The soldiers opened fire on the crowds massed outside The Castle Inn, killing at least sixteen people and Lewis and a man named Richard Lewis, aka Dic Penderyn, were arrested for stabbing a soldier named Donald Black.

The two men were tried for murder and, found guilty, both were sentenced to death. Yet the only real evidence against Richard Lewis came from a local barber, who was known to have a grudge against him and had been heard to threaten to get even with him. Richard was wearing a blue coat and trousers at the time of the murder but several witnesses testified that Black's murderer wore a drab coat. Furthermore, numerous people swore that Richard was elsewhere in the town when Black was stabbed. Even though almost 11,000 people signed a petition for a reprieve for Richard, he was hanged at Cardiff on 13 August 1831. His last words were, 'I suffer unjustly. God who knows all things knows it is so.'

Lewis Lewis was reprieved, his sentence commuted to transportation for life. There is anecdotal evidence that, in America, in1874, a man named Ieuan Parker made a death-bed confession to Black's murder.

**1874** Commercial traveller Henry Leyshon needed to go to Caerphilly on business and decided to take his wife and seven-year-old daughter along for the ride. He approached cab proprietor James Marks to hire a phaeton but Marks only had one thoroughbred mare available, a bad-natured beast that he was reluctant to hire out.  **4 JUNE**

Leyshon was persuasive, pointing out to Marks that he would be accompanied on his journey by his pregnant wife and daughter and would therefore be driving extremely carefully. Eventually he overcame Marks's misgivings.

As Leyshon approached the hill on the Cardiff side of Caerphilly, he touched the mare with the whip, using it several times to urge her up the steep slope. As the horse reached the top it bolted. Leyshon fought to control the phaeton as it careered along the lane, gouging huge scars in the roadside banks with its wheels. Finally, he dropped the reins, which became entangled around the mare's legs, driving her into a frenzy. She kicked and plunged until the phaeton overturned, spilling its three occupants onto the road.

They were found almost immediately and taken to The Old Station Inn. Both Mr and Mrs Leyshon were unconscious and Mr Leyshon died later that day. His wife survived for thirty-six hours, dying without regaining consciousness and leaving four children orphans.

Leyshon's daughter received only minor cuts and bruises in the accident that killed her parents and the contemporary newspapers were pleased to report that Mr Leyshon had insured his life for a considerable sum of money, which it was hoped would provide a secure future for his children.

**5 JUNE** **1869** Forty-nine-year-old John Lane had a grievance with his brother-in-law, William Richards, and went to have it out with him. Arriving at Richards's farm in Kilgwrrwg, he found that he and his wife had gone to Chepstow market.

Lane turned their servant out of the farmhouse and locked the door. He then drove his brother-in-law's cows into a field of standing clover and, when farmer William Nicholls (or Nicholas) protested, Lane shot him in the head, killing him instantly. As butcher James Davies rushed to help Nicholls, he too was shot. His right arm was later amputated and he lost the sight of his right eye.

Several people saw Lane leaving the scene of the murder and when he was arrested the next morning at the home of a relative, he accused people of stealing cattle from his farm and cheating him out of money, saying he had only done what was written in the Bible.

Lane was tried for murder at the Monmouthshire Assizes. There was little doubt that he was not in his right mind at the time of the shootings and, after hearing that his mother had spent time in a lunatic asylum and his brother was 'sometimes curious', the jury acquitted Lane on the grounds of insanity and he was ordered to be detained during Her Majesty's Pleasure. He was sent to Broadmoor Criminal Lunatic Asylum, where he is believed to have died in 1898.

**6 JUNE** **1878** The steamer *Chrysolite* was berthed at the Alexandra Dock, Newport, loading coal bound for Lisbon. Most of the crew were on shore leave, leaving the captain, mate, second mate, watchman and some coal trimmers on board when, just after midnight, the ship exploded.

Four bodies were recovered and eight injured men rescued, most suffering from burns and broken bones. Several others were missing, presumed dead, either 'blown to atoms' or propelled into the water and drowned.

The cause of the explosion was believed to be the ignition of accumulated coal gas and it was assumed that the nightwatchman went into the hold with a candle. At a later enquiry, it was pointed out that safety lamps were as necessary on board coal ships as they were in the most dangerous of mines.

*Alexandra Dock, Newport. (Author's collection)*

**1909** John 'Jack' Edmunds appeared before Mr Justice Ridley at the Monmouth
Assizes charged with murdering Cecilia Harris at Abersychan.

On 20 February, fifty-nine-year-old Cecilia saw Edmunds hanging around outside her isolated farmhouse, carrying a gun. She ordered him to go away and he retreated a few yards, lighting a cigarette and eyeing her defiantly. When Cecilia repeated her request for him to leave, he pointed the gun at her and she retreated indoors and locked the door.

As she watched from her bedroom window, Edmunds approached the house and broke a window. Cecilia managed to escape but only got as far as her garden gate before Edmunds shot her in the mouth and brutally raped her, as she lay bleeding,

Afterwards, Edmunds offered to bandage Cecilia's wounds and courteously assisted her indoors. Anxious to get rid of him, Cecilia offered him all the money

*Mr Justice Ridley. (Author's collection)*

in the house if he would go and Edmunds pocketed 5s 6d and her watch, before cutting her throat with a breadknife. As he attempted a second cut, Cecilia begged for her life, urging Edmunds to think of his mother. Only then did he leave.

Cecilia staggered three-quarters of a mile to a neighbour's house. As she waited for the doctor, she scribbled a note: 'Jack Edmunds shot me and cut my throat he got my money.' [*sic*] In spite of her horrific injuries, Cecilia lived until 5 May.

At his trial, Edmunds denied having been anywhere near Cecilia's farm on the day in question. However, five witnesses testified to seeing him in the area and blood, semen, hair and fibres were found on his clothes.

The jury found him guilty but twenty-four-year-old Edmunds immediately appealed his death sentence. Cecilia's post-mortem revealed heart disease and bronchitis and Edmunds maintained that she died from these illnesses, rather than as a direct result of the attack on her. His appeal was dismissed and he was executed at Usk on 3 July by Henry Pierrepoint.

**1869** A post-mortem examination was carried out on seven-year-old Arthur
Mottram.

Arthur lived with his aunt at Aberkenfig and, a week earlier, complained of pains in his head and stomach. Soon, he was vomiting and, although a doctor was called and medicine prescribed, Arthur was so sick that he was unable to keep it down. At the inquest, coroner Mr H. Cuthbertson learned that Arthur's mother had lost another son a year earlier. Two-year-old Edwin was perfectly healthy until, exactly like Arthur, he suddenly developed sickness and diarrhoea. Edwin was insured by a burial society and his mother received £3 18s on his death – now a second son, who was also insured, had died under suspicious circumstances.

Cuthbertson requested a post-mortem examination and doctors found that Arthur had softening of the brain and intestinal disease but were unable to find any traces of poison. The inquest jury returned a verdict of 'death from natural causes' and Cuthbertson pointedly informed Arthur's mother that he would be watching her family very closely from then on.

**9 JUNE**    **1898** Gamekeeper Robert Scott was patrolling the Margam Abbey estate with under keeper Mr Kidd and estate policemen Mr Hawkin, when their attention was drawn to a man walking on the mountainside. After watching him through binoculars, they heard shots being fired and headed towards them. Scott became separated from his companions and was later found in a ditch, his face destroyed by two gunshot wounds.

An appeal for information brought forth a witness who heard shots and saw a man with a shotgun walking towards Taibach. The police questioned villagers and established that Joseph Lewis from Maesteg had spent the night there with a couple named Williams.

Lewis was arrested but released after implicating a Mr Jones. However, Jones had an unshakeable alibi and Lewis was eventually charged with Scott's murder.

The evidence against Lewis was circumstantial but the case against him was strengthened by Jones and another man named Griffiths, both of whom testified that Lewis had confessed. Their testimony was persuasive and the jury at the Glamorganshire Assizes found Lewis guilty. He was executed at Swansea on 30 August.

**10 JUNE**    **1924** Eighteen-year-old John Peacock of Swansea got into difficulties in rough seas at Langland Bay. Seeing Peacock in trouble, John Evans went to his aid, without even pausing to take off his boots. However, conditions were so bad that Evans vanished beneath the waves. A third man, Clifford Harcourt, tried to rescue both men but he too disappeared.

Leighton Dunbridge managed to reach Evans, who told him, 'Thank God you've come. I am a married man with kiddies.' Dunbridge towed Evans most of the way to the shore but became exhausted and had to release his hold.

Dunbridge was pulled from the water unconscious but eventually revived by artificial respiration. Peacock, Evans and Harcourt drowned, their deaths witnessed by hundreds of visitors to the beach, including their families.

*Langland Bay.*
*(Author's collection)*

**1920** Fifteen-year-old Katherine Alice Primrose Whistance, who lived with her aunt Sarah Ann White at Llanvetherine, cycled to her mother's house about two miles away, arriving before six o'clock in the morning. 'Katie' was vague about the purpose of her visit, although she mentioned that she thought Mrs White was going out of her mind and that her aunt had given her some money.   **11 JUNE**

By 7.30 a.m. Katie was at the police station in tears. She again mentioned her aunt going out of her mind, begging, 'Please come down at once.' When the police arrived at Mrs White's isolated cottage, they found her bludgeoned to death and days later Katie admitted, 'I did murder my auntie.'

At Katie's trial at the Monmouth Assizes, the prosecution maintained that she didn't want to live with her aunt anymore. This would not normally be an adequate motive but the accused '…was approaching an age when girls frequently could not control themselves and were unable to resist impulses.' The defence ridiculed this, saying that, with the exception of a minor disagreement six weeks before the murder, Katie and her aunt lived happily together. Neither prosecution nor defence considered insanity as a factor in the killing, which the defence maintained was more likely to have been the work of a man than a young girl.

Katie was found guilty and, under the Children's Act of 1908, could not be sentenced to death. She was ordered to be detained during His Majesty's Pleasure.

**1869** An inquest was held on the deaths of three men killed in a railway accident at Maesycwmmer on 10 June. After repairs were carried out on a train, it was taken for a test run on the Brecon and Merthyr railway. The train pulled several wagons of iron ore and carried railway superintendents Mr Kendall and Mr Simpson, traffic manager Mr Crane, driver Mr Stokes and fitter Mr Pollard.   **12 JUNE**

The trial was going according to plan until the train reached Maesycwmmer, when the train failed to negotiate a curve and went off the rails, falling 16ft onto the road below a bridge. Stokes, Kendall and Simpson were buried in the wreckage, while Crane and Pollard were thrown clear and, although injured, survived the disaster. When the bodies were finally extricated from the rubble, it was found that Stokes and Kendall had been 'smashed to atoms' and Simpson boiled alive by steam.

The inquest jury returned a verdict that all three men were 'accidentally killed through the engine running off the line.'

**13 JUNE** **1832** Mrs Powell died in Crickhowell and her body was laid out and left in her house overnight. The following morning, it was evident that her home had been burgled, the heartless thief even trying to prize the rings from the corpse's fingers.

The burglar gained entry by smashing a pane of glass at the rear of the house then reaching through and unlatching the window. Fortunately for the magistrates charged with tracing the culprit, he or she had been cut by the broken glass. There were large drops of blood throughout the house and a trail clearly leading to the house next door. Having followed the trail, magistrates searched the adjacent house, finding all of Mrs Powell's missing items there.

*Crickhowell.*
*(Author's collection)*

**14 JUNE** **1875** Twelve-year-old Elizabeth Jones returned home to Briton Ferry, having been missing for several days. She told her parents that she was now a married woman.

Some months earlier, Elizabeth had caught the eye of street missionary Mr Lely. Believing Lely to be a good, Christian man, Elizabeth's parents did not prevent their association but objected when Lely offered to put her in school and educate her at his own expense until she reached marriageable age.

Now Elizabeth told her parents that she and Lely went by train to Newport, where they were married in church. Lely's sister was invited to be a witness but fainted when she found out that her brother intended to take a child bride and refused to participate in the ceremony.

When Elizabeth returned home, her father gave her 'a good thrashing', expressing shock that a clergyman would marry so young a child without the consent of her parents. Evan Jones was keen to punish both Lely and the minister as strongly as the law would allow but Elizabeth threatened to cut her throat if her father tried to keep her from her husband. Elizabeth's mother was more relaxed about her daughter's nuptials, saying that it was best to let the matter rest. She believed that, given time, her daughter might outgrow her obsession and knew that any objection from her parents was likely to force the child into the arms of her new husband.

**1872** At the Cwmbach Colliery near Pontypridd, miners were raised and lowered in two carriages that counterbalanced each other, one rising as the other descended. They were connected by a chain passing over a revolving drum, which was powered by an engine controlled in the surface engine house.

15 JUNE

Miners communicated with the engine house by coded knocks and, on 15 June, William Davis was ascending, when he realised that the speed of the carriage was increasing. Davis knocked to alert the engine house but the carriage went ever faster, until it reached the drum, where it was wrenched from the chain and fell back into the depths of the pit. A worker at the pit bottom dodged the falling car and, when the dust settled, found Davis dead in the rubble.

Meanwhile, the banksman who should have been operating the carriages had momentarily left the engine house to collect some new tackle. As he returned, he noticed the carriages in motion and raced back to see who was working them. He was confronted by a complete stranger running the engine at full pressure and, although the banksman pushed him aside and tried to stop the engine, he was unsuccessful.

William Thomas insisted that the colliery superintendent had sent him to the engine house but the superintendent denied doing so – indeed Thomas didn't even work at the pit. He was found guilty of manslaughter at the Cardiff Assizes, where it was suggested that Thomas was insane and the presiding judge deferred sentencing while enquiries were made into the state of his mind. Thomas was ultimately sentenced to six months' imprisonment with hard labour.

**1928** Collier Trevor John Edwards of Cwmaman loved Annie Protheroe. However, when Annie moved to Swindon, Trevor began seeing Elsie Cook and made her pregnant.

16 JUNE

He wrote to Annie, telling her that by the time she came home he would either have a wife or a coffin. Then, on 16 June, he took Elsie for a walk on the mountain at Llanwenno, having first bought a flagon of beer from a pub.

Edwards smashed the flagon over Elsie's head. When her felt hat protected her from serious injury, he tried to throttle her with his bare hands and, when that still didn't kill her, he cut her throat with his razor, almost severing her head from her body. He then made a half-hearted attempt at committing suicide, before handing himself in to the police.

Tried at the Assizes in Swansea, twenty-one-year-old Edwards was found guilty of wilful murder and sentenced to death, although the jury added a recommendation for mercy. In spite of this, Edwards was executed at Swansea on 11 December.

**17 JUNE** **1919** The funeral of twenty-year-old Harold Smart took place at Cardiff. Days earlier, Harold, who was wounded in the First World War, staggered up to a police officer and complained that a 'coloured' man had cut his throat. He was rushed to hospital in a cab but died shortly after arrival.

In the aftermath of the First World War, men returning from the front grew resentful of 'coloured' men, who were seen as taking jobs from British war heroes. This attitude was especially prevalent in areas such as Cardiff, where foreign seamen and dock workers had integrated into the community. On 11 June, the racial tension in the area exploded into a riot, which was to last for several days and claim the lives of another two men besides Smart. Dozens more were injured.

*The Times* of 13 June reflects the appalling attitudes of the period. 'There are a thousand coloured men out of work in Cardiff, most of them sailors and it has to be remembered to their credit that during the war they faced the perils of the submarine campaign with all the gallantry of the British seaman...The negro is almost pathetically loyal to the British Empire and he is always proud to acclaim himself a Briton. His chief failing is his fondness for white women.'

At the Swansea Assizes in July, ten men were convicted of rioting and were awarded various prison terms ranging from three to twenty months, all with hard labour.

**18 JUNE** **1868** Martha Thomas and William Protheroe had been courting for some years when Martha fell pregnant. The pregnancy became a source of argument and Protheroe beat Martha, for which he was given a short prison sentence. While he was incarcerated, Martha gave birth and obviously believed that Protheroe would marry her on his release but Protheroe had other ideas and she had to summon him to force him to acknowledge paternity.

On the evening of 18 June, Martha slipped out of her home in Breconshire, having told her sister-in-law that she wanted to go to Rhymney. Four days later, the smell of decomposing flesh led to the discovery of her body at the bottom of an abandoned mineshaft.

Her arms and legs were shattered, her face and head smashed to pieces and her neck bent forward as though she had fallen headfirst into the pit. A post-mortem examination was ordered and the doctor given the almost impossible task of finding any marks of violence on the body. Although there were no indications of any struggle at the mouth of the pit, the doctor thought that there might be fingertip bruises on Martha's neck.

Believing that he was suspected of killing Martha, Protheroe went to the Glamorganshire police and satisfied officers that he was elsewhere when she died. However, although Martha's body was found just on the Glamorganshire side of the border with Breconshire, the inquest was held in Breconshire and the coroner ordered the Breconshire police to arrest him.

When the case came to trial – at the Brecon Assizes – the prosecution called a number of witnesses who claimed to have seen Protheroe in the vicinity, while the defence called no witnesses at all. Even so, presiding judge Mr Baron Piggott's summary of the case was favourably biased towards Protheroe and the jury found him not guilty.

**1893** Police Constable's Green and King of Cardiff were approached by a man with a knife, who told them, 'I give myself up to you. I have done it.' When King asked him what he had done, the man elaborated, 'I have murdered Mary Sheen.'

Twenty-five-year-old Mary Sheen (aka Sweeney) lived with Thomas Collins. However, she was not averse to visits from her estranged husband, creating jealousy between the two men.

On 10 June, Collins was released from prison after serving six months for felony and went with Mary to his mother's home. They argued constantly and Mary accused Collins of having an incestuous relationship with his mother. On 17 June, Collins attacked Mary with a knife, causing wounds that needed hospital treatment. She refused to press charges but, two days later, Collins attacked her again and this time her wounds were fatal.

When Collins appeared at the Glamorganshire Assizes, the question for the jury was his mental state at the time of the murder. Collins had been drinking and was known to react badly to alcohol. He claimed to have been incensed by Mary's allegations, even though doctors suspected that Collins might have been delusional and imagined Mary's accusations of incest.

The jury believed Collins sane and found him guilty, leading to the mandatory death sentence. However, the sentence was immediately appealed and two doctors were sent from London to examine him. He was reprieved and transferred to Broadmoor Criminal Lunatic Asylum.

**1886** As William Haddis was riding his bicycle at Magor, he was held up by William Davies, who had stopped his horse and cart in the middle of the road while he lit his pipe.

When Haddis politely asked to pass, Davies grumbled that he paid a licence for using the road, whereas cyclists didn't and consequently had no business on the public highway. Davies then drove off at a snail's pace, forcing Haddis and his brother, John, to crawl along behind him. When the Haddis brothers finally passed the cart on a bend, Davies called, 'Look out, or I will ride over you,' and deliberately drove the cart at William, cutting his head and severely damaging his bicycle.

John grabbed the horse's bridle, bringing the cart to a halt, at which Davies threatened to run him over too unless he let go. Davies failed to appear at Newport Petty Sessions to answer to charges of damaging a bicycle and injuring its owner but was fined 20s plus costs in his absence and ordered to pay £3 15s compensation to Haddis.

**1894** Having spent most of the day drinking at the Dunraven Hotel, Bridgend, twenty-four-year-old Evan Williams argued with the landlord about bread and cheese.

The petty spat quickly blew over and Williams left the hotel at closing time. Soon afterwards, the landlord and his family were rudely awakened by an explosion and the collapse of their bedroom ceiling. Somebody had thrown

*Dunraven Place, Bridgend, c. 1950. (Author's collection)*

dynamite through a cellar grating, lighting it by means of a long fuse and, although the ten occupants escaped without serious injury, the explosion blew out most of the hotel windows, causing more than £300 worth of damage.

The police found that the door of the explosives store at a nearby quarry had been kicked open and dynamite stolen. Williams worked there and the police were able to follow a trail of footprints to his home, where he was arrested in his bed. By then, he had sobered up and was appalled at what he had done. Since the explosion occurred immediately before the Glamorganshire Assizes, Williams was sent for trial for 'causing an explosion likely to endanger life.' He pleaded guilty to what his defence counsel referred to as a motiveless act, committed when the accused had 'given way to intemperance'. In spite of his previously excellent character, Williams was sentenced to seven years' penal servitude.

22 JUNE    **1869** Eighteen-year-old Mary Ann Hoare appeared before magistrates at Swansea charged with assaulting her father.

Mary Ann started a drunken argument with her mother and, when her father intervened, Mary Ann flew at him like a wild animal. She bit his thigh, ripping large holes in his clothes with her teeth, before seizing his tie and throttling him. Fortunately for Thomas Hoare, his neighbours pulled Mary Ann away before she killed him.

Magistrates committed her to prison for fourteen days. Her father begged them to send her to a reformatory on her release but the magistrates informed him that they would have no control over Mary Ann once she had served her sentence.

**1917** Forty-six-year-old farm labourer Arthur Stokes died from gunshot wounds in the kitchen at Penywern Farm, near Pontypridd, and sixteen-year-old servant Alice Roberts confessed that she was responsible for his death.    23 JUNE

She appeared at the Glamorganshire Assizes on 20 July, charged with wilful murder. The court heard that, prior to the shooting, Alice had complained that Stokes had behaved improperly towards her and had been advised to keep her bedroom door locked. According to Alice, on the morning of Stokes's death, she was alone in the house, apart from her mistress's deaf mother. Stokes came into the kitchen and tried to kiss Alice, who struggled and managed to fend him off. Stokes then lit his pipe and asked Alice to fetch the farm gun, saying, 'If you love me show duty; if not shoot me,' at which Alice pulled the trigger.

Having heard all the evidence, Mr Justice Sankey summed up the case for the jury, telling them, '... a woman's virtue is a pearl of great price' and Alice was legally entitled to defend hers by any means. The jury found her not guilty and she was discharged.

**1894** In the early hours of the morning, boilermaker Morris Jones of Cadoxton was awakened by his wife Margaret making a strange noise beside him in bed. Margaret was unable to speak and her husband sent their servant for a doctor.    24 JUNE

Initially, Dr Treharne was unable to establish what was wrong with Margaret until it was noticed that her false teeth were not in the glass at her bedside. The doctor was unable to save Margaret and an inquest later determined that she had died from suffocation as a result of swallowing her teeth while sleeping.

**1830** Workers at a colliery in Cwm Carno, Glamorgan, drilled a hole in the mountainside, to allow fresh air to ventilate the mine.    25 JUNE

On 25 June, the area was visited by a terrific thunderstorm. The hole was situated close to a small brook, which soon burst its banks following the deluge of rain. Thousands of gallons of water poured down the air pipe into the mine below, where six men and a woman were working.

One man struggled to the mouth of the mine, where he was rescued as the flood water reached his chin. The remaining six people were drowned.

**1886** As David Jeans and his fiancée Ellen Merchant (or Marchant) walked across fields near Cardiff, they were approached by five men demanding money. The couple ran and were pelted with stones until, with the robbers hot on their heels, Jeans pulled out a revolver and fired several shots, wounding three of the men.    26 JUNE

Jeans reported the incident to the police, assuring them that he acted in self-defence. However, the police recalled a previous occasion, when Jeans appeared at Roath police station claiming to have been attacked by two men. The men also reported the incident but gave a very different account, alleging that Jeans shot at them without provocation. With no way of proving either account, the police were unable to press charges.

Once again, both parties were telling completely different stories. Interviewed independently, George Mills, James Hawker, John Williams and Thomas Kellow stated that Mills politely told Jeans and his girlfriend that they were walking on private land and Jeans pulled his gun from his pocket and opened fire. The fifth man, John Carey, was shot in the head and gave a dying deposition corroborating his friends' statements. When Carey died, Jeans was charged with wilful murder.

He appeared at the Glamorganshire Assizes on 2 August. Ellen claimed that she and Jeans were in fear for their lives and that the five men used disgusting language, demanded money and threw stones. Ellen admitted that Jeans fired his gun but said that he fired into the air or the ground. If the jury accepted Ellen's evidence, the crime was reduced to one of manslaughter and the jury found Jeans guilty of the lesser offence, recommending mercy on account of the provocation he received before the shooting. He was sentenced to twelve months' imprisonment.

27 JUNE   1894 Margaret Ann Jenkins appeared at the Glamorganshire Assizes charged with the murder of her seven-week-old daughter, Lizzie.

Margaret lived in Treherbert with her husband, David, who worked nights at Ferndale Colliery. When Margaret woke David on the afternoon of 18 May, she remarked conversationally, 'I have finished the baby,' and when David asked what she meant, she pointed to the pantry where she had placed Lizzie's body, having decapitated her with an axe.

Margaret had borne eleven children, four of whom had died in infancy or childhood. She suffered from depression and was described as being 'strange of manner'. Judged unfit to plead at her trial for 'feloniously and of malice aforethought killing and murdering Elizabeth Ann Jenkins', Margaret was ordered to be detained until Her Majesty's Pleasure be known.

28 JUNE   1858 One of three interconnected boilers at the Victoria Iron Works Company malfunctioned. Three men climbed on top, one of whom was seen to put his hand on the safety valve lever and press it down, before engineer Thomas Price sat on it. Less than thirty seconds later, the boiler exploded.

David Nunnery and Thomas Rees were blown sky high, their badly maimed bodies found almost 60 yards away. Price and Jonathan Woodford were also killed instantly and several men were injured, most suffering severe scalding.

Fortunately, the chimney stacks above the boiler fell away from the work sheds, otherwise the death toll would undoubtedly have been much higher.

At an inquest held by coroner Mr Brewer, the jury were told that Price was a reliable, careful, trusted employee, who was sober at the time of the accident. The only reason anyone could think of for his recklessness in sitting on the safety valve was that the boiler was deficient in power and he was trying to prevent it letting off steam. The jury returned a verdict of 'accidental death' on each victim.

Note: The explosion is variously reported to have occurred on Saturday and Monday (26 or 28 June).

**1882**  John Jeffries was an elderly, crippled shoemaker, whose second wife, Ellen,    **29 JUNE**
led him a dog's life. So frequent were their arguments that the couple were given notice to leave their Newport lodgings.

On 29 June, their landlady heard John yelling 'Murder!' and found that Ellen had slashed him with a knife as he lay in bed, cutting his neck and chest.

The police were called and Ellen was arrested, in spite of her insistence that John had injured himself to get her into trouble. She appeared before magistrates, but they didn't believe her story either and sentenced her to twenty-eight days' hard labour.

**1870**  After arguing with her husband, William, about money, Maria Gay    **30 JUNE**
returned to her parents, who kept The Lamb and Flag Inn at Eglwysilan. She was sharing a bed with her stepmother, when William burst into the room and attacked her with a large hammer.

Maria snatched the hammer from her husband, who then hacked at her with a knife or razor. Her hand was badly cut and, when she fainted due to loss of blood, William fled. He was later found by police hiding in a pig sty, very drunk and sobbing that he only wanted to persuade Maria to come back.

William appeared at the Assizes charged with three counts of feloniously stabbing and wounding his wife, one with intent to murder her, one with intent to do her grievous bodily harm and one with intent to disable her.

Both Maria and her stepmother testified that William was a kind husband and Maria blamed herself for the vicious attack. 'It was my temper that did it,' she insisted. 'I drew him into a bad way and left him. It was my own fault.'

The jury found William guilty of the lesser offence of unlawful wounding and William threw himself at the court's mercy, saying that he and Maria were reconciled and pointing out that he had already been in prison for seven months awaiting trial. He was sentenced to a further twelve months' imprisonment with hard labour.

# JULY

*Newport Docks. (Author's collection)*

**1871** Patrick Sullivan was employed as a blast furnace stoker at the Abernant Works in Aberdare and, given permission to go to the office to collect his wages, he didn't return to the engine house for eight hours, by which time he was blind drunk. Foreman James Price ordered him to go home but two hours later, Sullivan appeared back in the engine-house, still intoxicated, and Price again ordered him home.

It is not certain whether Sullivan disobeyed him or whether he went home and returned to the Works a third time but at 2.30 a.m. on 2 July, he was found dead under a large revolving crank, which had obviously hit his head and killed him instantly.

**1909** A dam at the mouth of the Ebbw suddenly collapsed, inundating construction work on an extension to the Alexandra Dock, Newport.

At least sixty-six men were digging a massive trench, 50ft deep and 30ft wide. The rush of water caused the trench to cave in, toppling cranes and railway wagons into the excavation and burying the men under tons of earth.

By midnight, eight had been brought out alive and four dead. It proved impossible to estimate the number still missing, since many who were not injured had simply wandered home in shock. By the following morning, twenty-six more men had been rescued alive and one further body recovered, but it was feared that at least twenty were still entombed.

The final death toll was thirty-nine, although ten days after the disaster, labourer John Knight turned up alive. He somehow managed to crawl out of the landslide unnoticed almost twenty-four hours after it occurred and spent the next few days wandering around in a daze.

**1874** Former soldier Patrick Riley argued with his wife, Rose Ann, when she moved their mattress off the bedstead onto the floor. The couple shared one room in Herbert Street, Cardiff, with their four sons, aged nineteen, sixteen, fourteen and eight years old.

When Rose was found dead the following morning, Patrick reported to the police that she had died through drinking. However, a post-mortem examination suggested otherwise, revealing numerous bruises and a fractured skull.

The police interviewed Rose's sons, the three eldest of whom stated that, after their father took the mattress off the floor, their mother staggered towards the fireplace and fell. However the youngest, Thomas, told a different story, telling police that he saw Patrick kick Rose several times in the head with his heavy boots.

Patrick was committed for trial for wilful murder. At the Cardiff Assizes on 18 July, the doctor who performed the post-mortem stated that Rose's injuries could not have resulted from a fall and Thomas stuck to his story, which contradicted his brothers' evidence in almost every respect.

The jury told Mr Justice Quain that they wished to return a verdict of manslaughter but Quain was unwilling to accept it, asking the jury to continue deliberating. Although Quain eventually relented, the jury failed to reach an agreement, leaving the judge no option but to defer the case until the next Assizes. Riley languished in prison awaiting the Winter Assizes of 1874 but they were postponed and it wasn't until March 1875 that he came to court again.

Although Thomas stuck to his story, his three brothers now remembered their mother falling a few days before her death and complaining of pain in her head. (Asked why they failed to mention this before, they explained that nobody had ever asked them!) With this new evidence, Riley was found not guilty and discharged from court to spontaneous applause. As compensation for his lengthy spell in prison, he was paid his army pension, although the money was put towards the cost of his defence.

**4 JULY** **1875** Two hundred feet below ground at the Western Colliery in the Rhondda Valley was an airshaft that discharged both foul air and steam from a nearby engine. The steam softened the roof of the tunnel hence a special watch was kept on it at all times.

A check on 3 July showed that the roof was in urgent need of repair and five miners were sent down next morning to attend to it. Due to the proximity of the engine, it was very hot and the men could only work for short periods before retreating to a cooler part of the workings for a few breaths of fresher air.

As Isaac Williams and John Prosser worked on the roof, there was a sudden fall, which buried both men in rubble. The roof was creaking ominously and, according to the contemporary newspapers, '... with true heroism, only David Morgan advanced through the darkness to the very jaws of death in his anxiety to assist his friends.'

There was no sign of Prosser and Williams was completely buried from the neck downwards and calling desperately for help. Morgan grasped his head, while Williams wriggled his body to try and extricate himself. Suddenly, a deafening roar signalled a further fall. Morgan ran to safety but Williams and Prosser were buried beneath a ton and a half of rock and earth.

It took six hours to recover their bodies.

**5 JULY** **1904** Margaret Evans of Senghenydd was left babysitting her ten-month-old granddaughter, Mabel, but, when the child's mother returned home, she found Margaret deliberately holding the baby over the fire. Mabel died from shock and burns, leading to her grandmother's arrest for wilful murder.

That Margaret killed the baby was beyond doubt. Thus, when she appeared at the Glamorganshire Assizes, the main task for the jury was determining her mental state at the time.

Margaret was devastated, telling police that she did not know what had come over her. Prone to bouts of drinking, after which she was known to suffer from delusions, she had strong premonitions that she and her relations were doomed to die by fire. She also heard voices and imagined that the tea kettle and clocks spoke to her. As expected, the jury found her guilty but insane and she was ordered to be confined as a criminal lunatic until Her Majesty's Pleasure be known.

**6 JULY** **1882** At the shipbuilding works at Pembroke Dock, Isaac Bristow stepped onto a workbench, where an enormous circular saw was running. Unfortunately, his foot slipped and he fell across the saw, severing one of his legs.

*Pembroke Dock.*
*(Author's collection)*

The fifty-nine-year-old carpenter tried to stand up, managing to partially raise himself on his arms. However, weak from loss of blood, he fell again, this time landing stomach first on the revolving saw. His body was cut almost in two.

Bristow left a wife and several children to mourn his loss.

**1898** Ship's fireman Henry O'Neil (aka Price) was a steady and sober man who, **7 JULY** when he was not at sea, lived happily with his wife, Margaret, and their three children in Swansea.

He returned from a tour of duty on 3 July. It was an eventful trip, since his ship struck an iceberg off Newfoundland and Henry was delighted to be home safe and sound. However, the shipwreck seemed to have unhinged his mind as, on 7 July, he stabbed Margaret eight times and ran away, leaving her bleeding to death on their bed.

The alarm was raised by one of the couple's children and Margaret was rushed to hospital, where she died within minutes. Henry was discovered hiding in a nearby lavatory and confessed to having stabbed his wife, before making a dash for the canal and flinging himself in.

The jury at the subsequent inquest found a verdict of wilful murder against O'Neil, followed by suicide while temporarily insane.

**1916** Daniel Sullivan of Dowlais was a mean drunk. Having spent the night of **8 JULY** 8 July drinking at The Antelope Hotel, he purchased a bottle of rum before leaving.

Arriving home, he shouted for his wife Catherine to make him some food. Told by his nine-year-old stepdaughter that her mother was asleep, Daniel dragged Catherine out of bed and kicked her from the bedroom to the kitchen.

A coker at the Iron and Steel Works, Daniel wore hobnailed boots, which inflicted terrible injuries on his wife. 'There'll be a corpse leaving the house tonight,' he yelled at his stepdaughter and stepson, who fled the house in terror. They ran to the neighbours for help and, when there was no response, went to the police station. The police arrived to find Catherine lying dead in a pool of blood and her husband hiding in the chicken coop.

Tried and found guilty at the Swansea Assizes, Sullivan's only reaction to his death sentence was to calmly state, 'I am not guilty.' He was refused leave to appeal his conviction and was executed at Swansea Prison on 6 September. Daniel Edwards, the landlord of The Antelope Hotel, was fined £20 and sentenced to twenty-eight days' imprisonment for selling him alcohol out of hours.

**9 JULY    1929** Two British submarines, H47 and L12, collided about twenty miles off the Welsh coast. The H47 was holed and sank with all crew. Only three survived, all of whom were on the conning tower at the time of the collision. One jumped off the H47 and clung to the landing stays of the L12, maintaining his hold even as the L12 was dragged under water.

Immediate search and rescue attempts were initiated from Pembroke Dock but since the watertight doors of the H47 were open at the time of the collision, there was no hope that any of her crew had survived. Three men from the L12 were also killed in the incident, making a total of twenty-four fatalities.

**10 JULY    1844** An inquest was held into the death of twenty-three-year-old servant Mary Anne Lewis, who died near Bridgend the previous day.

Mary Anne was prone to sudden fainting spells and, on the morning of her death, had risen early to milk the cows. Since her cap was found on a rock on the bank, it was supposed that she had gone to a nearby stream to wash her face and fainted while kneeling, falling face down and drowning in the shallow water.

The inquest jury returned a verdict of 'accidentally drowned.'

**11 JULY    1864** Twenty-two-year-old Mary Prout appeared at the Haverfordwest Assizes charged with murdering her nine-week-old illegitimate daughter, Rhoda.

On 22 May, the body of a baby girl was found at the bottom of a disused coal pit in Roath. A post-mortem examination showed that she died from extensive fractures to her skull, resulting in a build up of blood on her brain. She also had a broken thigh and numerous bruises on her body, which occurred while she was alive. Mary, who was visiting her family nearby, insisted that Rhoda died at the Narberth Workhouse but when questioned on 23 May, she admitted to the police, 'If they hang me for it, I'll tell the truth. I threw it and ran away a short distance and then returned and found there was no noise.'

Mary's counsel tried every possible defence for his client, suggesting that there was no proof that Rhoda was alive when she left the Workhouse, or that she may have died from convulsions and finally that Mary Prout was insane but the jury found her guilty. Her mandatory death sentence was later commuted to life imprisonment and she was sent to the Knaphill Female Convict Prison in Surrey.

**12 JULY    1869** A wanton act of malicious cruelty was perpetuated on eighteen young turkeys belonging to a farmer at Crickhowell. During the hours of darkness, some unknown person or persons attacked the birds with a knife, cutting one leg from each.

All of the birds survived and it was reported that the farmer intended to fit each with a custom-made wooden leg, so that they could continue to be fattened for the Christmas market.

**1911** Henry Phillips was a violent husband and his wife Margaret left him several times during their thirteen-year marriage, always returning for the sake of their four children. However, after a beating on 13 July 1911, Margaret took three of the children and went to her mother in Knelston. She charged Henry with persistent cruelty and he was summoned to appear before magistrates on 8 December.

13 JULY

Margaret found rooms in Knelston and, on 26 July, her sister Ann went to fetch water from a well and bumped into Margaret on the street. The sisters chatted for a few minutes before Ann walked on but she had not gone far when Margaret screamed, 'Oh, Harry! Harry!'

Ann rushed to fetch her mother and her lodger, Thomas Casement, then ran back to Margaret, arriving just in time to see Henry slashing her throat. Henry fled, with Casement chasing him, but when Henry stopped running and asked, 'Is the bugger dead yet?' before threatening to kill Casement too, the lodger abandoned his pursuit.

Henry then walked into The Welcome to Town Inn and bought a pint of beer, ordering four bottles to take away. On leaving, he calmly announced to landlord John Thomas, 'I've just killed my wife.'

By then, the police were on Henry's trail and after following a track through a cornfield they found him sleeping off the effects of his beer. Since Margaret's mother, sister and Thomas Casement witnessed Margaret's violent death, the jury at the Cardiff Assizes on 11 November had no hesitation in finding Henry guilty and he was executed at Swansea on 14 December.

**1875** Heavy rain fell throughout Monmouthshire, with more than five inches recorded in twenty-eight hours. The weight of the water in the one-acre reservoir at Cwmcarn became too great for the sand and gravel retaining banks, which burst, sending a tidal wave of water rushing down the valley.

14 JULY

The water demolished everything in its path. Bridges, walls, roads and buildings were swept away, including a cottage and its three occupants. A flannel factory and adjoining cottage were completely destroyed. The owner, John Hunt, was caught in the torrent but managed to grab a branch and was later rescued. One of Hunt's apprentices held onto a piece of floating machinery and he too was saved. Sadly, Hunt's wife, four children, two servants and a second apprentice drowned.

**1856** As 160 men descended to begin their shift at the Cymmer Colliery near Pontypridd there was an explosion of such ferocity that it was feared that none could survive. Fortunately some miners were still close enough to the shaft to be rescued but, by that evening, 112 bodies had been recovered. A final body was brought out of the pit the next day and one of those rescued alive died on 17 July.

15 JULY

Thirty-four of the 114 fatalities were aged under sixteen and fifteen of those under twelve. Most households in the area lost at least one family member and one family lost a father and three sons, aged ten, thirteen and sixteen.

An inquest was opened and adjourned several times before concluding that the safety precautions at the mine were woefully inadequate, with poor ventilation and frequent use of naked lights, even though pockets of gas were common. The inquest jury eventually returned verdicts of manslaughter against managers Jabez Thomas, Rowland Rowlands and Morgan Rowlands.

All appeared at the Swansea Assizes on 24 February 1857, where they were acquitted.

**16 JULY** **1921** Swansea Sunday school teachers Myrddin Lavis and Thomas Davies organised a picnic for their classes at Three Cliffs Bay. Just before leaving the beach to go home, the two men decided to bathe and, watched from the beach by their pupils and by Davies's mother, were swept away by a strong current and drowned.

When their bodies were recovered the following day, twenty-four-year-old Lavis and twenty-two-year-old Davies were clutched in each others' arms. An inquest later returned a verdict of accidental death on both men.

*Three Cliffs Bay in the 1950s. (Author's collection)*

**17 JULY** **1878** William and Elizabeth Watkins and three of their children, Charlotte, Alice and Frederick, were found brutally murdered in their cottage at Langibby At first, police believed that William had killed his family and then committed suicide but all five victims had been brutally murdered, their cottage ransacked and then set on fire.

Several people had seen a tramp in the area and, when police heard that a man with a scratched face and bloodstained clothes had begged a lift to Newport in the mail cart, they put a watch on the town and quickly apprehended a suspect.

Spanish sailor Joseph Garcia was discharged from Usk Prison on the morning of 16 July, having served a sentence for housebreaking. When arrested, he was wearing William Watkins's boots and some of his clothes and he carried a bundle of women's clothes and part of a clock, later identified by eldest daughter Mary Ann Watkins as belonging to her mother. Garcia's own clothes were recently washed, but still bore traces of blood.

Although largely circumstantial, the evidence against twenty-one-year-old Garcia was persuasive and, at the Usk Assizes on 30 October, the jury found him guilty and he was sentenced to death. He made no confession before his scheduled execution date of 18 November, when he fainted as William

Marwood was preparing to execute him. His last words were a declaration of his innocence.

Having spent a two-week holiday with her parents, fifteen-year-old Mary Ann left her family home on the morning of the murder to return to her position in service. But for that, Garcia would probably have claimed six victims.

**1887** The three sons of Monmouth tobacconist James Jennings lost their lives in a devastating fire.    18 JULY

The boys were asleep in the living quarters, two floors above the shop, when their parents realised that the building was on fire and, although Jennings, his wife and her sister managed to escape, five-year-old Reginald James, three-year-old Cyril Arthur George and one-year-old Edgar William perished in the conflagration.

At the inquest on their deaths, the jury found it impossible to establish the cause of the fire, although they didn't discount Mr Jennings's theory that it was started by Lucifer matches stocked in the shop. The jury bemoaned the fact that no ladders were available since, by the time the fire escape arrived on the scene, the smoke and flames were so intense that it proved impossible to reach the children. Had ladders been stored with the more cumbersome fire escape, it was widely believed that all three would have been saved.

**1890** Twenty-year-old servant Elizabeth Watts appeared at the Breconshire Assizes charged with the wilful murder of her illegitimate son and with concealing his birth. Since the Crown decided not to proceed with the former offence, she was tried only for concealment and pleaded guilty.    19 JULY

On 13 May, Elizabeth complained of diarrhoea and was given whisky and hot water, then gin and hot water by her mistress. Within fifteen minutes, Elizabeth secretly gave birth to a baby boy, whose body she placed in a patch of stinging nettles in the garden of her mistress's home at Llanspyddid. The body was discovered and, when Elizabeth was questioned, she said that she had accidentally trodden on her baby and killed him.

In passing sentence, Lord Chief Justice Coleridge remarked that he viewed Elizabeth's story with great suspicion. He 'hoped with all his heart' that her statement was true and that no murder took place, but said that her conduct had such a disagreeable resemblance to murder and was so entirely consistent with murder that he felt bound to pass a heavier sentence than he might normally consider in such case. He then sentenced Elizabeth to nine months' imprisonment with hard labour.

**1888** Maude Neville Williams died at Cardiff and Mary Jane Florence Rees and Louisa Wilson later appeared at the Swansea Assizes charged with her wilful murder. It was alleged that the two women caused Maude's death by using instruments with intent to produce an abortion.    20 JULY

Almost the only evidence against them was a statement taken from Mrs Williams before her death. There was considerable argument in court over whether this was a deposition – in other words, whether Mrs Williams believed at the time that she was dying. If it were a deposition, there was a legal requirement to notify the accused that it was taking place.

Mr Justice Charles decided not to allow the statement as evidence, without which the case immediately collapsed. However, the defendants were then charged with using instruments or other means on June Collier with intent to procure an abortion on 1 June. This time the prosecution were able to prove that Mrs Collier visited Louisa Wilson's home in response to cryptic newspaper advertisements offering 'important and valuable information' to married ladies. Mrs Collier paid £2 to undergo a surgical procedure carried out by Mrs Rees, the day after which she miscarried.

The jury found both prisoners guilty and Mrs Rees was sentenced to ten years' penal servitude, Mrs Wilson to five. The court concluded by trying Rees's husband, John, for performing a similar operation on a girl named Alice White. Having paid £1 for her operation, Alice demanded her money back when it failed to produce the desired result. The jury found Alice's evidence 'untrustworthy' and Rees was acquitted.

**21 JULY**   **1892**  Six-year-old Walter Hibbard of Neath died from the effects of an injury received in May. An inquest on his death was held on 25 July by coroner Mr Cuthbertson, at which Walter's mother, Elizabeth, was committed for trial at the next Assizes, charged with his manslaughter.

Elizabeth had only a few days to wait before her trial, where she pleaded guilty. The court heard that, during an argument with her husband, Elizabeth aimed a blow at him, accidentally striking Walter on the head.

Mr Justice Lawrence described Walter's death as 'as close to an accident as possible,' adding that he did not believe Elizabeth intended to hurt her child. Humanely, Lawrence passed a sentence of one day's imprisonment, saying that he hoped that Elizabeth and her husband could live happily together from then onwards. Having been incarcerated while awaiting her trial, Elizabeth left the court a free woman.

**22 JULY**   **1862**  The daughter of farmer Henry Collins married and, to celebrate the happy occasion, Collins allowed his farm labourers to leave work early. Sixteen were working in a hayfield adjacent to the South Wales Railway near Newport and, in order to return to the farm, had to cross the line at a level crossing.

They were travelling in a large waggon, pulled by three horses, and as the first horse reached the railway line, the workers heard a train approaching. Those riding on the waggon shouted a warning to the man leading the horses, who just had time to fling himself out of the way before the train sped past. It hit the back two horses, killing them instantly and ripping away the side of the waggon.

By a miracle, the two horses were the only fatalities and the labourers were left shocked but unharmed. Had the waggon been just 2ft further across the line, all would almost certainly have been killed.

**23 JULY**   **1870**  An explosion of fire damp took place at the Charles Pit, Llansamlet. The pit was thought of as a safe one, so much so that it was worked with naked lights rather than safety lamps and this was the first such incident for thirty years. There were fifty miners below ground at the time, nineteen of whom lost their lives. A further five were badly burned.

The bereaved relatives included two sisters, each of whom lost a husband and son in the disaster, and a family who lost a father and two sons. One victim, twenty-six-year-old William Williams, was due to have married on the day after the explosion.

**1868** Coroner Mr E.D. Batt held an inquest at Pontypool on the deaths of nine victims of a boating accident the previous evening.    **24 JULY**

A party of fourteen went for a pleasure trip on Glyn Pond and were within a few yards of the shore when their boat struck an underwater stake and was holed. As the boat filled with water, the young women aboard panicked and began rushing around.

*Pontypool & District Hospital, c. 1912. (Author's collection)*

Someone stuffed a shawl into the hole but it did little to stem the leak. One man asked if they should jump out and was told that it would lighten the load but, as he clambered out, the boat overturned, throwing its occupants into the water.

Luke Sanger and James Essex launched an iron punt from the shore but the people in the water seized the edge and overturned it. Sanger was trapped underneath and drowned, while desperate, grasping hands prevented Essex from swimming and he eventually had to be rescued himself. One of the victims was his daughter, Eleanor, while the Edwards family lost four members in the tragedy.

The inquest jury returned verdicts of accidental death, recommending that life saving equipment should be sited at the pond and that the stakes in the bottom preventing people from using fishing nets should not be more than fifteen inches tall.

**1870** Twenty-six-year-old William Evans appeared at Swansea Police Court charged with a criminal assault on eight-year-old Anne Louisa Gwynne.    **25 JULY**

Anne was the oldest of three daughters of James Gwynne from Mumbles. Gwynne separated from his wife due to her loose morals and she took the girls to live in a brothel in Swansea. Evans cohabited with Mrs Gwynne and, arriving home at two o'clock one morning, found her out with some sailors. Her three daughters were sleeping peacefully in their bed until Evans climbed in with them and raped Annie.

The little girl gave a clear account of what transpired, positively identifying Evans as her rapist. Two neighbours recalled finding Annie in a state of hysteria and testified to seeing Evans leaving the house on the day in question. However, having examined Annie soon after the incident, surgeon Ebenezer Davies stated that, although there was no question that violence had been used against her, she was physically too small for penetration to have taken place and so young that the capital offence of rape could not possibly have been completed.

Evans insisted that he was innocent and, at the Glamorgan Quarter Sessions on 18 October, the jury found him not guilty of indecent assault.

**26 JULY** 1893 Caradog Price and Samuel Riley argued at Neath Fair and Price shook Riley by the collar. When PC Merryman intervened, Price let Riley go and the elderly man fell backwards, banging his head on the ground and knocking himself unconscious.

Merryman stayed with Riley until he came round, when Riley assured him that everything was fine and the dispute was '...only a bit of bother.' The constable ordered both men to leave the fair and they went their separate ways.

Soon afterwards, another policeman noticed that Riley seemed drunk. As the constable spoke to him, Riley suddenly fell and was caught by the policeman before he could hit the ground. Still thinking that Riley was drunk, the policeman took him to the police station in a handcart and, when he was still unconscious several hours later, called in a doctor. Riley was taken to the Workhouse Infirmary, where he died the next day.

Price was arrested but insisted that Riley struck him first and that he didn't hit the old man, merely pushed him. Meanwhile, a post-mortem examination on Riley identified the cause of his death as a large blood clot beneath his skull. There were no marks of violence on his body, although Dr Davies maintained that only considerable violence could have caused the blood clot.

Price appeared at the Glamorganshire Assizes charged with feloniously killing and slaying Samuel Riley. Riley's daughter testified that her father suffered a fit almost twelve months earlier and had complained of pains in his back shortly before his death. Price's defence counsel pointed out that Riley was not under constant supervision in the seven hours that he was in custody and therefore it couldn't be assumed that he was unconscious throughout that entire period. Price had no animosity towards Riley and there was nothing to suggest that the push witnessed by PC Merryman was sufficiently violent to cause Riley's death. Mr Justice Charles concurred and suggested that the jury gave Price the benefit of the doubt. He was found not guilty and discharged.

**27 JULY** 1896 Coroner Mr M. Roberts-Jones held an inquest at Nash on the death of Louisa Maud Evans, alias Mademoiselle Albertina.

Fourteen-year-old Louisa's adopted parents were friendly with the proprietors of Hancock's Circus and agreed to Louisa acting as Mrs Hancock's companion. When Louisa met French aeronaut Auguste Gaudron at Torquay, she told him that she was Grace Parry, a twenty-year-old acrobat. She also told him that it was her ambition to do a parachute jump and, learning that Gaudron had a contract at the Cardiff Exhibition to perform a series of jumps from a balloon, Louisa ran away from the circus and met him there. On 21 July, in spite of terrible weather, Gaudron sent Louisa up in a balloon to make her first ever descent.

Her parachute was caught by strong winds and she was seen drifting helplessly towards the Bristol Channel. When her body was found on 24 July, a post-mortem examination showed that she drowned, in spite of wearing a cork lifejacket. It was believed that Louisa fainted and was unconscious when she hit the water, becoming embedded in mud and unable to extricate herself.

The inquest returned a verdict of 'accidentally drowned', adding that although it had ultimately been Louisa's decision to jump, they held Gaudron morally responsible for allowing someone so young and inexperienced to make the jump in such inclement weather.

**28 JULY** **1890** Robert Smith of Garndiffaith took his three sons to Abergavenny on the pretext of bidding farewell to a friend who was emigrating. When they reached the station, Smith and two of his sons boarded the train. The third boy – a cripple – was sent home with a message for his mother that her husband was off to America and would send money when he could. With no money and no means of support, Mrs Smith and her remaining three children were forced into the Workhouse.

*Abergavenny and Holy Mountain. (Author's collection)*

Smith had booked three passages to America on board the *Germanic* and was arrested as he and his sons were about to embark for their new life. Magistrates at Pontypool later found him guilty of abandoning his wife and children and causing them to become chargeable to the Pontypool Union and sentenced him to one month's imprisonment with hard labour, ordering him to pay the costs of his arrest and prosecution.

**29 JULY** **1882** Thomas King appeared at the Swansea Assizes charged with the wilful murder of Elizabeth Bridley at Merthyr Tydfil.

King and Elizabeth lived together as man and wife, although theirs was a violent relationship, fuelled by excesses of alcohol. On 19 June, Elizabeth went to visit a neighbour. She was drunk and, on arriving at her neighbour's house, sent the neighbour's child back to her own home with a message for King – he was to make her a cup of tea.

King took exception to being ordered about and immediately went to the neighbour's home, where Elizabeth sat on a stool in the kitchen. King swore at her, knocked her off the stool and kicked her several times as she lay on the floor.

Elizabeth died almost immediately and a post-mortem examination showed that the kicks had fractured her 11th and 12th ribs, driving them into her spleen and causing fatal internal bleeding.

When King appeared at the Assizes, his defence counsel maintained that the offence was manslaughter rather than murder. The judge told the jury that the difference between the two was intent and, if they believed that King had not intended to kill Elizabeth, the appropriate verdict would be one of manslaughter. The jury found King guilty of the lesser offence and he was sentenced to fifteen years' penal servitude.

30 JULY  1825 Newspapers reported a number of fatalities caused by a heatwave affecting most of South Wales. Among them were Reverend R. Thomas of Llandilo, who dropped dead after walking to Abergavenny, and Evan Jones of Newport and Thomas Strowbridge of Pwllgwenlly, who both died from drinking cold water after exposure to the sun.

A man and a woman haymaking in the fields near Pontardulais died within minutes of each other, while another haymaker, eighteen-year-old Richard Lewis of Llangefelach, suddenly clapped his hand to his head and said, 'I cannot work any more – I cannot see,' before collapsing. He died three hours later and a post-mortem indicated that he had died from the effects of the heat. The newspapers reported that, although there was only a matter of hours between death and the post-mortem, Lewis's body was already in a state of extreme putrefaction.

31 JULY  1862 The area around Merthyr Tydfil was so dangerous that the policemen usually patrolled in pairs. However, the danger to Sergeant William Thomas came not from villains but from two of his constables.

On 31 July, Thomas found PC William Rowlands drinking on duty. Thomas gave Rowlands a dressing down and reported him to the Superintendent, before resuming his beat. A little while later, as Thomas approached the canal bridge in Merthyr, he spotted Rowlands and his partner PC Stuart (or Stewart) waiting for him. The two constables savagely attacked Thomas, beating and kicking him senseless, before throwing him over the canal bridge into the water below.

The cold water revived Thomas, who was carried by the current to the opposite side of the canal. Rowlands and Stuart immediately crossed the bridge and began to pelt the sergeant with stones, knocking him unconscious again. Fortunately for Thomas, the commotion attracted the attention of a group of canal boatmen, who pulled him from the water.

Police Constable Stuart was later apprehended at Treforest, while Rowlands managed to evade capture until 5 August, when he was arrested at Bristol. Both were tried for attempted murder at the Cardiff Assizes and, found guilty, were each sentenced to penal servitude for life.

# AUGUST

*Chepstow Castle. (Author's collection)*

**1 AUGUST** **1889** When twenty-six-year-old Margaret Cantwell fell pregnant, it was naturally assumed that she would produce a baby after the customary nine months and, when there was no infant, people in Newport began to gossip. The rumours reached the ears of the police and Detective Inspector Thomas Henry Jones was sent to question her. When he asked the whereabouts of her child, Margaret admitted that it was upstairs.

Jones asked neighbour Mary Connors to act as a chaperone and she accompanied him upstairs to the bedroom that Margaret shared with her sister. Margaret moved the bed and, after rummaging around, removed a dead child wrapped in sacking from a box beneath it.

Jones arrested Margaret for concealing the birth of her child and, later that afternoon, police found two more mummified babies in the box. All three infants had skull fractures and, although it was impossible to establish whether they were born alive, surgeon Robert Cooke reasoned that, had they been dead, there would have been no need to fracture their skulls. When questioned, all Margaret would say was, 'I done it.'

The inquest jury decided that there was insufficient evidence to prove that the two mummified babies had been murdered but returned a verdict of wilful murder against Margaret in respect of the death of the most recently born child.

Margaret appeared at Monmouth Assizes on 1 August but the trial was postponed due to the illness of a witness. She made a second appearance on 28 February 1890, when Cooke told the court that he was unable to prove that her baby had ever led a separate existence. Without Cooke's testimony, the prosecution withdrew the charge of wilful murder and Margaret was advised to plead guilty to concealment of birth, which she did. Bearing in mind the delay in bringing Margaret to trial, Mr Justice Hawkins sentenced her to just three months' imprisonment.

Remarkably, in spite of the terrible stench emanating from beneath Margaret's bed, her sister, who shared her room and their two brothers, who lived with them, claimed to have noticed nothing unusual and had never questioned their sister about the outcome of her three pregnancies.

**2 AUGUST** **1892** Twenty-nine-year-old collier Edwin Pugh appeared at the Swansea Assizes charged with the attempted murder of Dr John Lloyd Edwards at Ynyshir.

Edwards was the colliery medical officer and, on 23 May, was walking to his lodgings at Ystradfodwg with two friends when he heard running footsteps behind him. He turned and saw a man with one arm raised – there was a flash and a loud bang and Edwards fell to the ground, shot in the left shoulder.

It was dark and the description of the shooter given by Edwards and his companions was sketchy. However, all agreed that the man was very tall and police soon heard that a miner under Edwards's care was missing. Edwin Pugh was very tall and was known to bear a grudge against Edwards, who refused him a certificate to claim sick pay. Since Pugh had frequently threatened to shoot Edwards, the police searched the area and he was eventually found in a nearby forest, having hidden for a week without food.

At Pugh's trial, the court heard from several medical witnesses, all of whom believed he was mentally unsound. The jury found him guilty but insane and Mr Justice Lawrence ordered him to be detained during Her Majesty's Pleasure.

Edwards was lucky to survive – had he not been turning when he was shot, the wound would almost certainly have proved fatal.

**1876** Hearing hysterical screams, neighbours rushed to nine-year-old Cecilia Nickels's home in Penarth, where the child sobbed that her stepfather had killed her mother.

Cecilia Tree's head had been smashed to a pulp by a heavy wooden sailmaker's fid and, although Dr Nell was called, she died within minutes of his arrival. Only then was the house searched for her husband, who sat in the bedroom, his throat slashed so deeply that his spine was exposed. Charles Tree lived until the following morning and, although unable to speak, he responded to questions by nodding or shaking his head and thus indicated that he killed his wife through jealousy.

Cecilia and Charles had been married for five years and, two years earlier, Charles, a ship's watchman, was involved in an explosion on his ship. He was so badly injured that he spent almost eighteen months on the *Hamadryad* Hospital Ship and, even after his discharge, still had open wounds on his leg. Charles became convinced that Cecilia was unfaithful and was particularly jealous of George Dawkins, the couple's lodger, who had lived with them for about six months. Although Dawkins insisted that these suspicions were groundless, there were frequent violent rows between Charles and his wife and he had previously attacked her with a knife and an axe. Even so, Cecilia refused to bring charges against him.

Dr Nell testified at the inquest into the Trees' deaths that he had treated Charles for his leg wounds for many months and had never observed any indication of insanity. The jury returned verdicts of wilful murder and suicide, adding that there was nothing to suggest that Charles was not in a sound state of mind at the time.

*The Promenade, Penarth, 1910. (Author's collection)*

**4 AUGUST** **1949** A double execution took place at Swansea Prison.

On 4 June, the body of sixteen-year-old Beryl Beechey was discovered on a railway embankment in Aberavon. The previous evening, Beryl was sent with a message for Mrs Mackintosh, who was out when Beryl arrived at her home. The Mackintosh household was the first port of call for the investigating officers and twenty-one-year-old Robert confirmed that Beryl had given him ten shillings, which he passed to his mother.

When fresh bloodstains were found in the kitchen and under Robert's bed, he changed his story, now stating that he invited Beryl in and remembered nothing more until he woke up and found her dead body lying half under his bed. He carried her to the railway embankment, where he dumped her over a low wall, cleaning the house prior to his mother's return.

Two days later, twenty-year-old Beatrice May Watts was found in a plantation near Nantybar. Like Beryl, she had been strangled and sexually assaulted, although when her killer Rex Harvey Jones handed himself into the police, he claimed that their intercourse had been consensual. Jones could not explain why he killed Beatrice.

The two men were tried on consecutive days at the Swansea Assizes and although efforts were made to gain reprieves for both, they kept their appointments with executioner Albert Pierrepoint.

**5 AUGUST** **1878** Coroner Mr H. Cuthbertson held an inquest at Neath on the death of twenty-three- month-old Alice Vincent.

Alice was attended by Dr Stephens for three weeks, after her mother reported that she was suffering from convulsions. However, it was blatantly obvious to Stephens that Alice was starving and, when she died, he refused to issue a death certificate. A post-mortem examination confirmed Stephens's conclusions, showing that there was nothing wrong with Alice apart from want of food. She weighed only 8lbs when she died, instead of the normal weight for a child of her age of 25-30lbs.

Alice's father was in California and, in his absence, Mrs Vincent lived with a man named David Morris, preferring to spend her money drinking than on feeding her children. Alice and her siblings survived solely on handouts from the neighbours and would regularly eat chicken food and potato peelings from rubbish heaps. Mrs Vincent never bothered to wash the children, or their clothes – including nappies – and sent them to school only occasionally.

The relieving officer testified that until June, Margaret (or Mary) Vincent received 11s parish relief every week, 2s in cash and 9s in groceries. He stopped the family's payments when he found out that Mr Vincent regularly sent money home to support them – between October 1877 and May 1878, this totalled almost £60.

The inquest jury returned a verdict of manslaughter against Mrs Vincent, who was committed for trial at the Glamorganshire Assizes where she was found guilty and sentenced to nine months' imprisonment. While awaiting her trial, she gave birth to twins, one of whom died.

**6 AUGUST** **1867** Coroner Mr W.H. Brewer held an inquest at the Workhouse Hospital at Newport on the death of farm labourer Henry Russell.

Russell was working at Bishton, forking hay and throwing it to the top of a rick when, without any warning, the horse pulling the cart on which he was standing took fright and bolted. Russell was thrown from the cart and landed on the tines of his pitchfork, which penetrated his eye and neck. He died from his injuries the following day.

*Haymaking, 1911.*
*(Author's collection)*

The inquest jury returned a verdict of 'accidentally killed.'

**1893** Thousands of visitors flocked to Aberavon beach, among them a Sunday school party from Ystrad.

7 AUGUST

Brothers William and John Bath and boatman John Cramp agreed to take the party out in an open boat, measuring just 20ft by 5ft 6in. Almost thirty climbed aboard, leaving the little craft overcrowded and riding low in the water. As it reached the end of the breakwater, heavy waves breaking on the seaward side caused panic among the passengers. Almost as one, they rushed to the opposite side of the boat, effecting its immediate capsize.

Most of the passengers were young people and many drowned in front of their families and friends, who watched helplessly from the beach as the catastrophe unfolded. Because nobody was sure precisely how many were on the boat, more than a week after the disaster, it was believed that some bodies were still missing.

At an inquest held by coroner Howel Cuthbertson, the jury returned a verdict of manslaughter against the Bath brothers, who owned the boat. At their trial at Cardiff Town Hall on 17 November, the Baths were charged with feloniously killing and slaying Gwenllian Llewellyn, Cecilian Hopkins, Margaret Harris and twenty-one others.

Although there was no doubt that there were too many in the boat, the defence maintained that because most passengers were women and children, although overcrowded, the boat's load was not overweight. The prosecution

*The beach at Aberavon in the 1960s. (Author's collection)*

countered that this made the trip even more perilous, since women and children were not usually able to swim.

Nevertheless, in order to prove a charge of manslaughter against the Bath brothers, the prosecution had to show that they had been criminally negligent to the point of recklessness and the jury evidently felt that this was not proven, since they found both defendants 'not guilty'.

**8 AUGUST** **1892** Evan Hughes, John Rowlands and William Davies spent the night cleaning a sump at the bottom of the new pit at Clydach Vale. The job finished, they were on the point of leaving the pit when a stone arch collapsed, burying all three men in rubble.

Rowlands and Davies were killed instantly and, although Hughes was alive when brought to the surface, he died shortly afterwards. Hughes left a widow and two young children, while Rowlands's funeral was held on the day that he was due to have married.

**9 AUGUST** **1875** George Richards appeared before Lord Chief Justice Coleridge at the Glamorganshire Assizes charged with the wilful murder of his wife, Mary Jane, at Cardiff on 27 March.

The court heard that ship's pilot Richards had been unemployed for nine weeks and became obsessed with the notion that he was unable to support his wife and their six children. Although the family were poor, they weren't starving – a collection had been made for them at the docks, which raised £2, and their relatives were helping financially until Richards could find another job. However, with a general strike in South Wales and a fall in the coal trade, many tug boats lay idle and Richards remained out of work.

On 27 March, Richards cut his wife's throat and was disturbed by a lodger while cutting his own. Mary Jane bled to death within minutes but her husband recovered sufficiently to stand trial for her murder and was found guilty and sentenced to death.

His sentence was appealed on the grounds of insanity and he was later reprieved. When the Richards' rooms were searched after the murder, police found plenty of food, as well as £1 10s in gold and 10s in silver.

**1891** Twenty-five-year-old William Walters appeared at the Glamorganshire **10 AUGUST** Assizes charged with the wilful murder of his wife, Ellen.

In the early hours of 3 May, William and Ellen argued about money. Although numerous people heard them quarrelling, only one person actually saw William beating and kicking his pregnant wife then dragging her onto the pavement outside their rooms in Cardiff.

The police and a doctor were called and Ellen was found to have numerous fresh injuries. Most seriously, she was bleeding from a wound just behind her vagina and Dr Byrne was unable to stop the haemorrhage. When Ellen died, a post-mortem examination showed that she bled to death and Byrne was of the opinion that the wound was caused either by Ellen sitting heavily on a jagged object or by a blow from a blunt object, such as the toe of a boot.

The lone witness who saw the murder was only nine years old and, although he gave his evidence in court clearly, the jurors were concerned about placing too much reliance on so young a child. They found Walters guilty of the lesser offence of manslaughter and he was sentenced to ten years' penal servitude.

**1877** Catherine Donovan and Mary Healey went shopping for faggots in **11 AUGUST** Newport. On their way they met Henry Elliott, and there was some larking about between the three.

At Daniel Guy's butchers, Henry picked up a knife from the counter. 'Now for murder,' he cried, swinging the knife and catching Mary on her breast and again on her left-hand side.

'Oh, Kate, I am stabbed,' Mary complained, but, not realising the seriousness of her injury, she stood chatting to Catherine for fifteen minutes before going home and made no attempt to contact the police.

The wound on Mary's breast was a mere scratch but the one on her side had nicked her intestines, and she died from peritonitis three days later. Henry appeared at the Gloucester Assizes, charged with manslaughter. His defence counsel maintained that this was a case of homicide by misadventure and that his client was merely flourishing the knife to show off his dexterity and had never intended to stab anyone. When the jury found him guilty, the judge accepted that there was no malicious intent, describing Henry's crime as 'culpable negligence with a deadly weapon', before sentencing him to three months' imprisonment with hard labour.

**1893** While Margaret Agnes Williams was staying with her sister in Swansea, **12 AUGUST** the family went to bathe at Port Eynon Bay. Margaret waded out a little too far and found herself struggling against the outgoing tide. She shouted, 'I can't get in,' and watched as six other members of the party formed a human chain to try and reach her, but the chain was broken apart by the strong swell and servants Mary Ann Phillips and Mary Jane Cole were washed away.

Margaret's niece, Isabel, was a strong swimmer and managed to reach the two servants, who clung desperately to each other. Isabel tried to push them towards the shore but the current was too strong and she was forced to abandon the rescue attempt to save herself.

Several others tried to save the drowning women but failed. Eventually a punt was launched, which rescued Isabel and another lady. The two servants were brought to shore lifeless and, although artificial respiration was attempted for nearly three hours, it was unsuccessful.

At the subsequent inquest, coroner Mr Talfourd Strick recorded verdicts of 'accidental death', commending those who had put their own lives at risk to try and save the victims.

**13 AUGUST**   **1869** Coroner Mr Edward Strick held inquests at Swansea on three children, who died in separate incidents on 12 August. Seven-year-old William Ellery Perkins drowned in the Beaufort Dock while playing with friends. Eighteen-month-old William Henry Jones was run over and killed by a baker's horse and cart and seven-year-old Francis John Hallam drowned while fishing.

The jury returned verdicts of 'accidental death' on all three children, adding that they attributed no blame to the driver of the cart that ran over William, who was driving very slowly at the time of the accident.

**14 AUGUST**   **1913** Twenty-nine-year-old Hugh McLaren was hanged by John Ellis at Cardiff, having been convicted of murdering Spaniard Julian Biros.

Like many itinerant workers at Cardiff Docks, Biros had no fixed abode, sleeping at the Crown Fuel Works, as did Patrick McGuirk. On 23 March, McGuirk and Biros rose early, hoping to pick up some causal labour on the SS *Dee*, which was due to dock that morning. They were joined by labourer John Walsh and, as the three chatted on the quayside, McLaren approached and offered to make them some tea. He took a packet of tea from his pocket, which Biros immediately recognised as belonging to him. Angrily, he asked McLaren to give it back and McLaren responded by pulling out a knife and thrusting it into Biros's side.

Biros died in hospital later that afternoon and, since his murder was witnessed by McGuirk and Walsh, as well as by crewmembers from SS *Dee*, the police immediately charged McLaren. 'I got nothing to say,' McLaren said arrogantly, adding, 'I could kill a dozen dagos like that and they could not touch me for it.'

Mr Justice Coleridge was later to prove him wrong at the Swansea Assizes, sentencing him to death after the jury found him guilty of a murder that had no motive other than racial hatred.

**15 AUGUST**   **1900** The Dowlais Ironworks employed several Spaniards, two of whom lodged at The Bute Inn and, after celebrating a Spanish national feast, Gregorio Lasuen and Martin Savada began quarrelling. The argument led to a physical fight, which was broken up by landlady Mrs O'Shea, who insisted the two men shake hands. Minutes later, Savada collapsed into Mr O'Shea's arms, having been stabbed in the groin with a chisel. The tool severed an artery and he bled to death within minutes.

Lasuen was charged with wilful murder, appearing at the Glamorganshire Assizes in November. The foreman at the Dowlais Works had taken a shine to Savada, giving him less work to do than Lasuen, who was understandably jealous, since both men were paid the same. However, Lasuen insisted that he and Savada were 'like brothers' and swore that he hadn't stabbed his compatriot.

The chisel belonged to landlord John O'Shea, who worked as a carpenter and undertaker. By the time the case came to trial, O'Shea was in America and Lasuen's defence counsel tried to suggest that he had absconded. At Mr Justice Bigham's insistence, the defence was forced to withdraw the insinuation, but it had obviously raised doubts in the minds of the jury, who found Lasuen 'not guilty'.

**1930** As seventeen-year-old Evelyn Minty and her ten-year-old sister were bathing at Newton Bay, Porthcawl, the younger girl got into difficulties.    **16 AUGUST**

The girls were being watched from the beach by their parents and aunt and, seeing his daughters in danger, Revd Charles Stanley Minty from Cardiff dashed into the sea fully-clothed to save them. No sooner had he reached the water than he was knocked over by a large wave.

Evelyn assisted her younger sister to the beach then went back for her father, who was in the water for less than half a minute. However, by the time he was brought ashore, he was dead.

An inquest jury at Porthcawl found that Minty died from asphyxia due to drowning.

**1908** Patrick Noah Percy Collins stayed in bed at his lodgings in Abertridwr,    **17 AUGUST**
sending down a message that he wasn't going to work.

Nineteen-year-old Annie Dorothy Lawrence usually made breakfast for her brother, William, and her family's two lodgers, Collins and John Donovan, who were all miners. That morning, Annie's mother was woken by screams from downstairs. The kitchen door was locked against her and, having forced it, Mrs Lawrence saw Annie in a pool of blood on the floor. Before she could react, Collins pushed past her and ran out of the house.

As Annie bled to death, Collins handed himself in at the police station. He and Annie were once sweethearts but Annie had recently ended the relationship and was courting another man. Collins tried his hardest to persuade her to reconsider but Annie wouldn't entertain the idea.

According to Collins, he stayed at home that morning in order to talk to Annie alone. He asked her to kiss him, saying that, had she done so, he would have gone to work happy. Annie refused and told Collins to leave her alone or she would call her mother. She and Collins struggled and he stabbed her seven times.

Collins was tried for wilful murder at the Swansea Assizes on 11 December. His defence counsel pleaded insanity, showing that Collins came from a family of weak-minded people but when the jury returned their guilty verdict, they made no concession to Collins's mental state. He was hanged at Cardiff by Henry Pierrepoint on 30 December.

**1899** A heavy fall took place at Llest Colliery near Bridgend. The fall released a    **18 AUGUST**
volume of gas, which exploded when it came into contact with the naked flames used by the colliers. Although the explosion was described by one survivor as 'a puff – nothing more', nineteen of the fifty men working below ground were killed.

The colliery was considered a safe one, although the Government's Inspector of Mines had written to advise the managers that safety lamps were vital. The management made regular inspections and believed it safe to use naked lights and, even though there had recently been four minor explosions, only issued safety lamps when gas levels were unusually high. They also ignored suggestions that the pit should be better ventilated.

At the subsequent inquest, the jury ruled that the victims met their deaths by suffocation as the result of an explosion of gas, adding that they believed that the management had made an error of judgement in not introducing safety lamps.

**19 AUGUST**   **1876** Butler Henry Tremble was due to leave Dolaucothy House, Carmarthenshire. His relationship with his employer, seventy-five-year-old John Johnes, had been strained since Tremble applied for a licence to run a public house and local magistrate Johnes turned down the application because he didn't think Tremble a fit person. After several warnings about his conduct, Tremble was sacked, although he immediately argued that he was leaving of his own accord.

Whether he resigned or was fired, Tremble wanted revenge and at ten o'clock in the morning, he walked into the library at Dolaucothy House and shot and killed Johnes. He then went to the kitchen, where Johnes's daughter was talking to cook Margaret Davies. Seeing Tremble with a gun, Margaret bravely stood in front of Charlotte Cookman and refused to move until eventually, Tremble thrust the gun barrel past her and fired, hitting Charlotte in the thigh. (Although badly injured, Charlotte survived.)

Stopping only to shoot the family's dogs, Tremble then walked to The Caio Arms, which was run by John Davies, who had been awarded the licence that Tremble so desperately wanted. Fortunately Davies was out, so Tremble went home to the cottage he shared with his wife and their six children. Meeting his eldest daughter on the way, he gave her a letter to deliver to Reverend Charles Chidlow, then, with the police at his door, Tremble barricaded himself in his bedroom and shot himself.

The letter to Chidlow was a request for him to administer Tremble's financial affairs, so that his children would be taken care of after his death. It was dated 15 August, showing that the murder was premeditated and made no mention of Tremble's wife, Frances, suggesting that he may have planned to murder her too.

**20 AUGUST**   **1871** John Tallis Robinson was found dead at his house in Swansea.

The previous evening, Robinson and his daughter Caroline visited a neighbour, returning home just after midnight. As they arrived at their front door, they surprised William Morris on the doorstep.

Robinson asked Morris what he was doing and Morris punched him on the side of the head. He tried to hit Robinson a second time but Caroline deflected the blow and led her father indoors, bolting the door behind them. Morris made an ineffectual attempt to follow them before leaving.

Robinson fell against the parlour wall and slumped to the floor. Caroline tried to rouse him then tried to get him upstairs to bed but was unable to do either and eventually lay down on a sofa in the parlour and went to sleep. She was awoken by her stepmother, with the news that her father was dead.

Robinson was an epileptic but, since his position against the wall had not changed since the previous evening, doctors felt it unlikely that he had died during a fit. A post-mortem examination revealed that his heart was in an advanced state of fatty degeneration and this was given as the cause of his death. The doctors could find no signs that he had been hit but reasoned that, although a blow would have little effect on a healthy man, on a man with such extensive heart disease, any blow would be likely to have accelerated his death. William Morris was therefore charged with manslaughter.

He appeared at the Swansea Assizes in March 1872, where his defence counsel insisted that there was no case to answer, since Robinson died from natural causes. The jury disagreed, finding Morris guilty and he was sentenced to two months' imprisonment.

**1900** Jamaican William Augustus Lacey was executed by James Billington at Swansea, having been convicted of murdering his wife, Pauline.

21 AUGUST

William had a job at the Great Western Colliery but was so jealous that he often refused to go to work, believing that his wife would see other men in his absence. Nineteen-year-old Pauline struggled to make a go of her marriage but eventually wrote to her father, who suggested that she came home. The idea drove William into a fury and he threatened to kill her if she left, drawing a finger across his throat in case she had misunderstood him.

From then on, William refused to leave Pauline alone in the house. The couple argued almost constantly and, on 6 July, their landlady heard a desperate scream. Pauline was dead, her throat cut and a bloody razor by her side.

Soon afterwards, William walked into the police station and confessed to killing his wife because she was going to leave him. By the time he appeared before magistrates, he had changed his story, now claiming that Pauline begged him to kill her and, when he refused, she slashed her own throat. According to William, she asked him to finish the job, which he did.

At his trial at the Swansea Assizes on 2 August, William concocted a third version of events, insisting that Pauline had committed suicide because she wrongly believed that he had been intimate with her sister. The jury chose to believe his initial confession to the police.

**1825** John Evans was executed at Brecon, having been tried and convicted for a murder committed only two weeks earlier.

22 AUGUST

At two o'clock on the morning of 8 August, Margaret Williams of Llandulas was called from her bed. She slipped outside in her nightclothes and never returned. Margaret was expecting Evans's baby and already had another child by him, hence he became the prime suspect in her disappearance.

Evans fled on learning that he was a wanted man and was eventually found in a deep pool of water. Although it was never established whether he was hiding

*Brecon. (Author's collection)*

or if he meant to drown himself, as soon as he realised that he was about to be apprehended, he attempted to cut his own throat and, taken into custody, tried to bribe the constable to let him escape.

There was no trace of Margaret and Evans denied all knowledge of her whereabouts. However, the police were convinced that she had met with foul play and interviewed his brother-in-law, Daniel Rowlands.

Rowlands revealed that Evans had asked for help to bury a body but, while Rowlands was willing to lend his spade, he drew the line at any further involvement. He indicated the direction in which his brother-in-law went on the night in question and the police found Margaret buried in a shallow grave, her neck broken. The motive for her murder was thought to be Evans's desire to marry another woman.

23 AUGUST **1824** Richard Williams and Mary Morgan were tried at the Monmouth Assizes for the wilful murder of William Evans.

On 26 April, the men spent an evening drinking in Newport, before meeting prostitutes Eliza Nixon and Mary Morgan and walking with them along the banks of the canal. Eliza and William went into the saw pit of a nearby timber yard. As they petted, a 300lb slab of wood, which was leaning against the side of the pit, suddenly toppled onto them.

There was bad blood between Eliza and Mary and, when Eliza screamed, Mary ignored her and went home. It was left to Richard to heave the wood off Eliza, who later told Mary that she would never forgive her for not helping. Laughing, Mary calmly smoked her pipe and, when another prostitute asked why she had not helped, she replied that she had intended to murder Eliza as revenge for informing on her for keeping a disorderly house.

Everyone seemed to have forgotten Evans, who was crushed to death by the timber. (Williams was later to claim that he didn't see his friend when he rescued Eliza and assumed that he had gone home.) The wood could not have fallen accidentally, so Williams and Mary were charged with wilful murder.

At their trial, Mr Justice Park stated that that Evans indisputably met his death by a slab of wood being thrown on him and told the jury that they must decide if the prisoners threw it, adding that if something was used as a weapon and caused death, then the crime was murder. If the jury believed that Williams and Mary threw the wood, was there malice aforethought? Park said that he could see no malice on Williams's part and, as the defendants had not known in advance that Eliza and Evans would go to the saw pit and had not taken the weapon with them, he saw very little to prove aforethought. After twenty minutes' deliberation, the jury acquitted Williams and found Mary Morgan guilty of manslaughter. She was sentenced to fourteen years' transportation.

**1884** John Francis of Pembroke had shown signs of insanity for some time and arrangements were in hand for his admittance to Carmarthen County Asylum.

24 AUGUST

On 24 August, Francis picked up a hammer and told his wife to say her prayers. Mrs Francis protested that she had already prayed that morning but her husband gave her until the count of three to kneel down. He counted aloud 'One...two...' but, before he got to three, Mrs Francis clasped him in a bear hug and they tumbled downstairs locked together. Although her husband hit her on the head with the hammer, Mrs Francis managed to break free, running out of the front door shouting 'Murder!'

Her cries brought the congregation of the Calvinistic Methodist Chapel to her assistance and, while someone fetched the police, others restrained Francis, who was wearing only his blood-soaked shirt. When Sergeant David Evans arrived, Francis seemed calm and the policeman took him upstairs to get dressed. Once there, Francis fought like a man possessed and it took five men to hold him down. Such was his strength that Francis nearly managed to throw all five downstairs.

He was sent to Carmarthen Asylum the next day.

*Main Street, Pembroke. (Author's collection)*

**25 AUGUST** **1895** William Parker and David Hopkins were fanatical about pony racing and, meeting at Neath, their conversation turned to an upcoming race, in which both had entered ponies. Hopkins rated his mare's chances of winning very highly and, when Parker asked if he might see her, he proudly took him to The Lamb Inn, where the pony was stabled. The following day, the mare had a one-inch-long nail embedded in the underside of her hoof and the pub landlord's young son said that he saw William Parker drive the nail in with a stone.

Parker was found guilty of maliciously wounding the mare at the Quarter Sessions but when it came to sentencing, there was a flaw in the legal paperwork and the chairman decided to forward the case to the Assizes.

When the case came to trial, Parker's defence counsel stressed his respect-ability, suggesting that the nail got into the mare's hoof by accident. The trial jury overturned the verdict reached at the Quarter Sessions and Parker was dis-charged.

**26 AUGUST** **1893** A march in Pontardawe in support of striking tin plate workers and colliers attracted around 4,000 people. By and large, the demonstration passed peacefully, until a few men from the tail end of the procession slipped into The Colliers Arms.

At first, the conversation between John Davies and local resident Richard Davies (no relation) was amicable, until someone commented that they could smell burning. John put his hand in his pocket and found his handkerchief smouldering – he accused Richard of 'putting the fire in his pocket' and hit him. Richard stumbled backwards over a settle and immediately lapsed into unconsciousness.

*Pontardawe.*
*(Author's collection)*

The local doctor arrived within minutes but Richard had stopped breathing, although there was still a faint pulse at his wrist. Artificial respiration was at-

tempted for thirty minutes but failed and a post-mortem examination showed a three-inch-long blood clot on Richard's brain from a ruptured artery. The doctor found no evidence of disease and could only assume that a blow caused the rupture. However, he would have expected a blow to the cheek or chin to cause a clot at the top of the head, not at the base of the brain, thus it was possible that the clot came from ruptured capillaries.

John Davies was charged with manslaughter, appearing at the Glamorganshire Assizes in November. Richard Davies was an alcoholic, with only one leg. He was a particularly argumentative man and several people testified that he complained of feeling unwell before entering the pub and that he suffered from heart disease.

Mr Justice Collins asked the jury if they needed to hear any more evidence. The jury agreed that they didn't, finding John Davies not guilty.

**1900** Richard Hutt appeared before magistrates at Merthyr Tydfil charged with shooting James Mack, with intent to disable him. **27 AUGUST**

The Bench heard that Mack was on sick furlough from the Boer War in South Africa and was walking home on 25 August, having enjoyed a few drinks. As he passed through Tirphil, three men sitting outside a coffee tavern jeered at him. When Mack confronted them, they denied making fun of him but, as he walked away, they shouted after him several times.

Mack went back and hit one of the men, realising only after he had done so that the man was a cripple who walked with a crutch. Before Mack could apologise, one of the men pulled out a revolver and shot him in the groin.

Arrested for the shooting, twenty-three-year-old Richard Hutt handed over a revolver and around fifty cartridges. He made conflicting statements, first saying that the gun went off accidentally then admitting that he had fired to protect his friend, adding that he never intended to hurt anyone. Hutt was tried at the Swansea Assizes and found guilty, with a strong recommendation for mercy from the jury. The judge advised him to get rid of his revolver before he did any more harm with it and discharged him on his own recognisances.

**1848** Matthias Kelly, a private in the 14th Regiment of Foot, was executed at Monmouth. **28 AUGUST**

Although stationed at St Woollos, Kelly lived with a woman named Agnes Hill. A former member of the Irish constabulary, he was an exemplary soldier but on the evening of 25 May, he got drunk and, as punishment, was sentenced to six days' confinement to barracks, although he was permitted to walk around the yard.

On 26 May, Agnes appeared at the barracks asking Kelly for money. He handed over 2s 6d and Agnes went to the canteen, where she treated two soldiers to food. When Kelly realised how she was spending his money, he went in search of her, finding her in the yard, talking with a soldier named Dennis Doherty.

Kelly went back to his room and picked up his musket. He politely asked Doherty to stand aside before raising his musket and firing at Agnes. The ball hit her in the stomach, passing straight through her body and she died the next day. Kelly freely admitted shooting her, claiming that Agnes had been 'shamefully false' towards him.

There were several witnesses to the shooting and, with Kelly's confession, the jury at the Monmouth Assizes needed little time to deliberate, pronouncing him guilty. They did however recommend mercy on the grounds of provocation, although their recommendation was not heeded.

**29 AUGUST**    **1841** Nineteen-year-old prostitute Sarah Sophia Fleming and a friend were in Chepstow with Benjamin James, who lived off Sarah's earnings. They were joined by three young men, who escorted them to the top of Tutshill, where Sarah went off alone with one of them.

James was unaccountably jealous and called for Sarah to come back. When she didn't, he and Sarah's friend followed her and clearly saw Sarah in the moonlight, intimately touching Edward Jones. James raised his fist to strike her but was held back by Jones, who urged Sarah to go home. 'If I do, Ben will beat me worse when he catches me,' Sarah replied.

James eventually broke free and rushed at Sarah, punching her hard on her right side. Sarah fell to her knees and crawled over to him, begging, 'Don't do it any more, Ben.'

'I will murder you,' James replied.

Sarah kissed him and, although James continued to threaten her, he didn't hit her again.

Sarah, James and her friend spent the night in a barn, with Sarah complaining of pain in her right side and back. The next morning, James left the girls, saying that he was afraid that Sarah might die and he would be blamed. It was left to Sarah's friend to half carry her into Chepstow and find a lodging house willing to take them in. By the next day, Sarah was so ill that her father was summoned from Bristol and, unable to afford a doctor for his daughter, he sent her to Chepstow Workhouse.

*Chepstow from Tutshill. (Author's collection)*

James was arrested and taken to her bedside so that her deposition could be taken. Sarah just screamed, 'Take him away, he will kill me!' She later reconsidered and asked to make a deposition but by the time James was brought back, she was dead. A post-mortem examination showed the cause of death to be acute inflammation of her lungs and liver.

James was committed for trial but, at the Monmouth Assizes of March 1842, the Grand Jury reduced the charge from murder to manslaughter, since Sarah had fallen at Chepstow Castle a month before her death and there was no way of proving that her injuries were not sustained then. Found guilty, James was sentenced to twelve months' imprisonment.

**1893** A group of boys stopped at the clay pits in Carmarthen Road, Swansea, after school to play on some floating pieces of timber. Seeing a man approaching, they tried to scramble ashore and one makeshift raft tipped over, plunging three boys into the water. **30 AUGUST**

Leyshon Williams managed to get to the bank but Rhys Davies and Isaac Tucker sank. The man managed to pull both boys out of the water and, by chance, a doctor was passing in his trap at the time and, seeing a crowd of people, stopped to see if he could assist.

Isaac was brought back to life by artificial respiration and went on to make a full recovery but, although Dr Howell Thomas worked on eleven-year-old Rhys for more than an hour, he was unable to resuscitate him.

**1842** William Evans left The Red Cow Inn at Llantrissant early to collect the rent due on properties he owned. His wife, Mary, was already up but their six-year-old son, William junior, still slept peacefully in his bed. **31 AUGUST**

At about ten o'clock, a friend called for the boy to walk to school. Nobody answered his knocks and, when William returned five hours later, the doors and shutters were closed and a customer waited patiently outside. William let him in, calling for Mary but receiving no response and, on searching the building, the two men found her hanging from a beam in the bedroom.

William fetched his neighbours, who cut Mary down but she was beyond assistance. Worse still, when someone went into the downstairs parlour, which was in darkness due to the closed shutters, they tripped over young William, who lay in a pool of blood, his throat cut from ear to ear and a bloody razor by his side. Mary had tried to cut her own throat but, having failed to inflict more than a minor injury, had hung herself. It was not the first time that she had attempted suicide – some months earlier she strapped William to her back and waded into a river but was thwarted by a passer-by.

Mary suffered from depression and had repeatedly told her husband that he would be better off without her and the boy. She also had an irrational fear of poverty and it was concluded that, in a bout of temporary insanity, she killed her much-loved child to prevent him from suffering.

# SEPTEMBER

*Newport and Abercarne Colliery, Abercarne. (Author's collection)*

**1905** A woman arrived at Landore on the Cardiff train, carrying a baby in a ₁ SEPTEMBER white shawl. Several people saw her and, when a baby was found in a ditch later that night, were able to describe her to the police.

The baby, later identified as three-month-old Edna Lilian Thomas from Somerset, was taken to Swansea Workhouse. Her bonnet had been deliberately pulled down over her nose and mouth and tied tightly with a ribbon around the back of her head and doctors estimated that Edna would have suffocated within an hour. She eventually died from malnutrition on 2 October.

Meanwhile, police were investigating thirty-nine-year-old Henrietta Hunter, the woman last seen with Edna. They established that Henrietta, a housekeeper in Swansea, operated a lucrative sideline in baby farming, which she had practised for several years in Wales, Bristol and Scotland. Her usual method was to advertise her willingness to adopt a baby on payment of a fee then, having collected the child at a railway station, put it out to nurse and disappear, taking the fee and defaulting on her agreed payments to the nurse.

Henrietta was charged with attempting to suffocate Edna with intent to murder her and appeared before Mr Justice Lawrence at the Swansea Assizes. Found guilty, she was sentenced to ten years' penal servitude.

**1865** After collecting their wages, Robert Coe and Edward (or John) Davis left ₂ SEPTEMBER the iron works in Mountain Ash. An hour later, they were seen walking towards Dyffryn Wood, after which Davis was never seen alive again.

Four months later, a farmer found a decomposed corpse. The head lay a few yards away in undergrowth and, since Edward Davis was the only missing person in the area, his father was shown the remains. Mr Davis was able to identify the skull as Edward's by a distinctive chipped tooth and also recognised the remnants of clothing found with the body.

As the last person to be seen with Davis, Coe became the prime suspect in his murder. He had borrowed a hatchet around the time of the murder and, when it was examined, there were still faint traces of blood on the handle, although analytical chemist Dr Herapath was unable to determine whether it was human or animal in origin. There were also bloodstains on a coat that Coe was known to have worn on the night of Davis's disappearance.

Even though the evidence against eighteen-year-old Coe was entirely circumstantial, the jury at his trial found him guilty and he was sentenced to death. Although he requested that his confession was not published until after his execution, before facing executioner William Calcraft at Swansea Gaol on 12 April 1866, Coe admitted to murdering his friend for his wages of 33s.

Note: Some sources report the location of the execution as Cardiff.

**1876** Farm manager James Watkins of Whitchurch found a bundle in the ₃ SEPTEMBER kitchen and, noticing what appeared to be blood on the outside, contacted the police without unwrapping it. The parcel contained a dead baby, covered in coal dust.

Suspicion fell on eighteen-year-old servant Mary Peterson Mahoney who, when confronted with the body, immediately admitted, 'It's mine.' Asked if the child was born alive, Mary said that it wasn't. However, when questioned further, she said that she gave birth in the lavatory in the early hours of that morning and, when the baby cried, was afraid that the noise would rouse the household. She went to the shed for the coal pick, which she plunged into the infant's head, killing her instantly, before wrapping the body in an apron and concealing it under some coal sacks in the kitchen, to be disposed of later.

Mary was tried for wilful murder on 11 December and, found guilty, received the mandatory death sentence. She was later reprieved.

**4 SEPTEMBER** 1876 Joseph Jones appeared at Carmarthen Police Court charged with being drunk and disorderly and with threatening to drown a child.

On 2 September, someone informed Sergeant Hughes that a child had been thrown into the river. Hughes found Jones in the river drunk, his five-year-old nephew screaming on the bank. Hughes pulled Jones out of the water, but he tried to dash back several times, saying that he was teaching the boy to swim. He offered no excuses or apologies for his actions and couldn't comprehend that he had endangered his nephew's life.

Daniel Griffiths told the court that he rescued the boy since Jones seemed incapable of assisting the drowning child. Other bystanders related Jones dragging the hysterical child towards the river and dangling him over the bank. When people remonstrated with him, he assured them that the boy was in no danger and he would save him if he fell in.

The magistrates decided that Jones had not intended to drown his nephew, saying that, if they believed he had, they would have indicted him for attempted murder. Even so, they considered his treatment of the boy most brutal and sentenced him to two months' imprisonment with hard labour.

**5 SEPTEMBER** 1898 An inquest was held at Merthyr General Hospital on the death of Cole Thomas, who committed suicide, following an unsuccessful attempt to murder his wife, May.

Thomas married in March 1897, then seemed to become mentally unhinged, insisting that his first wife was displeased with him for remarrying after her

GENERAL HOSPITAL, MERTHYR.

*Merthyr General Hospital, 1920. (Author's collection)*

death. He was cruel and violent towards May, who eventually left him. However, she was about to give birth to the couple's baby and was persuaded to return by her husband's doctor, who assured her that Thomas had agreed to seek treatment for his delusions, hallucinations and increasingly bizarre behaviour.

Remarkably, Thomas told his doctor and a male cousin that he had taken an intense dislike to May and that it was only with great difficulty that he refrained from killing her. His doctor suggested that Thomas should seek treatment and then left Thomas to arrange his own admission into an institution, while encouraging May to return to him.

On 2 September, as she nursed their baby, Thomas hit May three times over the head with a poker. He then went upstairs, climbed into the bath and cut his throat with a table knife. The inquest jury determined that Thomas '...died from cutting his throat whilst in a state of temporary insanity.' They joined the coroner in expressing incredulity that May had been permitted to return to live with a deranged man, with self-confessed murderous intentions towards her.

**1873** It was pay day at the coal and iron works in Sirhowy and Jeremiah **6 SEPTEMBER** Buckley's wife Johanna went shopping.

When she was late returning, Jeremiah went in search of her, returning home with her at eight o'clock at night. He sent out for a six-quart barrel of beer, which he drank with a neighbour and then began to beat his wife in front of their twelve-year-old son, Timothy.

Johanna was punched several times in the face, hit over the head with a poker and had a chamber pot thrown at her. Bleeding heavily from a wound on her left temple, she was then turned out of the house with Timothy and the door locked against them.

It was a cold, rainy night and after sheltering in the hen house for an hour, Johanna was determined to get her son back indoors. She banged on the door until Jeremiah answered, when she was beaten again.

It was three days before a surgeon was called to examine Johanna's head injury, by which time she was suffering from partial paralysis of her tongue and right arm. Dr Coates was able to insert his finger into the wound, which was an inch deep and, although he treated Johanna for several days, her symptoms worsened. Eventually Coates and another doctor cut into Johanna's skull, finding that it was fractured, a piece of detached bone driven into her brain.

When Johanna died on 16 September, Buckley was charged with her wilful murder, appearing before Lord Chief Justice Coleridge at the Monmouth Assizes in March 1874.

The Buckleys had been married for sixteen years and the police were regularly called to stop Buckley from beating his wife. According to Timothy, his father beat his mother almost every Saturday night when drunk and had hit her with a poker before and frequently threatened to kill her.

To the astonishment of the judge, the 'most merciful' jury deliberated only briefly before pronouncing Buckley guilty of manslaughter. Coleridge announced that he was going to award the maximum sentence possible and sentenced Buckley to penal servitude for the rest of his natural life.

7 SEPTEMBER 1844 Private Thomas Dando of the 41st Welsh Infantry, who was stationed at Brecon, went with a friend to bathe at Punch's Hole in the river near Usk. The water was very deep and, although Dando was a good swimmer, he got cramp half way across the river and suddenly sank. Although his friend immediately ran for help, by the time Dando was pulled from the water, all attempts to revive him failed.

At the subsequent inquest, held by coroner Mr T. Batt, the jury returned a verdict of 'accidentally drowned.'

8 SEPTEMBER 1877 The illegitimate son of thirty-four-year-old charwoman Frances Roberts died from starvation in Cardiff.

Thomas was born on 15 August and, within a week, Frances returned to work, leaving him in the charge of twelve-year-old Margaret Smith. Unfortunately, Frances failed to leave any food with her babysitter, apart from oatmeal and water. When Thomas died, he weighed less than half the normal weight for a baby of his age and Frances was charged with manslaughter by neglect.

At the Winter Assizes in Swansea, her landlady told the court that Thomas was well fed and cared for until the nurse attending Frances left, when Thomas was placed in a box and kept in filthy conditions. 'The poor little lamb cried until it could cry no more,' stated Mary Dunscombe, who made Frances take Thomas to the doctor on 29 August, by which time he was almost skeletal.

In her defence, Frances stated that she earned only 1s 3d a day and had several children to care for. 'I did all I could for the child,' she claimed tearfully, adding that she was simply too poor to purchase the milk he needed.

The trial jury treated her extremely sympathetically, finding her not guilty.

*Victorian memorial card. (Author's collection)*

9 SEPTEMBER 1832 A Llanelly man died from *cholera morbus* – an acute form of gastroenteritis, characterised by stomach cramps, vomiting and diarrhoea.

He was washed and laid out in an open coffin, so that people could come and pay their last respects. As a crowd of friends and relatives viewed the body, the 'corpse' very slowly sat up and gazed around in a bemused fashion. Realising his situation, the man leaped out of his coffin shouting, 'I am not dead yet' and bolted from the house stark naked, leaving behind him a group of hysterical mourners and a very red-faced doctor.

**1907**  As Margaret and Rebecca Leyshore walked back to school after lunch, they glimpsed something perturbing through the window of a house in Bridgend Road, Pontycymer. The sisters crept to the window for a closer look and saw a woman lying on the floor, with a much younger man kneeling over her.

Terrified, the girls fled to the other side of the road and, moments later, the front door of the house opened and the man came out, his hands coated in blood. He shouted something in Welsh at the girls, who ran off in fear for their lives. The man went back indoors, emerging a few minutes later dragging an apparently dead body, which he unceremoniously dumped in the street before going back inside.

Neighbours recognised the body as seventy-year-old Rachel Hannah Stills. As they bent to check her, Rachel's thirty-year-old son George threatened to kill them, before slamming the door shut again. The women could do nothing for Sarah apart from pulling down her skirts to preserve her modesty and calling the police.

Officers suspected that Rachel had been beaten and kicked to death and, on entering her house, found her two sons, John and George. The latter was wiping blood from his hands with a piece of rag and immediately told the police, 'I'm the one you want.'

George admitted hitting his mother but insisted that he had only struck her once before dragging her outside. Nevertheless, he was charged with wilful murder, appearing before Mr Justice Sutton at the Cardiff Assizes in November.

When witnesses testified that George was drunk at the time of his mother's murder and stated that Rachel often sported cuts and bruises, the jury found him guilty and he was sentenced to death. Friday 13 December proved an unlucky day for George Stills, who kept an appointment at Cardiff Prison with executioner Henry Pierrepoint.

Note: Some contemporary newspapers report that Rachel's throat was also cut.

10 SEPTEMBER

**1911**  At three o'clock in the morning, the hamlet of Cuckoo near Haverfordwest was shaken, as if by an earthquake and, as day broke, villagers realised that John Vaughan's house had exploded.

Forty-seven-year-old Vaughan was found dead in an outbuilding, the bottom part of his face completely blown away. John was a cripple and had long believed that his forty-four-year-old wife, Jane, was unfaithful. A notebook found in the shed recorded his suspicions: 'Jas Lewis done all this, Jas Lewis caused all this. Hang him, hang him.' An order for gelignite was written on an adjacent page.

Several hours later, what remained of the bodies of Jane and the couple's ten-year-old son, John, were recovered from the wrecked cottage.

11 SEPTEMBER

**1878**  In the early hours of the morning, a decision was made to flood the Prince of Wales Colliery, Abercarne. After an explosion on 11 September, the management

12 SEPTEMBER

faced a terrible dilemma – if they continued ventilating the pit to supply fresh air to any survivors, they would fan the flames of the underground fires.

Eighty-two men working in close proximity to the pit mouth were rescued, six of whom later died from their injuries but when it became apparent that there could be no more survivors, the mine was flooded with around thirty-five million gallons of water from a nearby canal.

The official death toll was 268 but some reports suggest that there could have been up to a hundred more fatalities. (It was reported that one woman dropped dead from shock when told that her son had died.) It proved impossible to determine the cause of the explosion and only twelve bodies were ever recovered.

**13 SEPTEMBER** **1863** James Sumption and Diana Williams ran a brothel in Merthyr Tydfil, although Sumption often took his 'girls' to fairs and race meetings. It was on such a trip to Kirving that he became involved in a fracas with a group of local men. Sumption had the well-deserved reputation of being a violent bully, with a string of convictions for various offences but on this particular occasion, he came off worst in the fight, which ended with the gang throwing lime into his eyes.

On 12 September, John Evans of Aberdare was paid and instead of taking his money home to his wife, he went on a drinking spree and, the next day, he found himself at Sumption's brothel. Diana Williams recognised Evans as one of the men involved in the fight at Kirving and, when she shared this information with Sumption, he became enraged, asking Evans if he remembered the incident. When Evans admitted he did, Sumption kicked him to death with his heavy hobnailed boots.

Magistrates sent Sumption for trial at the Assizes charged with wilful murder. However, at his trial on 21 December, the jury found him guilty of the lesser offence of manslaughter and he was sentenced to four years' imprisonment.

**14 SEPTEMBER** **1894** The owners of The White Hart Inn on the outskirts of Llandeilo (Llandilo) woke shortly after midnight to find the premises on fire. Mary Edwards rushed

*Llandilo. (Author's collection)*

to the bedroom window, shouting for her two daughters Mary and Elizabeth and her servant to follow her as she lowered herself 10ft to the road below. Meanwhile, John Edwards went to the bedroom at the back of the premises, where his four sons were sleeping.

As soon as Edwards entered the bedroom, the floor collapsed, pitching him and his sons into the kitchen below. The kitchen door was locked and Edwards was unable to escape, eventually collapsing against the door.

Mrs Edwards woke her neighbours and, while one went to raise the alarm, David Thomas smashed the lock on the kitchen door with a hatchet. Since Edwards had fallen against it and was now unconscious, it took Thomas some time to force the door open and drag him outside. His lower body was terribly burned, the flesh falling away from his limbs and he died a few hours later.

The fire was thought to have been started when clothes airing by the kitchen fire caught light, the flames fuelled by melting fat from a flitch of bacon, hanging from the kitchen ceiling. Although the fire brigade were quickly on the scene, there was no water to douse the flames and all they could do was to form a bucket chain to a brook almost 200 yards away. The bodies of Rees (9), Joseph (6), Henry (3) and William (15) were recovered when the fire burned itself out.

**1895** Arthur Vaughan and Henry Lewis agreed to settle a minor dispute with a prize fight, to be held on Llanwonno Mountain. The fight attracted around ninety spectators, who watched as the men fought for three-quarters of an hour, before it became apparent that the smaller and lighter Vaughan was losing. Although Vaughan was keen to continue, it was decided to end the bout and the two men shook hands and headed home.

Vaughan walked only 600 yards before complaining of feeling faint and vomiting. His brother went to find a cab and a doctor but by the time he

15 SEPTEMBER

*Llanwonno Church. (Author's collection)*

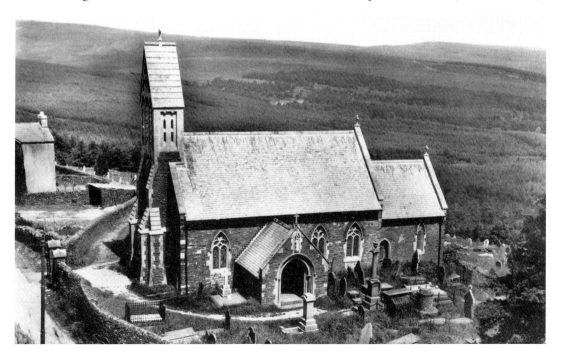

returned Vaughan was unconscious, dying later that afternoon. A post-mortem examination determined the cause of death as severe shaking of the brain.

Ten men were charged with manslaughter in connection with Vaughan's death, three of whom were later discharged by magistrates due to lack of evidence. The remaining seven were committed for trial at the next Glamorganshire Assizes.

Only six actually appeared at Cardiff Town Hall in November 1895, one being unwell at the time of the trial. Henry Lewis was charged with feloniously killing and slaying Vaughan, while the four seconds, the timekeeper and the stakeholder were charged with aiding and abetting him.

It was emphasized throughout the trial that Vaughan was willing, if not anxious, to continue fighting, even though he was losing. Both his brother and brother-in-law testified that they asked Vaughan several times if he wanted to stop and were told that he wished to continue. It was also stressed that the fight was a perfectly fair one and that the combatants had shaken hands afterwards.

Mr Justice Lawrence told Lewis that he was technically guilty as charged and, in law, his fellow defendants were equally liable. However, he accepted that Lewis had not intended to take Vaughan's life and that the other defendants had taken no active part in the fight. Lawrence therefore bound all of the defendants to appear for judgement if called upon to do so in future, adding that he hoped that this would prove a lesson to them all.

16 SEPTEMBER **1851** A reward of £50 was offered for information leading to the conviction of the murderer(s) of seventeen-year-old servant Ruth Jones, whose body was found in Linkparkmain Pond, near Conwil on 9 August.

Ruth was last seen alive between nine and ten o'clock on 8 August, when she was asked by her mistress to put some loaves in the oven before retiring for the night. The next morning, her body was found face down in the pond, which was less than 3ft deep.

Although fully dressed apart from her cap, she had been raped and hit several times on the back of the head with a blunt instrument. Police found numerous spots of blood around the pond and a man's footprints in the mud at the edge.

Ruth was known to have an admirer, who sometimes visited her at night and, although they did not know the man's identity, her employers testified to occasionally hearing footsteps and a male voice outside their home. However, nothing was heard on the night of 8/9 August and Ruth had given no indication that she was intending to go out, although her bed had not been slept in.

At the inquest on Ruth's death held by coroner George Thomas, the jury returned a verdict of 'wilful murder against some person or persons unknown'. In spite of the reward and an assurance by Home Secretary Sir George Grey that a pardon would be granted to any accomplice who was not the killer but was prepared to give information, the case remains unsolved.

17 SEPTEMBER **1886** Eleven-year-old Edith Beatrice Mary Williams was playing with friends in Cardiff when they came across an unattended bonfire. The flames proved an irresistible draw for the children and, before long, Edith's skirts caught fire and her legs and lower body were badly burned. She lingered in agony for almost two weeks, before dying from the effects of the burns.

At the inquest on her death held by coroner Mr E.B. Reece, it was alleged that a boy was pulling burning sticks out of the fire and throwing them and that one such missile was responsible for setting fire to Edith's clothes. If this were the case, then the coroner's jury were justified in returning a verdict of manslaughter against the child but they decided that the fire could have resulted from a chance spark or from Edith getting too close to the bonfire and returned a verdict of 'accidental death.'

**1842** As people made their way to St Mary's Church, Swansea, for evening service, William Kneath ran out into the street shouting that his wife had just died. One of the churchgoers was surgeon Mr Bevan, who accompanied Kneath back to his rooms, where he found Mrs Kneath on the bedroom floor, her body still warm. Noticing some bruises on her head, he suspected foul play and contacted the police.

18 SEPTEMBER

*St Mary's Church, Swansea. (Author's collection)*

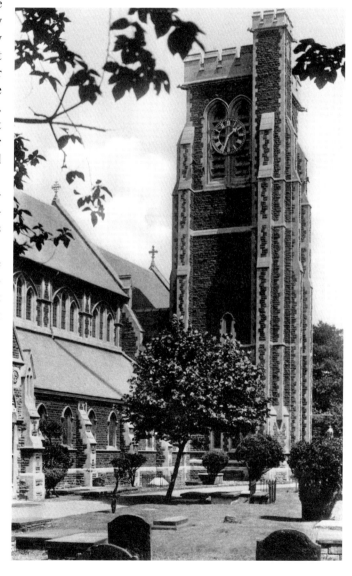

Kneath told the police that he and his wife spent most of that day in bed, drunk. He woke in the early evening to find that she had wet the bed and, in disgust, gave her a hefty shove. She landed on the floor with a tremendous thump, which, to Kneath's surprise, didn't wake her and, as he peered over the edge of the bed, she gasped twice then died.

Coroner Charles Collins instructed Bevan to conduct a post-mortem, which revealed that Mrs Kneath had died from apoplexy, brought on by 'the intemperate use of intoxicating liquors.' Witnesses at the inquest testified that the Kneaths were a very loving couple, especially when drunk, which they usually were on Sundays. Only an hour before her death, Mrs Kneath stole a shilling from her husband's pockets and, leaving him sleeping, went to the pub and spent the whole amount on spirits.

On hearing this, the inquest jury returned a verdict of death by visitation of God and Kneath was released from custody.

**19 SEPTEMBER**  **1878** Swansea draper John Jenkins missed a cigar case, in which he kept his shop takings. Having last seen the case at 9.30 a.m., it was five hours before he noticed it was missing and reported its theft to the police.

Meanwhile, thirteen-year-old Susan John had come into some money, which she said was a legacy from her uncle. Susan and her school friends counted out £29 10s 6d, which Susan wrapped in a rag and hid in a hedge.

For the next few weeks, Susan treated her friends to unlimited sweets and even paid for a tea party, all the while stressing that the money must remain a secret. Susan's best friend, Catherine Rees, was given £2 4s 6d and told to say that she had found it – she was also given a purse containing £5 to keep for Susan. However, Catherine's mother became suspicious at her daughter's unexpected windfall and spoke to Susan's mother and the police.

When questioned, Susan insisted that another girl, Ellen Thomas, gave her the money, having found it in Swansea Market. When Ellen denied this, Susan was arrested on suspicion of theft from John Jenkins and committed for trial at the next Assizes.

The only real evidence against Susan was that the missing money contained two crown coins, as did that recovered from Susan's stash. Jenkins had not seen Susan in his shop on the day of the robbery, although he had not been there all the time. Thus the Grand Jury, whose job it was to consider the prosecution's evidence and determine whether there was a strong enough case to be tried, found 'no bill' against Susan and she was discharged without penalty.

**20 SEPTEMBER**  **1857** The prospect of followers of the Mormon faith gaining a stronghold in Llansamlet seemed to engender near panic among the villagers, who viewed them as a 'fanatical sect', saw their founder Joseph Smith as 'an imposter' and branded their sermons as 'disgusting, profane and preposterous.' Thus, when the Mormons arrived in Llansamlet on Sunday 20 September, intending to preach their own version of the gospel, they were ambushed by a crowd of hostile villagers numbering almost 300, who jeered, hooted and pelted them with cabbages, potatoes, apples and eggs and forced them to beat a hasty retreat.

**21 SEPTEMBER**  **1865** Eleven-year-old Edwin Beach, an inmate of the Workhouse, was sent with two other boys to dig potatoes near Monmouth Gaol.

As the boys returned to the Workhouse, they lost control of the overloaded truck on which they were carrying the potatoes on a steep slope and it ran over Edwin, who died from his injuries a few hours later. A post-mortem examination revealed the cause of his death to be 'concussion of the brain.'

At the inquest on his death, his companions told coroner Mr E.D. Batt that they had asked a man to help them pull the truck down the hill but he refused. The jury returned a verdict of 'accidental death', recommending that a man should accompany the boys in future to prevent further accidents.

**22 SEPTEMBER**  **1884** When Catherine Rees of Neath kissed Thomas Smith in the street, her husband, David, took exception and punched Smith, who retaliated. Soon they were brawling, with neighbours taking sides and becoming involved in the ruckus.

The police were called and Catherine, David and Thomas were arrested. All three were taken before magistrates charged with obstructing the street by fighting.

Smith and Catherine were each sentenced to fourteen days' imprisonment with hard labour but the magistrates discharged David Rees without penalty, saying that, under the circumstances, he was entirely justified in acting as he did.

**1890** The steamship *Harrogate* was undergoing repairs in dry dock at Cardiff 23 SEPTEMBER when three workmen went into a storage tank to remove some damaged plates. Before long, one shouted for help and James Airs, who was working nearby, raised the alarm and went to see what the matter was. He was immediately overpowered by noxious fumes and fell headfirst into the tank.

The foreman sent for a doctor and began the difficult process of getting the unconscious men out of the tank. Airs was dead but artificial respiration was started on the others and, as they regained consciousness, all three became hysterical and violent – it took six men to restrain one of them.

There had been a serious fire on the ship a few days before and it was theorised that carbonic acid had been produced in large quantities and seeped into the tank, affecting the labourers when they inhaled the fumes.

**1832** A woman from Kidwelly was targeted by a confidence trickster, who 24 SEPTEMBER knocked on her door claiming to have found a parcel. He opened it, revealing a sealed envelope amongst its contents, which contained a folded piece of official-looking paper.

'It's a £50 note!' the man exclaimed in apparent surprise, generously offering to share his spoils with the woman. However, neither had any change.

The man ascertained that she had eight sovereigns in the house and offered to let her keep the note in exchange for her money, promising to come back the following day with change for the large note and return her sovereigns. His offer was eagerly accepted but, when he failed to return, the woman showed the bank note to a literate neighbour, who revealed that she had been left a worthless piece of paper.

**1892** Police Constable King came across nine-year-old Charles Morgan 25 SEPTEMBER wandering the streets of Cardiff. The child told King that his mother put him out of the house three days earlier, since when he had been sleeping in gardens. He was dirty, inadequately clothed and alive with vermin, with a large, suppurating abscess beneath his ear, along with another wound on his neck.

Recollecting that Charles had been apprehended before for sleeping rough, King took him to the police station, from where he was sent to the Workhouse. His mother was traced and told police that Charles was the son of her first husband, her second husband being a marine engineer.

Sarah Briggs later appeared at Cardiff Police Court charged with neglecting to provide sufficient clothing for Charles and allowing him to get into such a state of filth as to cause unnecessary suffering. She was smartly and fashionably dressed and took little interest in her son beyond grumbling that she couldn't control him.

Although Sarah was ultimately discharged with a caution, she had a previous conviction for beating her son and the magistrates concluded that she was

*Queen Street, Cardiff, c. 1910.*
*(Author's collection)*

'a dissolute and negligent parent.' They sent Charles to an Industrial School, ordering his mother to pay 4s a week until his sixteenth birthday.

26 SEPTEMBER    **1898** Railway guard John Jones appeared at Barry Police Court charged with behaving in an unseemly way in a railway carriage on the Vale of Glamorgan Railway.

Alfred Henry Lanfier told the Bench that he and his aunt were travelling by train from Bridgend to Barry on 25 September. Jones was very drunk and, shortly after leaving Rhoose, he exposed his genitals to Lanfier's aunt. Jones vehemently denied having done any such thing but Lanfier's accusation was corroborated by another passenger, Charles Tamlyn.

Magistrates fined Jones £5 plus costs or one month's hard labour in default.

27 SEPTEMBER    **1861** Although in his eighties, the Lord-Lieutenant of Monmouthshire, Capel Hanbury Leigh, was a sprightly man, until a fall downstairs left him confined to bed.

On 27 September, Mrs Leigh noticed that her husband had finished the bottle of his daily tonic. The doctor was expected that afternoon and Mrs Leigh, who was going out, told her husband to stay in bed until he came.

Mr Leigh had other ideas and decided to get up just before lunch. He asked his valet William Jennings Riddesdale, to pour him a dose of tonic but, as soon as he swallowed it, Leigh realised that Riddesdale had mistakenly given him the embrocation prescribed for the after effects of his recent fall. Neither appreciated the seriousness of the mistake and it wasn't until fifteen minutes later that the valet sent for a doctor. By chance, Leigh's own doctor arrived minutes later, several hours early for his appointment. By then, Leigh was coughing up bloody mucus and, although the doctor gave him an emetic, the lining of Leigh's stomach and oesophagus were completely destroyed and he died the next day.

At the inquest, the jury accepted that Leigh had directed Riddesdale to the wrong bottle and that the valet, who was not wearing his glasses, had simply made a tragic mistake. They returned a verdict that 'death resulted from the effects of a poison accidentally administered.' Tragically, although Leigh's doctor was early for his appointment, he was actually delayed by a bridge repair that forced him to make a detour of four miles and had also had to wait for over an hour for his transport to be made ready. Without these delays, he would have been at his patient's bedside before the fatal dose was administered.

**1878** Navvy Michael Harney lodged with Mrs Sullivan and her two teenage sons at Dowlais and had formed such a strong attachment to his landlady that the couple planned to marry. It was not a match that sixteen-year-old Cornelius Sullivan and his eighteen-year-old brother Joseph approved of and there were frequent quarrels. 　　　　28 SEPTEMBER

One squabble broke out as the family ate supper on 28 September and Harney tried to put Joseph out of the house. Cornelius waded in to help his brother and the table was upset, knocking over and extinguishing the lamp.

In the confusion, Cornelius rushed at Harney with a knife. He was restrained by his mother but, as Harney walked past, Cornelius lashed out, stabbing him on the left-hand side of his neck. The knife severed two major blood vessels and Harney bled to death within minutes.

Cornelius and Joseph were arrested and Cornelius freely admitted having stabbed Harney, saying that he didn't care if he swung for it. They were brought before magistrates charged with wilful murder and, while Joseph was discharged due to lack of evidence, his brother was committed for trial at the next Assizes.

His trial took place at Swansea on 2 November, where he was found guilty of the lesser offence of manslaughter and sentenced to fifteen years' imprisonment.

**1927** Dai Lewis earned his living by offering services to bookmakers at racecourses – those who hired stools and chalk from him protected themselves against unforeseen 'accidents' that might otherwise befall their stalls or even their persons. 　　　　29 SEPTEMBER

Although Dai normally worked Monmouth racecourse, on 28 September he muscled in on the Cardiff racecourse 'owned' by brothers John and Edward 'Titch' Rowlands. John, Titch and their entourage of heavies were outraged at Dai's intrusion onto their territory but Dai chose to ignore their wrath.

On 29 September, he was drinking in The Blue Anchor public house in St Mary Street, when he found himself surrounded by the Rowlands' gang. Dai ignored their presence and the gang eventually retreated to a café across the road. When Dai emerged from the pub, they jumped him, stabbing him in the throat.

He was rushed to Cardiff Royal Infirmary, where three anonymous calls were made, inquiring about his welfare. The police were alerted after the second and managed to trace the third to the Colonial Club, where they arrested John and Titch, Daniel Driscoll, John Hughes and William Price and charged them with attempted murder. All were taken to Dai's bedside to witness his deposition but Dai stubbornly insisted that they were his good friends.

When Dai died and the charge was elevated to one of wilful murder, John Rowlands confessed. Hughes was released due to lack of evidence but the remaining four men were tried at the Glamorganshire Assizes on 29 November.

*Two views of St Mary Street, Cardiff. (Author's collection)*

Price was acquitted, while Driscoll and the Rowlands brothers were found guilty and sentenced to death.

Edward Rowlands and Daniel Driscoll were hanged at Cardiff Gaol on 27 January 1928 – John Rowlands was certified insane and sent to Broadmoor. In the aftermath of what became known as 'the Hoodoo murder', a series of misfortunes befell some of the key participants. John Hughes died within the year and a prostitute who had appeared as a prosecution witness committed suicide. William Price was blinded in one eye with a butcher's hook and four of the police officers involved died very young, one committing suicide and the other three dying from cancer, tuberculosis and a stomach disorder.

**1891** Eight miners at New Glyncorrwg Colliery, Abergwynfi climbed into a bowk **30 SEPTEMBER** – a large bucket – and were pulled upwards by a steel rope, drawn by a revolving iron wheel. As the bowk reached the surface, it failed to stop and was pulled over the top of the wheel. All eight men were thrown out and killed

The steam engine powering the winding wheel was driven by David Davies, an experienced driver who was just about to be relieved by John Jones. As Jones was hanging up his coat, Davies shouted for help shutting off the steam.

Colliery rules stipulated that there should be no more than six men in a bowk at any one time and, at the inquest on the eight deaths, it was alleged that Jones smelled strongly of drink. Although it proved impossible to pinpoint the precise cause of the tragic accident, it was suggested that either Davies stopped the engine a moment too late or that there was a mechanical problem with the engine's throttle valve. The inquest jury returned eight verdicts of accidental death.

# OCTOBER

*High Street, Swansea, 1920s. (Author's collection)*

**1891** Shoe-black Thomas Ingram appeared before magistrates at Newport charged with being drunk and disorderly and with assaulting the manageress of The Tredegar Arms public house. He was further charged with wilfully damaging a door.

It was alleged that Ingram pulled a brass bar from the pub door and hit the manageress over the head with it. When arrested, he threatened to use a knife on her next time, for 'showing him up' in front of other drinkers in the bar.

It was forty-year-old Ingram's seventy-second appearance before magistrates on charges relating to drunkenness and he was sentenced to six months' imprisonment in Usk Gaol.

**1884** At Howell's Pottery in Landore, Swansea, a large quantity of clay had been spread out to dry on the floor of a room in an upper storey. The weight of the clay proved too great and the floor gave way, falling into the rooms below where a number of young women were working.

Fifteen-year-old Mary Ann Doyle and seventeen-year-old Margaret Gordon were buried beneath the clay and, when they were extricated, Mary Ann was dead. Margaret was seriously injured but is believed to have survived.

A later inquest returned a verdict of 'accidental death' on Mary Ann Doyle.

**1828** Edward Barnett was arrested in Liverpool on suspicion of having murdered Esther Stephens (or Stevens) in Monmouth on 28 September.

Although Esther was married, she and Barnett were having an affair. When Barnett's ardour cooled, he decided to leave England for good. With his life savings of £32, he made for Bristol, where he tried to find a passage to America, returning to Monmouth when he was unsuccessful.

Esther was not prepared to let him go. She found out where Barnett was staying and sent him a letter, telling him that her husband would shortly be leaving for his work as a bargeman and asking Barnett to meet her.

Barnett was seen arriving at Esther's lodgings and, in the early hours of 28 September, the occupants of the rooms below heard banging and shouting coming from her apartment. Thinking that William Stephens was beating his wife, William Pearce shouted upstairs, 'What the devil are you about, Stephens? Are you going to murder the woman?' There was a final crash, then silence.

The following morning, Esther's body was discovered in her bedroom, which was awash with blood. There was no sign of Barnett, who left behind his jacket, hat, boots and almost £30 when he fled.

The inquest returned a verdict of wilful murder against Barnett and a large reward was posted for his capture. Knowing that he was intending to sail to America, police put a watch on all ports and he was apprehended in Liverpool and brought back for trial at the Monmouth Assizes.

Barnett explained that he was dozing drunkenly in Esther's bed when she leaned over him, a knife in her hand. Thinking that she planned to steal his money, he managed to disarm her and cut her throat.

The evidence against him was highly circumstantial, the case relying on what William Pearce claimed to have heard. Neither of the two knives found in the room belonged to Barnett and, when arrested, he had a deep cut on his thumb, suggesting that he might have wrenched a knife away from Esther. However, the jury took less than ten minutes to find him guilty and he was executed at Monmouth on 24 August.

**4 OCTOBER**    **1902** Although they weren't legally married, Jeremiah Callaghan and Hannah Shea had four children together. Callaghan only worked sporadically and was unable to provide a home for his family, so Hannah and the children lived in Bedwellty Workhouse.

On 4 October, Hannah and the children walked to Tredegar to meet Jeremiah, who was working as a stonemason's labourer. By the time her boyfriend finished work, Hannah had visited several public houses and as soon as she met Jeremiah, he angrily accused her of drinking. Hannah denied having drunk anything, at which Jeremiah gave her a violent shove, sending her sprawling on the ground. They soon made up their quarrel and visited several more pubs before walking back to the Workhouse.

Jeremiah was so drunk that he kept falling over. The children walked on ahead, while Hannah helped him and, as they reached the Workhouse, she stopped to talk to a woman named Jane Hannam. As they chatted, Jeremiah suddenly pushed Hannah against a wall and cut her throat. She staggered a few yards before collapsing and dying from loss of blood, while Jeremiah calmly smoked his pipe and was later seen dancing.

Forty-two-year-old Callaghan was tried at the Monmouth Assizes and insisted that he had no recollection of Hannah's murder and could remember nothing before waking up in prison after his arrest. His defence counsel suggested that Callaghan was suffering from *delirium tremens* but the prosecution countered by calling Dr Boulton from Cardiff Prison. Boulton had known Callaghan for several years and believed that he was of sound mind. Boulton's testimony proved the more persuasive and the jury found Callaghan guilty. He was executed at Usk Prison by William Billington on 12 December.

**5 OCTOBER**    **1887** Twenty-five-year-old Cornelius Callaghan appeared at Cardiff Police Court charged with setting fire to his wife, Julia.

Cornelius came home drunk in the early hours of the morning of 24 July and demanded something to eat. When Julia refused to get up, Cornelius threatened to 'burn the ******* bed' if she didn't and, moments later, she realised that her nightclothes were on fire.

As she jumped out of bed, Cornelius pulled the burning clothes off her, telling her that he was sorry he hadn't burned her ******* head off and pushing her out onto the landing. Roused by Julia's shouts of 'Fire!' other occupants of the house found her naked at the foot of the stairs, her back and legs badly burned. She spent six weeks in hospital, while her husband absconded and was eventually arrested weeks later in Newport.

Magistrates committed Callaghan for trial at the next Assizes, which opened on 3 November. Since Julia Callaghan failed to appear, the Grand Jury found 'no true bill' and he was discharged.

Although he wasn't hurt, the Callaghans' infant son was in the bed with his mother when his father set fire to it. Perhaps surprisingly, censuses indicate that Cornelius and Julia stayed married and went on to produce several more children.

**1853** An inquest was held at Abertillery on the death of engine driver James Anstice from Brighton.

**6 OCTOBER**

Between Aberberg and Abertillery was a hilly stretch of line, with sharp bends. There was a mandatory speed limit of nine miles an hour but, although an experienced and very careful driver, Anstice negotiated the awkward track at between forty and fifty miles an hour.

His engine ran off the rails near Abertillery, smashing into eleven trucks in a siding and then skidding for almost 100 yards, dragging a tender behind it. The stoker and another crew member clung on to the tender for dear life, somehow escaping serious injury. Anstice wasn't so fortunate. He was thrown from the train and his head was cut in two, his abdomen ripped open and his intestines scattered along the track.

The inquest jury returned a verdict that 'The deceased came by his death through furiously driving a railway engine.'

*Six Bells, Abertillery. (Author's collection)*

**1893** Fifteen-year-old William Harris was a member of a junior football team at Birchgrove, Swansea, and, as he and his team were practicing, William was hit behind the ear by a football.

**7 OCTOBER**

The boy shrugged off the incident but later complained of numbness in one leg and ringing in his ears. After walking home, he felt so unwell that he went straight to bed and, not long afterwards, he suffered a fit. In spite of the efforts of Dr Jones from Llansamlet, William died the following day from a ruptured blood vessel near his temple.

When questioned, the members of the football team gave conflicting statements. William's brother and another player, Samuel Davies, insisted that a boy named Dudley had deliberately thrown the ball at William, with the intention of hurting him. Dudley and several other players were equally insistent that William simply failed to catch the ball when it was thrown to him.

The inquest jury gave Dudley the benefit of the doubt and recorded a verdict of 'accidental death.'

**8 OCTOBER**　**1881** At 8.30 a.m., farmer David Jones and his wife Anne left Llangadock for a regular trip to Llandovery market. Although Jones was the son of a Methodist preacher, he was addicted to drink and had a couple of convictions for drunkenness. Having recently spent five weeks in Carmarthen Asylum, he was supposed to have been completely cured, although his family noticed that he seemed depressed.

Less than an hour later, their bodies were found on the roadside, their throats cut from ear to ear. David Jones still had a pocket knife clasped in his right hand and the fact that it had been very recently sharpened indicated that the deaths were planned in advance.

At an inquest held by corner Mr J. Prothero Lewis, the jury returned verdicts of wilful murder and suicide while of unsound mind.

**9 OCTOBER**　**1869** Thirteen-year-old Dennis Kelly was employed at the Ebbw Vale Iron and Steel Works and, as he walked across the shop floor, his shoe accidentally caught between two enormous rollers and his leg was crushed. The rollers had reached the boy's thigh before the machinery was stopped and he could be extricated.

Dennis was taken to his father's home, where he was treated by Dr Laxton until his death the next morning. A later inquest attached no blame to anyone for Dennis's demise and coroner Mr Brewer's jury returned a verdict of 'accidental death.'

**10 OCTOBER**　**1949** William Llewellyn cycled to meet Albert Edward Jenkins at his farm near Haverfordwest. When he didn't return for lunch, Llewellyn's wife and daughter went to see Jenkins, who told them that he left hours earlier. Mrs Llewellyn reported her husband missing and, the following afternoon, police found his tarpaulin-wrapped body in a clay pit on Jenkins's farm.

Jenkins was a tenant of Llewellyn's and had asked him to meet him to discuss buying the farm. According to Jenkins, he gave Llewellyn £1,050 in cash but when the police examined his signed receipt, they found that it was dated 29 September.

Jenkins had a ready explanation, claiming that £50 was for overdue rent, due on 29 September. Asked where he kept so much cash, Jenkins indicated a beam in his bedroom and said that the money had been on top of it. When the police saw that the dust on the beam was undisturbed, they charged Jenkins with wilful murder.

At Jenkins's trial at the Pembrokeshire Assizes, the prosecution maintained that he was at the point of financial ruin. His rent was overdue, as were payments on his tractor and his bank account was overdrawn. It was theorised that Jenkins murdered his landlord, hoping to prove that he had bought the farm but the receipt was an obvious forgery. Llewellyn's boots were found hidden beneath some manure in a calf stall, which had blood spots on the wall and the boot laces were found in Jenkins's pockets.

Jenkins stuck to his story. He had paid Llewellyn £1,050 in cash for the purchase of the farm and they parted on friendly terms. He recalled a couple of gypsies hanging about at the time and suggested that they had robbed and killed Llewellyn.

When the jury heard that the police tried to put £1,050 in bank notes in Llewellyn's wallet but had found it impossible, they found Jenkins guilty. He was hanged at Swansea Prison on 19 April 1950.

**1927** Sixty-eight-year-old Evan Davies and his wife were found in a bedroom of their gas-filled house in Powell Street, Swansea. Mrs Davies was dead and her husband was rushed to hospital, unconscious.

**11 OCTOBER**

No gas taps were turned on inside the house and it was surmised that the main gas pipe running under the road outside had fractured, allowing the escape of gas into the bedroom. This was most probably caused by the weight of a heavy steam roller, recently used to repair the road.

Evan Davies is believed to have died in hospital.

**1930** As twenty-nine-year-old Dorothy Hilda Narbett was preparing Sunday lunch at the cottage in Llangadock she shared with her husband and their two children, a couple of neighbours dropped in. When they left, Oswald Narbett went to fetch some milk.

**12 OCTOBER**

The last visitor, farmer William Jones, had walked about 200 yards when he heard a scream and saw one of the Narbetts' children running towards him. He rushed back to find Dorothy cradling her husband, who lay in their garden, bleeding from a wound in his chest. Narbett bled to death before help could be summoned and when a post-mortem examination later revealed that he had been stabbed through the heart, Dorothy was charged with wilful murder.

From the outset, Mrs Narbett insisted that Oswald's death was a tragic accident. She was rushing outside with a knife to cut some leeks and collided with her husband on the doorstep, the impact knocking her over. Mr Narbett immediately clutched his chest and, when she saw blood on his hand, Mrs Narbett thought she had cut his finger, claiming not to have felt the knife entering her husband's chest.

At the Glamorganshire Assizes, the court heard from Dr William Thomson Lawson, who believed the stab wound was more consistent with direct violence than accident, although he conceded that Narbett's death could have resulted from the circumstances described by Mrs Narbett. When the jury heard testimony from both of the Narbetts' visitors, stating that the couple seemed perfectly happy just minutes before the alleged murder, they immediately pronounced Mrs Narbett not guilty.

**1895** Norah Brian took her ten-week-old baby, Alice, to visit Mrs Harris in her room at the house in Cardiff, where they both lodged. As the women chatted, Thomas Harris came home and started an argument with his wife. In a temper, Mrs Harris hit her husband on the head with a pair of tongs. Harris immediately snatched up a poker and threw it at his wife but his aim was poor and the poker struck Alice, fracturing her skull.

**13 OCTOBER**

She was rushed to Cardiff Infirmary but died within minutes and Harris consequently appeared at the Glamorganshire Assizes in November 1895, where he was found guilty of manslaughter.

The jury tempered their verdict with a recommendation for mercy and Harris was given excellent character references. Mr Justice Lawrence told Harris that Alice died more through misadventure than malice, her death a tragic accident rather than a deliberate act. He therefore bound Harris over in his own recognisance to appear for judgement if called upon to do so in future.

**14 OCTOBER** **1886** The *Malleny* sank with the loss of twenty crew and, by 17 October, twelve bodies had been washed up between Ogmore and St Donat's.

Four were taken to The Greyhound Inn at St Brides Major to await the attentions of the coroner. Jenkin Powell stationed himself at the door of the room where the bodies lay in coffins and charged people 3*d* each to view them. When challenged, Powell insisted that he was collecting money towards the sailors' burial expenses.

Powell was charged with obtaining money by false pretences and sent for trial at the Swansea Assizes where, in his address to the Grand Jury, Mr Justice Wills expressed grave doubts about the strength of the prosecution's case. In order to demonstrate false pretences, it must be proved that the money collected was not used for burying the sailors and Powell was arrested before the money was distributed. His real offence was committing a gross outrage on public decency but that was not the offence he was charged with.

The Grand Jury shared Wills's concerns and returned 'no true bill' against Powell, who was discharged.

**15 OCTOBER** **1934** Coroner Mr E. Charles Jones held an inquest at Newport on the death of fifty-six-year-old John Fleming.

The inquest heard that John was given some mushrooms by a friend. Mrs Fleming cooked them but told the coroner that she hadn't liked the look of them and tried to persuade her husband not to eat them. At his insistence, she tried a tiny piece, which she spat out, saying that it tasted 'funny'. Her husband cleared his plate but collapsed shortly afterwards and was rushed to hospital unconscious, dying soon after arriving.

The mushrooms were identified as the highly poisonous species *Cortinarius*. In recording a verdict of 'death from natural causes' the coroner remarked that it was a good job that Mrs Fleming had not found them to her liking.

**16 OCTOBER** **1887** Forty-three-year-old Elias Davies of Llanwonno was very unhappily married. Between them, Davies and his son earned £10 a month but Lucy Davies spent almost every penny on drink, staying out late and neglecting her husband, their children and her household duties.

Her dissolute behaviour was the cause of frequent violent rows between the couple, and, on 16 October, one fight led to Lucy's death. A post-mortem examination carried out by Dr Davies (no relation) showed that she was in such a poor state of health due to excessive alcohol consumption that she would have died soon. Still, in the doctor's opinion, the assault by her husband had accelerated Lucy's death and Elias was charged with feloniously killing and slaying her, appearing at the Swansea Assizes on 3 November.

The jury found him guilty but recommended mercy on the grounds of extreme provocation from Lucy and Elias was sentenced to just two months' imprisonment with hard labour.

**1856** During the night of 16/17 October, jewellery worth £200 was stolen in Swansea. The police had plenty of leads and soon arrested two men in Bristol.

17 OCTOBER

Whereas Thomas John was prepared to come quietly, William Smith (aka John Duggan) fought tooth and nail to avoid arrest. He hit PC Bowden several times with a lifebelt before flinging himself into the Floating Harbour, from where he was eventually pulled almost drowned. When the Floating Harbour was later searched, most of the stolen jewellery was retrieved, with the exception of one gold ring, found on the boat on which Smith was placed after being dragged from the water.

Smith and John were tried at the Cardiff Assizes on 1 December. There was insufficient evidence to convict John, who was acquitted and discharged but Smith was found guilty. Being a ticket-of-leave convict, who had only been released from a previous prison sentence on a guarantee of his future good behaviour, Smith was sentenced to be transported for life.

Smith decided that he would rather die and, in the hope of being hanged, attacked a warder with a large piece of firewood that he managed to secrete in his prison cell. When his attempt at murder failed, Smith tried to hang himself from the window bars with his handkerchief but was cut down and revived.

A couple of days later, Smith's eyes were weeping and sore. Prison surgeon Mr Evans noticed that the eyeballs appeared to be scratched and treated Smith for several days but, rather than improving, his eyes worsened until Smith was in danger of losing his sight. Only then was he searched and a tiny fragment

*The Floating Harbour and tramway centre, Bristol, 1920s. (Author's collection)*

of glass found in his pocket. Under questioning, he admitted that he had been systematically scratching out his own eyeballs in the hope of going blind and avoiding transportation.

His efforts were in vain, since he departed for Western Australia aboard *Nile* on 18 September 1857.

18 OCTOBER **1890** A group of boys were cleaning Great Western Railway trains at the Landore engine shed at Swansea. Two boys were under one of the trains but were still to complete their work when the driver was mistakenly given an 'all clear' whistle. As the train pulled away, one boy scrambled out from underneath but the second was crushed, dying instantly.

At an inquest held by deputy coroner Mr T. Strick, the jury returned a verdict of 'accidental death' on fifteen-year-old William John Jenkins, absolving the driver of all blame. They did however suggest that better safety precautions should be taken in future to prevent such tragic accidents.

19 OCTOBER **1887** Nineteen-year-old William Longman appeared before magistrates at Cardiff charged with breaking and entering a shop in Cowbridge Road.

Among the items stolen was a quantity of sugar and the police were able to follow a trail of loose sugar from the shop to Longman's house next door. A search of the premises revealed the other stolen items – three tins of lobster, two of salmon, a bottle of sauce and three jars of apricots.

Longman was committed for trial at the Assizes, where he was found guilty and sentenced to four months' imprisonment with hard labour.

20 OCTOBER **1888** Five-year-old John Harper went missing at Pontardawe and, when a search by his parents and neighbours failed to locate him, his disappearance was reported to the police. John was seen earlier that day with eighteen-year-old Thomas Lott and that evening, the police found his body in a wood. His throat had been cut and he had been disembowelled.

The police went straight to the cottage where Lott lived with his mother. Lott readily confessed to killing John, telling the police that his knife was on the windowsill of a nearby slaughterhouse, to which Lott, who occasionally worked as a butcher's boy, had ready access.

By the time Lott was tried at the Swansea Assizes, several doctors had examined him. Lott's head was unusually small and irregularly shaped and Dr Pegge classed him as an 'imbecile'. However, Pegge had questioned Lott in English and Inspector Giddings of the Pontardawe Police pointed out that Lott testified in Welsh at the inquest and appeared perfectly sane. Another medical witness, Mr Price Jones, agreed with Giddings – he questioned Lott in Welsh and said that he appeared sane when spoken to in his native language but struggled to comprehend English, making him seem dull and stupid.

Since Pegge was more experienced, the jury accepted his opinion and pronounced Lott unfit to plead. He was sentenced to be detained until Her Majesty's Pleasure be known and sent to Broadmoor Criminal Lunatic Asylum.

No motive was ever discovered for Harper's brutal murder, although some contemporary newspapers alleged that the little boy had complained on previous occasions that Lott had tried to take him into the woods and make him take his clothes off.

**1966** As morning assembly finished at Pantglas Junior School in Aberfan and the children dispersed to their classrooms, there was a thunderous roar as the school was engulfed by a massive landslip of coal waste, which slid down Merthyr Mountain swamping everything in its path. One hundred and forty-four lives were lost, 116 of them children, most between the ages of seven and ten years old. 21 OCTOBER

Hundreds of volunteers flocked to the school, joining the emergency services and local miners in digging through the coal waste to try and reach the children trapped beneath it but sadly, only twenty-five pupils survived the disaster, many of whom were terribly injured. No one was rescued alive after eleven o'clock that morning and it was almost a week before all the bodies were recovered.

The waste tip was built over natural streams and springs and this, coupled with several days' heavy rain, caused a tidal wave of mud, slurry and water. An enquiry into the tragedy chaired by Lord Justice Edmund Davies ran for seventy-six days and concluded:

> ... the Aberfan Disaster is a terrifying tale of bungling ineptitude by many men charged with tasks for which they were totally unfitted, of failure to heed clear warnings, and of total lack of direction from above. Not villains but decent men, led astray by foolishness or by ignorance or by both in combination, are responsible for what happened at Aberfan. Blame for the disaster rests upon the National Coal Board. This is shared, though in varying degrees, among the NCB headquarters, the South Western Divisional Board, and certain individuals.

The NCB were ordered to pay compensation to the bereaved parents, which was set at just £500 per deceased child. In addition, the villagers were forced to pay £150,000 out of a fund of public donations to have the remains of the slag heap removed. (The sum of £150,000 was refunded by the Labour government in 1997 although many argued that, after taking interest rates and inflation into account, the amount repaid should have been £1.5 million.)

The tragedy, which robbed the village of a generation, occurred on the day before the start of the half-term holiday.

**1876** As servant Susannah Courtney slept in her bedroom at The Shipping Hotel in Seabeach, Swansea, she woke to find her employer in her room, his hand under the bedclothes. Susannah leaped out of bed in a panic and Henry Aherns bolted from the room. 22 OCTOBER

The following morning, Susannah complained to Mrs Aherns about her husband's behaviour but her mistress refused to believe her. Susannah went to her father, who spoke to Mrs Aherns but the lady would not hear a word against her husband and accused Susannah of lying, ordering her out of the house. When Susannah confronted Mr Aherns about the incident, he claimed that she had either had a nightmare or that what she believed was his hand beneath the bedclothes was actually the family cat.

Undeterred, Susannah made a complaint to the police and Aherns was brought before magistrates at Swansea, charged with assault. The magistrates reasoned that he was most unlikely to attempt to attempt to take liberties with a domestic servant when his wife and children were asleep in an adjoining bedroom and dismissed the case.

**23 OCTOBER**   **1826** Twenty-six-year-old Sarah Jones of Bassaleg went into labour with an illegitimate child. Sarah believed that the child's father, John Flook, loved her and wanted to marry her, until she found out quite by chance that he had married another woman. From that moment on, Sarah determined to have her revenge on Flook by murdering his baby.

Sarah told none of her family of her pregnancy and, when her mother came upstairs, Sarah sent her to fetch clean linen. Then, as her baby was born, Sarah quickly slashed its throat with a penknife and hid it under her mattress. The baby remained there for four days until Flook came to visit her and Sarah presented him with the body, sewn into some sacking. Flook took it away but failed to hide it well enough.

The baby's body was found and an inquest returned a verdict of wilful murder against Sarah, who was tried at the Lent Assizes, as were her father, Thomas, her mother, Mary, and John Flook. The Grand Jury found 'no bill' against Thomas and the prosecution offered no evidence against Flook, and both were discharged. Mary Jones was acquitted but Sarah was convicted and sentenced to death. Sarah's main concern was that her parents were not blamed and, when her death sentence was passed, she stated that her only emotion was joy that her mother had been acquitted. She was executed on 11 April 1827 and her body released to her family for burial in Bassaleg churchyard.

**24 OCTOBER**   **1876** Police Constable Luddy saw a man creating a disturbance on the Customs House Bridge, Cardiff. Luddy recognised him as Irish labourer Michael Crowley, who, just days earlier, was released from Cardiff Prison after serving a two-month sentence for assaulting a police officer. True to form, Crowley fought like a man possessed and it eventually took seven constables to subdue him and convey him to the police station.

Crowley had a long list of previous convictions for drunkenness and violence and magistrates sentenced him to four months' imprisonment with hard labour, warning him that, if he appeared before them again, he would get six months.

**25 OCTOBER**   **1877** John Davies and John Welsh had a trivial argument at Rhymney. The dispute escalated and Davies hit Welsh on the head with a stone used for sharpening a chaff machine. The wound bled copiously and later, a doctor extracted a small piece of stone from beneath the skin on Welsh's scalp. Davies was found guilty of assault, serving fourteen days in prison with hard labour.

Meanwhile, Welsh apparently made a full recovery but then fell ill, dying on 25 January 1878. A post-mortem examination revealed that his skull was fractured in the fight, a small piece of bone pressing on his brain causing a fatal abscess.

Davies was charged with manslaughter and appeared at the Glamorganshire Lent Assizes, where the jury found him guilty. Although they initially recommended mercy for Davies, since Welsh struck the first blow, they withdrew the recommendation when they discovered that Davies had a previous conviction for robbery. He was sentenced to eight months' imprisonment with hard labour, followed by a similar period of police supervision.

**1921** David Thomas returned from work to his home near Pontypool, to find the **26 OCTOBER** doors locked. After shouting for his wife Margaret for some time, Thomas fetched a ladder and scrambled through an open bedroom window. He found Margaret dead in the kitchen, her head battered almost to a pulp.

Since Margaret was a very tidy woman, the presence of the breakfast dishes on the table led police to deduce that she was killed soon after her husband left for work at 6.20 a.m. House-to-house enquiries confirmed that there was a tramp in the area at the time and that the same man had called at the Thomas household some days earlier and been given bread and cheese by Margaret.

The police set out to trace the tramp William Sullivan, arresting him on 17 November, when he had in his possession a pair of trousers that Mr Thomas confirmed had been stolen from his house. The trousers were sufficient evidence against him for Sullivan to be charged with wilful murder.

MR. JUSTICE DARLING

At his trial before Mr Justice Darling at Monmouth on 7–8 February 1922, Sullivan stated that he had been with another man when the murder was committed. However, his supposed companion, Mr Stuart, was either unwilling or unable to confirm Sullivan's alibi and, although his defence counsel tried to suggest that David Thomas had killed his wife, the jury found Sullivan guilty.

*Mr Justice Darling.*
*(Author's collection)*

'I am not guilty and have always said so,' protested Sullivan as Darling pronounced the death sentence. Nevertheless, on 23 March, Sullivan became the last person to hang at Usk Prison, which closed just eight days later.

**1884** Helen Street in Cardiff was a notorious area, inhabited by a variety of **27 OCTOBER** misfits and social outcasts, where drunkenness, prostitution and debauchery were rife. One resident, Daniel Beddoes, was a shoemaker but often made his living by less honest means.

On 27 October, Daniel, his wife Anne and their two female lodgers, described as 'unfortunates', were sitting by the fire reading the newspaper aloud. Daniel and Anne were both drunk and, when Daniel, who had a severe speech impediment, complained that he was unable to read, Anne snatched his glasses off his nose, throwing them into the fire. Daniel retaliated by picking up a poker and throwing it at his wife, the tip penetrating a major blood vessel at the base of her throat.

Daniel tried to staunch the bleeding with a handkerchief but his wife died within minutes. Coroner Mr E.B. Reece told the inquest that there was no question that Daniel's actions caused Anne's death and told the jury that their verdict must be one of murder or manslaughter against him, depending on whether there was intent to kill.

Beddoes appeared at the Assizes charged with manslaughter. His lodgers swore that Beddoes threw the poker without aiming it and his defence counsel contended that, in a moment of passion, Beddoes picked up the poker and flourished it, only for it to accidentally slip from his grasp and hit Anne.

Since Beddoes had admitted to throwing the poker, the jury found him guilty, although with a strong recommendation for mercy and, after considering overnight, the judge sentenced him to six month's imprisonment.

**28 OCTOBER** **1870** Edward Daley and Margaret Rimlan (aka Joseph) appeared at the Cardiff Quarter Sessions charged with larceny. Both were acquitted and decided to celebrate their release from custody. They began drinking at The Bath Arms Hotel, moving to The Custom House Hotel, where they met George Harding, who worked with Daley as a boatman.

After drinking until midnight, the three headed for Harding's boat. On the way, Harding challenged Daley to a fight and the two scuffled drunkenly until they were out of breath before boarding the boat, when each stood on opposite sides. Suddenly, Harding rushed at Daley and tipped him over the side into the canal.

Margaret ran away in terror and, when Daley was later found drowned, she went to the police. Her story was corroborated by a woman who was visiting a nearby house and saw the quarrel through her bedroom window, but Margaret changed her statement several times, once saying that Daley's death had been a tragic accident.

When Harding was tried at the Cardiff Assizes for Daley's wilful murder, the defence cautioned the jury against relying too heavily on Margaret's evidence, given that she had changed her story and was a 'woman of abandoned character.'

The judge told the jury that he personally could see no reason why Margaret should perjure herself and reminded them that her evidence had been confirmed by an independent witness. He also pointed out that, if Daley's death were an accident, Harding made no attempt to rescue him.

The jury deliberated for an hour before finding Harding guilty of the lesser offence of manslaughter. When Harding said that he was very sorry, the judge remarked that he hoped he would be sorry for the rest of his life and sentenced him to twenty years' penal servitude.

**29 OCTOBER** **1856** Seventeen-year-old Frederick Waters worked as a night policeman for the Taff Vale Railway Company. On his way home to Stormstown from work, he attempted to hitch a ride on a luggage train.

He tried to scramble aboard the last but one truck but slipped and fell onto the rails. He was run over by the truck he was trying to board and the one following, his body almost bisected. The accident occurred near the Darran Dhu Colliery and, although assistance was quick to reach Waters, he died at the moment of impact. At a later inquest, the coroner's jury returned a verdict of 'accidental death'.

**30 OCTOBER** **1838** Joseph Jones from Carmarthen was taken ill on the eve of his marriage and since it was too late to cancel the ceremony, his bride received their invited guests alone. Sadly, Jones died on what should have been his wedding night.

*Carmarthen.*
*(Author's collection)*

He had been feeling unwell for some time and, eager to be fit for his nuptials, consulted a quack doctor, who mistakenly diagnosed his complaint as pleurisy and bled him extensively. Jones was actually suffering from smallpox but the quack drained so much of his blood that the characteristic rash associated with the disease didn't appear, thus preventing him from receiving a correct diagnosis and the treatment which may have saved his life.

**1884** Twenty-one-year-old John Phillips was tried at the Pembrokeshire Assizes **31 OCTOBER** for the manslaughter of fifteen-year-old Charley Eynon.

While Thomas Hancock was away, his servants played a series of practical jokes on one another. The young men decided that anyone not in their shared bedroom by nine o'clock at night would be shot at from the top of the stairs and, when Eynon broke the curfew, Phillips took aim and fired.

The gun was loaded with the scrapings from a tin of red paint and a little gunpowder, the idea being that there would be a loud bang and the target would be splattered with red paint, which he would believe was his own blood. Since the gun wasn't loaded with ammunition, the boys thought it harmless hence when Eynon yelped in pain, they were surprised to see a wound on his left thigh. A nurse was called to treat the injury, which was initially thought to be superficial but Eynon gradually grew feverish and weak. By the time a doctor was consulted, infection had set in and Eynon died from blood poisoning on 8 October.

At an inquest held by coroner Mr W.V. James, the jury returned a verdict of manslaughter against John Phillips. Phillips appeared before magistrates a few days later and was acquitted but still had to stand trial at the Assizes on the coroner's warrant. At his trial, the jury recognised that Phillips had never intended to hurt Eynon, finding him not guilty.

# NOVEMBER

*High Street, Cardiff, c. 1920. (Author's collection)*

**1906** An inquest was held at Cardiff on the death of seventeen-year-old William Henry Wiltshire.

The South African Rugby Union team was on a three-month long tour of England and Wales and to celebrate their arrival in Cardiff, a firework display was held in Sophia Gardens in their honour.

As Wiltshire watched the display, a rocket fell from the sky and set fire to his clothes. Although bystanders beat out the flames with their bare hands, Wiltshire was so badly burned that he died from his burns on the morning of 1 November. The inquest returned a verdict of 'accidental death.'

**1862** Servant Jane Lewis left Tyntila Farm in the Rhondda Valley to attend chapel half an hour after her fellow servant, Thomas Edmunds.

The farmer, Thomas Williams, who was also Jane's uncle, had been out with his brother all afternoon. He too attended the service and commented to his wife that Jane wasn't there. However, neither Thomas nor Maria Williams was unduly worried, since there was a tea party in the village and they suspected that Jane may have gone there.

A little later, Jane's boyfriend (also named Thomas Williams but known as Tom Screens) arrived at Tyntila looking for Jane – she was supposed to meet him at chapel and he was worried that she may have another sweetheart. Yet it wasn't until 11 p.m. that Mrs Williams persuaded her husband and Edmunds to go and search for Jane. She was found less than 200 yards from the house, her throat cut, a bloody razor and its case lying nearby.

Although her head was almost severed from her body by seven deep cuts, after a five-day inquest, the jury sensationally found that Jane, who was about ten weeks pregnant, committed suicide.

The police continued to treat Jane's death as murder. The razor belonged to Thomas Edmunds, who admitted to being intimate with Jane once but insisted that it was only a month before her death. Apart from a period of between five and fifteen minutes, Edmunds had an alibi for the whole afternoon and there was absolutely no blood on any of his clothes. In addition, he possessed a pistol and ammunition and, had he murdered Jane, would more probably have used his gun than his own razor. Yet someone had taken his razor from on top of a cupboard at the farm – if that person was Edmunds, why had he not replaced it?

Farmer Thomas Williams was with his brother all afternoon and Maria Williams was caring for the couple's six children. Tom Screens also had a reliable alibi for the entire period during which the murder was committed.

The police eventually charged Edmunds with Jane's murder but the case was dismissed by the Grand Jury due to a lack of evidence and the murder of Jane Lewis remains unsolved.

**1887** At the Swansea Assizes, Mr Justice Cave and his jury tried to untangle a complicated case that occurred on 11 September, when PC Vincent Jones found prostitute Janet 'Jenny' Rees semi-conscious on the canal bank at Neath, bleeding from a number of wounds. She was taken to hospital, where it was established that she had been beaten with a blunt object.

Jenny told the police that two Germans named Ferdinand Schimmel and Emil Burggraff followed her from The Railway Inn to the canal bank, where Schimmel attempted to rape her, knocking her down and hitting her with a walking stick. Jenny screamed and a passer-by came to her rescue. Mr Mellin grappled with the Germans and was twice thrown into the canal but eventually chased off her attackers, at which point she was found by PC Jones.

Schimmel was charged with 'beating and wounding Janet Rees' and Burggraff was called as a defence witness. Burggraff told the court that he paid Jenny 2s for her services but Jenny told him she would rather go with Mellin. Having paid good money, Burggraff insisted that she should oblige him first but Mellin followed them to the canal and kicked Burggraff when he lay down with Jenny. After a brief scuffle with Mellin, the Germans decided that Jenny was not worth the trouble and left her and Mellin together.

Mellin insisted that he was a respectable married man and that he had never met Jenny before he went to her rescue. However, in his summary for the jury, Mr Justice Cave pointed out several discrepancies between Mellin's statement and the prostitute's account, not least the fact that Mellin referred to Janet by her familiar name, Jenny.

The jury found Schimmel not guilty. He and Burggraff were then indicted for the attempted murder of Mellin by throwing him into the canal but the prosecution decided not to proceed and both men were acquitted and discharged.

4 NOVEMBER    **1862** Feeling unwell, Heinrich Kegebein consulted chemists Albert and Franz Reinecke of Bute Street, Cardiff, who recommended purgative tablets and a mixture for purifying the blood. Albert Reinecke made up the prescriptions and Kegebein took his first dose.

*Absinthe jar.*
*(© N. Sly)*

Shortly afterwards, he complained of stiffness in his limbs and vomited several times. Kegebein died that afternoon and, when a post-mortem examination revealed that he had been poisoned, his medicine was analysed and found to contain aconite.

Albert Reinecke admitted accidentally adding extract of aconite to the pills instead of absinthe. The Reinecke brothers could not recall ever ordering aconite and it did not appear on any of their suppliers' invoices – nevertheless, it was found in the jar clearly labelled 'extract absinthii'.

Coroner Mr R.L. Reece told the inquest jury that the poison was obviously used in error and they must decide whether such carelessness constituted a crime or whether it was '...one of those deplorable accidents which might sometimes happen in the case of a well-qualified man.' The jury returned a verdict of 'accidental death', asking the coroner to unofficially censure the Reinecke brothers and caution them to be more careful in future.

**1961** Pot-holers Graham Jones, John Gerke and Chris Macnamara found a sack containing a human skeleton in a disused mine shaft at Brandy Cove on the Gower Coast.

Home Office pathologists determined that the body was that of a young woman, dressed in 1910s-style clothes, who had been cut into three pieces. The police were aware of a missing person fitting that description and, by superimposing a photograph of former chorus girl Mamie Shotton (*née* Stuart), onto a picture of the skull, they finally discovered her whereabouts after more than forty years.

In March 1920, police were handed a portmanteau abandoned by a guest at the Grosvenor Hotel, Swansea. It contained two shredded dresses and a pair of shoes, along with a Bible, manicure set and jewellery. There was also a scrap of paper bearing the address of Mamie's parents, who positively identified the items as having belonged to their missing daughter. Meanwhile, at Mamie's last known address, a cottage named 'Ty-Llanwydd', overlooking Swansea Bay, a cleaner discovered a handbag in the garden containing a few pounds and Mamie's ration book.

The police traced Mamie's 'husband', Edward 'George' Shotton, who was living with his wife and child, less than two miles from Ty-Llanwydd. Shotton admitted to living with Mamie but insisted that they had never married, since he already had a wife. They parted after a quarrel in December 1919 – he returned to his wife and had no idea where Mamie went.

The police discovered that Mamie had not been faithful. Yet she was frightened of George, writing to her parents that he was 'not all there' and saying that she didn't think they would be together long. George was arrested for bigamy and tried at the Glamorganshire Assizes on 29 May 1920. He offered a bizarre explanation, saying that Mamie was married to someone who was impersonating him, but was found guilty and sentenced to eighteen months' imprisonment with hard labour. In spite of exhaustive enquiries, the police were unable to locate Mamie, either alive or dead, and the case was shelved.

*Brandy Cove and Caswell Bay, Gower. (Author's collection)*

At an inquest held on the skeletal remains, the jury decided that Mamie met her death during November or December 1919, at the hands of George Shotton, who died in Bristol in April 1958 and so escaped justice.

Ironically, the English translation of 'Ty-Llanwydd', the house where Mamie Stuart apparently met her death, is 'The Abode of Peace'.

6 NOVEMBER    **1869** When work at Garndiffaith quarry finished for the day, everyone assumed that quarryman John Cross had gone home. In fact, unbeknown to anyone, there had been a fall of earth and Cross was trapped beneath it.

Cross clawed his way out but, even when he gained his freedom after several hours of scrabbling, a broken rib and a severe injury to his scalp left him unable to seek help. In bitterly cold weather, he bled to death during the night, his body lying undiscovered until midday on 7 November.

At an inquest held by coroner Mr E.D. Batt, the jury returned a verdict that Cross was 'killed by a fall of earth'.

7 NOVEMBER    **1868** John Morgan lived alone on an isolated farm at Velindre. A creature of habit, he was last seen alive on 7 November, locking himself in his cottage, as he usually did after finishing work for the day.

On 10 November, his concerned neighbours broke in, finding the old man dead in a pool of blood on his kitchen floor, a gunshot wound in his head. Since his pockets were turned out and his purse stolen, it was assumed that he was killed in the course of a robbery, although his killer failed to find Morgan's life savings of £40 in gold.

Suspicion fell on Morgan's nephew, twenty-six-year-old Henry Evans, who lived nearby with his parents and, although the evidence against him was entirely circumstantial, he was tried at the Swansea Assizes on 19 March 1869.

The court heard that Evans was seen carrying a gun on the day of the murder. He had borrowed a charge of gunpowder and a percussion cap from a neighbour and, when a post-mortem examination was carried out on Morgan, the shot removed from his brain was made from window lead, similar to some given to Evans by a neighbour shortly before the murder.

Spots of blood were found on Evans's clothes and there were also bloodstains on his dog, which followed him everywhere. Samples of this blood were sent to Dr Taylor of Guy's Hospital but Taylor was unable to determine whether they were human or animal. Finally, the key to the back gate of Morgan's cottage was found hidden in a hole over the front door of Evans's home.

Even though the evidence against Evans seemed damning, the jury gave him the benefit of the doubt and found him 'not guilty'. Nobody else was ever tried in connection with Morgan's murder.

8 NOVEMBER    **1847** An inquest was held by coroner Mr Davies on the death of seventeen-year-old Maria Evans.

Managers at the Dowlais Iron Company supplied miners with gunpowder for blasting and, on 6 November, a group of miners collected their allowance from the powder house then waited for the arrival of the iron trams. When the trams arrived, the men threw their powder onto the wagons so carelessly that one cask rolled straight off, burst and exploded.

A number of people had their clothes set alight or were blown over by the force of the explosion. (Only the quick thinking of a woman, who threw a bucket of water over the gunpowder remaining on the wagons, prevented a far more serious catastrophe.)

Eleven people were seriously injured and at least two died. At Maria's inquest, the jury returned a verdict of 'accidental death', adding that they believed that the accident was entirely attributable to the 'loose way' in which the miners handled their powder.

**1883** Twenty-eight-year-old Thomas Allen was bosun aboard SS *Farnley Hall*. **9 NOVEMBER** In order to disembark at Penarth Harbour, a ladder was positioned from the ship to the jetty and, as Allen crossed it, he missed his footing and fell 32ft onto the Gridiron – a raised platform used for loading coal.

His fall was witnessed by German Karl Arnold, who rushed to render what assistance he could. Finding Allen barely alive, his head completely smashed and most of his brain some distance away, Arnold carefully replaced Allen's brain and reconstructed the shattered fragments of skull, binding them with his handkerchief.

Not surprisingly, Allen died within minutes and the jury at the subsequent inquest held by coroner Mr E.B. Reece reasoned that his injuries would have been fatal even without Arnold's efforts at first aid.

**1905** William Arthur Smith returned home to Ogmore Vale, after a night shift at **10 NOVEMBER** the Aber Colliery, and went to bed after eating breakfast. As he slept, his cottage was shattered by an explosion that claimed the lives of his wife, two young children and lodger.

It was customary for miners to purchase the gelignite used in their work, the cost of which was deducted from their wages. Smith was never given any instructions on the use of gelignite but knew that it had to be kept from freezing to remain workable. While most miners kept their gelignite warm by putting it inside their clothes, Smith placed his in the oven at home and promptly forgot all about it.

Although Smith sustained no physical injuries, his nerves were completely shattered and, when he appeared at the Cardiff Assizes in March 1906, charged with the manslaughter of his wife, he had been unable to return to work. Although the deaths had obviously arisen from a tragic oversight on Smith's part, the crux of the case against him was that he had contravened the 1875 Explosives Act, by storing gelignite in non-registered premises and had consequently acted with gross negligence and recklessness.

The court took the view that this was a case of forgetfulness. There was little evidence that Smith had ever known that gelignite should not be heated and, if he had not been warned against any particular danger, he could not have acted negligently. The jury found Smith not guilty and, since the prosecution declined to offer any evidence on the charges pertaining to the children or lodger, twenty-four-year-old Smith was discharged.

**1929** A howling gale was causing a garden gate in Swansea to slam repeatedly **11 NOVEMBER** and eventually sixteen-year-old Henrietta Violet Gorman went out to close it. As she put her hand on the gate, she was electrocuted.

A neighbour had built an extension to a shed behind his house, running a flexible cable from his home to supply the shed with the power. The fierce wind blew the bare wires and, when they made contact with the metal railings surrounding the houses, the fences and gates became live.

The inquest jury returned a verdict of 'death by misadventure'.

**12 NOVEMBER**   **1825** Master mason Morgan Saunders went to the pub in Trevethin to pay his labourers. While he was there, one of the labourers got involved in a scuffle outside the pub and, in response to his cries of 'Murder!', Saunders and the other labourers went to his assistance. They found him lying on the ground, with Abraham Owen straddling him, his hands wrapped tightly around the man's throat.

As soon as Saunders came out of the pub, Owen released his stranglehold on the labourer. 'Do not strike me,' Saunders warned him, adding, 'I am not a fighting man and, if you do I will make you repent it.' Owen took no notice. He knocked Saunders off his feet then strangled him with his bare hands.

The other labourers tried to pull Owen away but he shook them off. With Saunders dead, Owen leaped over a precipice, dropping several yards into a brook below and when later dragged from his bed by the police, he was still wearing his wet stockings.

Tried for wilful murder, Owen said the labourer's dog bit him, and, when he kicked out at the animal, its owner and the other masons attacked him. Owen claimed that he was being severely beaten and was acting in self-defence. The jury didn't believe him, finding him guilty and he was hanged on 30 April 1826.

**13 NOVEMBER**   **1887** Thomas Davies died in hospital, having been found unconscious on 12 November in a field near Llanelli. Davies was a messenger at the Dafen Tinplate and Galvanizing Co. Ltd and every Saturday, he collected the wages from the bank, carrying them in a leather bag.

Davies had eight wounds on his head, which had evidently been inflicted with a hanger – a tool similar to a machete, used for separating tin plates. The hanger lay near the body, along with Davies's purse, which was still locked but had been slashed open and relieved of £245 of the £500 that it should have contained.

Although Davies died without making a statement, the police had an eyewitness. An eleven-year-old boy collecting rabbit food saw two men attacking Davies, one striking him over the head with the hanger, the other cutting open his purse. The child's description fitted David Rees, who was in the area at the time of the attack on Davies. Other witnesses had seen Rees hanging around the tin works on the day before the murder, when he had plenty of opportunity to steal a hanger.

Rees was arrested and appeared at the Carmarthen Assizes in February 1888. The court was told that, shortly before the murder, Rees tried to borrow money from a number of people, including a woman named Mrs Hughes, who testified that Rees threatened to kill her if she didn't let him have some. According to Mrs Hughes, Rees also spoke about attacking Thomas Davies but, until she heard about the murder, she assumed that his comments were meant as a joke.

Although the defence counsel cast doubts on the testimony of the young eyewitness, the jury found twenty-five-year-old Rees guilty and he was hanged at Carmarthen on 13 March. His accomplice was never identified.

**1899**  At the Glamorganshire Assizes, the court heard an application from the
Director of Public Prosecutions to order the discharge of Minnie Jane Hayter,
who was charged with the wilful murder of her husband at Bridgend.

The charge against her arose from the evidence of Dr Spreat, who told
magistrates that Hayter had died from a broken neck and that a bump on
the side of his head may have been caused by a billhook found lying near his
body. Mrs Hayter insisted that her husband was suffering from a bad cold
before she found him dead in bed on 6 October. Hayter's body was exhumed
by order of the Home Office and a post-mortem examination was carried out
in the presence of three surgeons. All were in complete agreement that Hayter
died from acute pneumonia. There was no broken neck and death was due to
natural causes.

If there had been no murder, then there was obviously no murderer and
Mrs Hayter was immediately released. The judge suggested that Spreat should
compensate her for his terrible blunder or, at very least, make a public apology.

**1876**  Chemist's assistant George Williams appeared before magistrates at
Cardiff charged with the manslaughter of Archibald Hayward.

Archibald was a sickly baby, who suffered from fits. Having had other
similarly afflicted children Archibald's father went to Cardiff chemist Mr Yorath
to purchase some syrup of rhubarb, with a little added laudanum.

Assistant George Williams had no syrup of rhubarb in stock, so substituted
spirit of poppies, telling Hayward that all syrups were the same. He made up
the medicine, labelling it 'Syrup of Poppies – Poison' and fixing the dose at half
a teaspoonful. However, he cautioned Hayward to give Archibald less than the
recommended dose, since he was so young.

Archibald's parents dosed him for several weeks, but his health did not
improve. Mr Hayward went back to the chemists' shop and told Williams that,
when his other children were taking the medicine, the chemist gradually
increased the amount of laudanum in the mixture. At Hayward's insistence,
Williams increased the laudanum from ten to twenty drops. After five months'
treatment, Archibald died on 6 November, when a post-mortem examination
suggested that death was probably caused by opium poisoning.

The magistrates committed Williams for trial and he appeared at the Cardiff
Assizes in March 1877. Doctors treating Archibald since before he began taking
Williams's prescription had always doubted that he would survive and, with
the doctor who performed the post-mortem not prepared to swear to opium
poisoning as the definitive cause of death, the judge instructed the jury to acquit
Williams.

**1900**  James Flynn appeared at the Swansea Assizes charged with attempting to
murder his wife, Mary, on 1 August.

Mary endured several years of ill-treatment by her husband before finally
plucking up the courage to summon him for assault. She left the papers on
the mantelpiece and when Flynn returned for his dinner, only his ten-year-old
daughter was at home. Flynn asked Mary Ellen to read the documents out to
him. 'I'll kill her before the night is out,' he threatened ominously.

When Flynn finished work that evening, Mary was at home. Flynn tried to drag her upstairs but Mary escaped and ran to the nearest police station, where she asked for police protection against him. She was sent home.

When she arrived, James was in bed asleep and, not daring to disturb him, Mary lay down on the rug in the front room. Just after midnight, James came downstairs, threw paraffin over her and set light to it.

A passing policeman, PC Higginson, saw the fire and broke down the front door of the house. As he beat out the flames, Flynn stood watching, making no effort to assist.

At his trial, Flynn insisted that he had no intention of setting his wife on fire. He had been very drunk at the time and had no idea that there was paraffin in the bottle. As for striking a match, he had only wanted to see where his wife was so that he didn't trip over her in the dark.

He failed to convince the jury, who found him guilty.

**17 NOVEMBER**　**1882** Workers at the Pembrey Explosives Works in Burry Port were thawing out dynamite, which froze at a relatively high temperature. There were strict regulations permitting only two people to be in the thawing sheds at any one time. Yet, when an explosion demolished one of the sheds, Jane Evans (16), Jane Williams (24), David Erasmus (15), John Jones (14) and Sarah Morse (13) were blown to pieces, while Mary Hughes (20) and William Ray (14) were terribly maimed. Ray had both hands and one leg blown off and was pulled from the debris begging, 'Kill me, kill me.' He and Mary died that afternoon, bringing the final death toll to seven.

It proved impossible to determine the cause of the explosion. The Explosive Co. Ltd blamed the victims, suggesting that they had carelessly flouted safety rules but the company were subsequently successfully prosecuted for several offences, among them allowing more than two people to work in the shed at any one time and employing persons under sixteen years old without adequate supervision.

**18 NOVEMBER**　**1892** A fire broke out overnight at the Merchants' Exchange at Pier Head in Cardiff, which caused an estimated £60,000 worth of damage to the buildings and the stock within. Fortunately, since the buildings concerned were business premises, there were only caretakers and nightwatchmen on site at the time, although one woman was rescued by portable fire escape.

Although the fire itself caused no fatalities, it drew a crowd of thousands of interested spectators and one boy, William Cahill, was accidentally run over by the fire engine and later died from his injuries.

**19 NOVEMBER**　**1893** Fifteen-year-old Mary Jane Jones of Carmarthen told her aunt that she was going to chapel but instead spent the afternoon and evening with a friend before setting off to walk home. Some time later, Sergeant James Jones was patrolling his beat in Carmarthen, when he was approached by twenty-five-year-old George Thomas saying, 'Sergeant, I want to speak to you. I want to give myself up for the murder of a girl.'

Thomas explained that, after attending chapel, he waited for Mary Jane in a quiet country lane near her aunt's home and cut her throat with a razor. He indicated where the body might be found and seemed so calm that Jones and his colleagues firmly believed he was sane.

It was thought that Mary Jane died after rejecting Thomas as a suitor but when he was tried, his defence was one of insanity. The medical witnesses seemed unable to agree although prison warder Mr J.W. Forbes was adamant that Thomas had been completely rational throughout his incarceration in Carmarthen Prison, and that the only thing remarkable about him was his callousness. The jury found him guilty of wilful murder, adding that they believed that he was in a perfectly sound mental state at the time.

With Thomas sentenced to death, immediate steps were taken to secure a reprieve on the grounds of familial insanity. However the Home Secretary declined to intervene and Thomas was executed at Carmarthen on 13 February 1894.

**20 NOVEMBER**    **1900** Cornelius Driscoll appeared at the Glamorganshire Assizes charged with murdering his sister, Catherine Kelly.

Catherine was a widow, who lived with her father and brother in Russell Street, Cardiff. She relied on parish relief and handouts to support herself and her children but, more often than not, her money was spent on drink.

On 16 October, after collecting her weekly relief money, she returned home so intoxicated that she had to be put to bed by her fifteen-year-old daughter, Margaret. Having argued with her brother already that morning and tried to hit him with a hammer, Catherine got up and rekindled the quarrel, calling Cornelius a lunatic and threatening to have him put out of the house. Another sister, Julia Driscoll, saw Cornelius push Catherine and went to fetch a policeman but, being drunk herself, was told to go home.

Margaret Kelly went out after putting her mother to bed but returned to find Catherine on the floor, shouting, 'Don't kill me,' and Cornelius standing over her, holding a poker. As Margaret watched, Cornelius hit her mother once on the head and then kicked her.

Catherine later died at the Cardiff Infirmary, and doctors noted that she had a fractured skull, giving the cause of death as inflammation of the brain, due to dirt getting into the wound on her head.

Cornelius was charged with wilful murder and, although he didn't deny hitting Catherine with the poker, he insisted that she hit him first. Taken to prison, he was described as 'excitable, perfectly confused and incoherent' and, on 29 October, the prison surgeon placed him '...on the borderline between sanity and insanity, if not over it.'

At Driscoll's trial, a deposition made by Catherine before her death was read out, in which she denied hitting her brother. (She also denied being drunk.) Margaret told the court that her uncle only hit her mother 'a soft blow' with the poker and that he was wearing 'soft boots' when he kicked her. Driscoll's defence counsel maintained that Catherine's death was nothing more than a tragic accident and that Driscoll was provoked into hitting his sister, never imagining for one moment that the blow would kill her. Recognising that there was provocation and no intent, the jury found Cornelius guilty of the lesser offence of manslaughter and he was sentenced to seven years' penal servitude.

**21 NOVEMBER**  **1836** An eighteen-ton boiler at the Dowlais Iron Works exploded and was blown 10 yards from its moorings. One end landed 50 yards away in the garden of

Dowlais House, which was occupied by J.J. Guest MP and another large section fell through the roof of another house, in which there were seven people.

Fortunately, the occupants escaped without injury but not everyone in the vicinity was quite so lucky. Fireman John Howe and two boys, John Jones and David Thomas, were killed by the blast and several passers-by were injured by flying debris, one woman very seriously.

Investigations showed that the disaster was caused by the rupture of a plate on a boiler and an inquest on the deaths of the victims ruled the explosion an accident.

*Furnaces at Dowlais Works. (Author's collection)*

**22 NOVEMBER**  **1870** Mary Evans and Evan Rees lived together in Neath, although Mary continually accused Evan of being attracted to other women.

On 22 November, Mary asked Evan to take her out but Evan protested that he was too tired. Mary threw a tantrum and Evan hit her two or three times before locking her out of the house. Mary immediately launched a barrage of stones at the windows and, when Evan went to the door to stop her, a large stone hit his forehead and fractured his skull.

Although badly injured, Evan survived until 21 January 1871. At his inquest, doctors testified that he died from purulent gangrene of the lungs and were of the opinion that, although he would have died from the disease anyway, the head injury accelerated his demise.

The inquest jury returned a verdict of wilful murder against Mary Evans, although magistrates later found a verdict of manslaughter. Thus, when she appeared at the Glamorganshire Assizes in March 1871, she was indicted for both offences.

Surgeon Mr Stephens testified that when Rees died, his skull injury had practically healed and that his death undoubtedly resulted from lung disease. The jury immediately acquitted Mary and Mr Justice Mellor remarked that she had had a very narrow escape.

**23 NOVEMBER**  **1887** Gwenllian 'Gwenny' and Evan Davies went to visit neighbours at Glanamman. The evening of socialising seemed to mark the beginning of the end of a difficult time for Gwenny, who had been ill for several weeks with 'weak blood'. Although her illness was not life threatening, Gwenny was depressed and, on 13 November, she suffered a severe fit. Her health and melancholy mood gradually began to improve and, although she still complained of pains in her head and chest, Evan believed that she was recovering.

On 24 November, Gwenny saw Evan off to work before tackling the laundry. A neighbour saw her at around ten o'clock and, minutes later, Gwenny sent her two oldest children to her mother's house, with a message that she wanted to see her.

Gwenny's mother returned with the two children. The newly washed clothes were drying on hedgerows around the house but there were no signs of Gwenny or fourteen-month-old Evan junior. After much searching, Gwenny's seven-year-old daughter found her mother and brother hanging from a roof beam in the loft.

Her grandmother sent her to the nearest neighbours for assistance and their lodger Thomas Thomas hurried to see what he could do. Unable to loosen the dog chain around Gwenny's neck and thinking she might still be alive, Thomas lifted her body, supporting her weight for some time. His efforts proved fruitless and Gwenny and Evan were pronounced dead by Dr Rees.

Gwenny was a good wife and mother. She had obviously killed herself and her son on impulse, since she broke off her chores to do so and, at the subsequent inquest, the jury returned verdicts of wilful murder and suicide, while in a state of temporary insanity.

**1920** Twenty-six-year-old Griffith Thomas appeared at the Swansea Assizes charged with the murder of twenty-year-old Elizabeth May Davies.

24 NOVEMBER

While Elizabeth was visiting Thomas in a police cell in Pontardawe, where he was detained for being a deserter, they ate some food that she brought with her. Within minutes, both were rolling around the floor in agony.

Fortunately, there was a doctor on the premises and, although Elizabeth died, he was able to save Thomas. In an apparent suicide pact, the newlywed couple left a note that read, 'Now our lives are ruined we die together rather than be parted.' A post-mortem examination found that Elizabeth had ingested twenty-seven grains of 'perchloride of mercury' [*sic*], a normal fatal dose being three to five grains.

Having survived, Thomas was charged with Elizabeth's wilful murder. The jury found him not guilty, much to the disgust of the presiding judge, who told them that they had not done their duty and had encouraged people to commit suicide together. A new jury was assembled to hear an additional charge against Thomas of attempting to commit suicide and, when they returned a guilty verdict, he was sentenced to nine months' imprisonment.

**1828** After several days of fog followed by a gale, the Captain of *La Jeune Emma* became disorientated and, mistaking the Lundy lighthouse for the French coast, grounded his ship on Cefn Sidan Sands. The passengers and crew rushed up on deck, where thirteen were washed overboard to their deaths by the mountainous waves.

25 NOVEMBER

Four of the crew grabbed pieces of wreckage and floated ashore. Two more owed their lives to the heroism of local residents. Theophilus Thomas swam his horse out to the wreck and rescued one man, while Joshua Griffiths risked his own life to pluck a young boy from the rigging, carrying him on his back for almost two miles to his home, where he was brought back to life from almost certain death. Sadly, not all of the locals were quite as gallant, as some tried to plunder the wreck.

Only six of the nineteen crew and passengers were saved. Among those who died were Lieutenant-Colonel Coquelin and his twelve-year-old daughter, Adeline, a niece of Josephine, the divorced wife of Napoleon Bonaparte. Father and daughter were buried together at St Illtud's Church, Pembrey.

**26 NOVEMBER**    **1900** Thirty-year-old Emma Hawkins of Roath went upstairs to bed with her eighteen-month-old son Robert George. Almost immediately, her husband heard a thump and a shout of 'John, I'm burning.' He found Emma lying at the bottom of the stairs, still holding Robert. Their clothes were on fire, as was the stair curtain and a broken paraffin lamp lay nearby.

John snatched up Robert and put out his burning clothes. He then pulled Emma clear of the fire and beat out the flames, using his hands, coat and a mat, all the while shouting for help. Neighbours summoned a doctor and Emma and Robert were rushed to Cardiff Infirmary, Robert dying soon after admission and his mother outliving him by three hours.

Although 'semi-conscious and delirious', Emma told the police that she overbalanced and fell backwards while walking upstairs. However, both she and John were drunk at the time of the accident and, at the subsequent inquest, neighbours recalled hearing sounds of a violent argument shortly before the fire.

Coroner Mr E.B. Reece was obviously suspicious about the extent of John's involvement in the deaths. He told John that he hoped there had been nothing more than 'high words' between him and his wife, suggesting that, if he was as drunk as witnesses suggested, he should treat this tragedy as a terrible warning to change his habits. In spite of Reece's misgivings, the jury returned verdicts of 'accidental death through burns' on both victims.

**27 NOVEMBER**    **1905** William Beavan appeared at the Monmouth Assizes charged with the wilful murder of his wife.

William was a master tailor and a sergeant with the Shropshire Light Infantry. When he returned home to Newport after a prolonged tour of duty in South Africa, he found that his wife had another man and had born him two children. In spite of Beavan's pleas, she refused to give up her lover and, when she was found with her throat cut, her husband was charged with her wilful murder.

The jury at his trial recognised that Mrs Beavan's extra-marital relationship amounted to provocation and found Beavan guilty of the lesser offence of manslaughter. He was sentenced to life imprisonment.

**28 NOVEMBER**    **1904** Eric Lange, aka Eugene Lorenz, appeared at the Swansea Assizes charged with the wilful murder of John Emlyn Jones.

Jones and his wife ran The Bridge Inn at Ystrad and, in the early hours of 11 September, Mary Jones was disturbed by an intruder in their bedroom. As she called out to her husband, the man struck her twice on the head with a blunt object, wrapped in brown paper.

John Jones grappled with the intruder, who rained blows on his head and body. Mary opened the bedroom door and called out to the cellar man but by the time Jack Carpenter had pulled on his trousers, the intruder had fled, leaving Jones slumped on the landing, having been both stabbed and battered with the paper-wrapped rasp left in the Jones' bedroom.

The police found a ladder outside, which the intruder had used to reach an open window. The cash register was open and a pair of brown shoes was left by the stairs. The police put out an alert for men without shoes and Lange was apprehended at half-past five that morning.

Although he identified himself as Eric Lange, many people knew him as Eugene Lorenz, the name he used when working at The Bridge Inn for a brief period in 1901.

Tried for wilful murder, Lange invented an accomplice named Harry and, while Lange admitted grappling with Jones, he maintained that it was Harry who actually stabbed and beat him. The jury didn't believe that Harry existed and found thirty-year-old Lange guilty. He was hanged by William Billington at Cardiff on 21 December.

**1878** Daniel Guy committed suicide in Swansea Gaol, while awaiting trial for the attempted murder of his wife and her brother. **29 NOVEMBER**

When Daniel returned to his Swansea home on 27 October, after an evening of drinking, his wife asked for housekeeping money and, when Daniel said he had none, Mary Guy bemoaned the fact that he had spent it all on drink.

Daniel pulled out a revolver, which Mary knocked from his hand before storming out, insisting that she would not return while her husband was armed. Two hours later, she changed her mind.

As she undressed for bed, Daniel shot her in the back. At least three shots were fired and, hearing the reports, Mary's brother, who owned the house, rushed into the bedroom. Daniel fired at John Phillips, the bullet grazing his neck and Phillips ran to the police station, returning with PC John Lewis. By then, Daniel had disappeared and, after fetching a doctor, Lewis went to look for him, finding him hiding in a yard. 'Is she dead?' Daniel asked, remarking, 'Damn her, the bitch, she ought to be,' when Lewis answered no.

Rather than face trial, Guy unpicked his hammock, fastened together two of the straps and hung himself from a water pipe in his cell.

**1877** Farm servant Mary Ann Evans summoned Edwin Pugh as the father of her illegitimate baby, born on 17 October. **30 NOVEMBER**

Four servants slept in the same room at Penrheol Farm, Bedwellty – Mary Ann and another girl in one bed and Edwin and his brother William in another. On 11 January, the second female servant left, leaving Mary Ann alone with the Pugh brothers.

Mary Ann told the court that she and Edwin were frequently intimate after 11 January and that she gave birth to a child nine months later. Edwin swore that he had done no more than speak to Mary Ann in the course of their work.

When a new female servant testified that she had interrupted Mary Ann having sexual intercourse with William Pugh on a sofa at the end of January, the court dismissed Mary Ann's claim for maintenance for lack of evidence.

# DECEMBER

*Margam Castle, 1960s. (Author's collection)*

**1887** Sergeant Lewis Hughes was called to a house in Blue Street, Carmarthen, where he found milk vendor Henry Jones nursing his daughter on his knee.

With difficulty, Hughes persuaded Jones to hand over the child. Seven-year-old Annie Jane Jones was dead, her throat cut so deeply that her spine was exposed. Distraught at what he had done, Jones wept bitterly and repeated in Welsh, 'I have killed my little child,' although he added, 'I would have done the same with the other child, if I had seen her.'

Jones remained devastated by Annie's death and was still beside himself with grief when he stood trial for wilful murder at the Carmarthen Assizes in February 1888. Asked how he pleaded, Jones sobbed, 'I did it.' Mr Justice Stephen suggested that he pleaded not guilty but Jones insisted, 'I did not know what I was doing at the time but I did it, My Lord, I did it.'

Stephen took this as a 'not guilty' plea, allowing Jones to be tried and his mental state taken into account. There seemed no rational motive for Annie's murder. Jones was a devoted father, who had been drinking at the time of the murder but was not drunk. However, it was shown that he once badly injured his head, since when he had suffered occasional epileptic fits.

The jury found him guilty but insane and he was sent to Broadmoor Criminal Lunatic Asylum.

**1938** At the Glamorganshire Assizes, twenty-seven-year-old sailor Henry Thomas Owens pleaded guilty to criminal assault on a girl aged fifteen years and ten months. He pleaded not guilty to charges of removing her from her father's possession and guilty to abandoning his three children, in a manner likely to cause them suffering.

While his wife was terminally ill, Owens hired the teenager to act as a housekeeper. When Mrs Owens died, he and the girl ran off to Bristol together, abandoning Owens's three children, aged seven, three and twenty-three months, in the house where their mother lay in her coffin.

Owens was found not guilty of removing the girl from her father's possession but sentenced to twelve months' imprisonment for each of the other two charges against him, the sentences to run concurrently.

**1842** Alexander Moxley went to Chepstow market, leaving his sister Mary alone in their cottage at Bantwn, St Arvans. While he was away, somebody beat Mary to death with a large stake, stealing the Moxleys life savings.

When the murder was discovered, a large crowd assembled at the cottage, among them Edward Rees, who lived nearby with his mother and his wife of only a few days. Rees had changed his clothes since that morning and, in the days following the murder he spent money freely, purchasing several items of furniture, redeeming pawned items and paying off his debts at the local pubs.

His unusual behaviour attracted attention and Rees was questioned. He was found to have several sovereigns and silver coins in his possession and his explanation of how he came by them was later proved untruthful.

A trail of footprints made by a man's bare feet led from Mary's home towards Edward's mother's cottage and, when Edward's feet were inspected, the soles were coated with clay and bits of fern, although the tops had recently been washed. Furthermore, a handkerchief was found at the Moxleys' cottage, which was very similar to one owned by Rees.

Rees was charged with wilful murder, appearing at the Monmouthshire Assizes in April 1843. When the jury found him guilty, Rees seemed unmoved by his death sentence, saying only, 'I am innocent and the Lord alone knows it.' He was hanged at Monmouth on 24 April.

4 DECEMBER     **1873** In Newchurch, Carmarthen, John Owen was out drinking with friends, including eighteen-year-old Edward Evans and, as the group left the pub to go home, Owen playfully tipped Evans's hat over his eyes. Evans objected and the two men began fighting.

Evans was punched several times and retaliated by picking up a large piece of wood, which he swung at Owen, hitting him across the back. Eventually, Evans ran home, with Owen in pursuit, although he failed to catch him.

None of the drinkers gave the fight a second thought until the following morning, when they heard that Evans had died during the night. A post-mortem examination confirmed that death was due to a ruptured artery in the brain, caused by a blow or a fall and the inquest jury reached a verdict of manslaughter against twenty-year-old John Owen.

Tried at the Carmarthen Assizes, Owen was found guilty of manslaughter, although the jury recommended mercy on the grounds of his youth and the circumstances of the case. He was sentenced to just four months' imprisonment with hard labour.

5 DECEMBER     **1864** Mary Ann Griffiths from Merthyr Tydfil went on an excursion with friends to Blaenavon. She was not accustomed to train travel and when her friends disembarked at Pontypool, one of them spotted Alfred Brown on the train.

Miss Phillips knew Brown as the station master at Hengoed and thought he would be the ideal person to shepherd her nervous friend back to Merthyr. Brown was happy to oblige, suggesting Mary Ann shared his first class carriage.

At first, Mary Ann and Brown chatted pleasantly about their mutual friend Miss Phillips. Then Brown began playing footsie with Mary Ann and when she indignantly snatched her feet away, he tried to kiss her.

Mary Ann begged him to keep his seat, telling him that she felt unwell and that she was engaged to be married but Brown began fumbling under her skirts. Mary Ann threatened to shout 'Murder' but he continued to indecently assault her until she fainted.

When she came round, her clothes were disarranged. As the train pulled in at Tredegar Junction, Brown offered to fetch some brandy but Mary Ann refused. The groping continued until Hengoed station, when Brown disembarked, saying, 'Miss Griffiths, I hope you will pardon me.'

Mary Ann arrived at Merthyr in hysterics and was persuaded to make a complaint against Brown, who was charged with indecent assault.

At the Usk Quarter Sessions in January 1865, the prosecution contended that Mary Ann had encouraged Brown's attentions, calling railway officials to testify that she was smiling pleasantly at him at Tredegar. (The station master there knew that Brown was engaged and assumed that Mary Ann was his fiancée.)

Mary Ann made no attempt to disembark, nor had she tried to alert anyone else to her plight and several witnesses testified to Brown's excellent character. Nevertheless, the jury found him guilty and he was sentenced to nine months' imprisonment with hard labour.

**1885** An inquest jury sitting at Swansea on the death of five-year-old Martha **6 DECEMBER** Ann Nash returned a verdict of wilful murder against her father, Thomas.

Nash was a widower with two daughters, Martha and Sarah, who was almost seventeen years old. On 16 November, he remarried, abandoning both girls with his landlady, Eliza Goodwin, and moving into different lodgings with his new wife.

Eliza tried numerous times to get Nash to collect the girls or pay for their upkeep and, on 4 December, her patience exhausted, she took Martha to her father's place of work and threatened to put her in the Workhouse if Nash didn't take her.

Later that evening, a group of men waiting for a boat saw Nash leading Martha onto West Pier, Swansea. The child was inadequately dressed against the cold wind, arousing the men's suspicions, and two of them followed Nash, meeting him walking back alone. When he saw them coming, Nash vaulted over the pier railing, landing on the sand below.

The men apprehended him and asked Martha's whereabouts. 'She's up there,' Nash replied and, when no trace of the little girl was found, he indicated the pier's lower level, suggesting that she was there. Unable to find Martha, the men took Nash to a nearby policeman and, soon afterwards, she was found drowned on the beach.

Nash appeared before Lord Chief Justice Coleridge at the Glamorganshire Assizes in February 1886. He explained Martha's death as a tragic accident, saying that he sat her on the pier rail intending to give her a piggy-back and a sudden gust of wind blew her into the sea. However, when the prosecution pointed out that he had made no attempt to rescue his daughter after her 'accident' and had made no mention of the tragedy to the men who were searching for the child, the jury found him guilty. He was executed by James Berry at Cardiff on 1 March 1886.

**1923** Fourteen-year-old Elsie Payne was given sixpence by a neighbour to buy **7 DECEMBER** some pasties and headed for the shop in Clifton Street, Cardiff, owned by her aunt and uncle. She arrived at about 8.45 p.m. and went straight into a back room, where her aunt Florence Lovatt was tending the fire.

'Oh, Auntie Florrie,' she moaned and, when Mrs Lovatt looked up, there was blood pumping from a wound in Elsie's throat. Before collapsing, Elsie said that a man had asked her for directions to Clifton Street.

She died at Cardiff Royal Infirmary that evening and at the inquest into her death, doctors disagreed on how she came to be injured. Even though a witness had seen a man run away after talking to a girl in Clifton Street, doctors were inclined to believe that the wound resulted from a fall onto spiked railings or broken glass.

The evidence was further complicated by a letter received by Elsie's parents, in which the writer, who signed himself 'John Davey', confessed to stabbing Elsie with a corkscrew. The police dismissed the letter as the work of an insane crank.

Unable to decide between accident and murder, the inquest jury returned an open verdict. Two further letters were received, one sent to Elsie's parents, one to her aunt. The letter to Florence Lovatt was postmarked 'Brixton, London' and covered three pages of foolscap paper, criticising the doctors' theories and raising numerous questions about Elsie's death.

**8 DECEMBER**    **1890** The new Vivian Pit at Abertillery had been blasted to a depth of 200 yards. Nine charges were fired on 8 December, before workmen were sent in to clear the debris. Unbeknown to anyone, one of the charges had failed to detonate and George Barrister unwittingly struck it with his pick. Barrister took the full force of the resulting explosion on his chest and was blown to pieces and Thomas Rees was also fatally injured. Between them, Barrister and Rees left ten fatherless children.

A further seven men were injured in the blast, including George Willard, who was dreadfully mutilated and is believed to have died from his injuries.

**9 DECEMBER**    **1832** The battered body of twenty-nine-year-old Eleanor Williams was found in the well at Llwyngwenno Farm in Llangyfelach. Eleanor, who was pregnant, had a fractured skull, as well as other injuries.

At an inquest on her death held by coroner Charles Collins, the jury returned a verdict of wilful murder by some person or persons unknown and despite painstaking investigations, the murder was never solved.

After Eleanor's funeral, villagers erected a gravestone inscribed:

1832 – TO RECORD A MURDER
This stone was erected by general subscription over the body of ELEANOR WILLIAMS, Aged 29 years. A native of Carmarthenshire living in this Hamlet in the parish of Llangyfelach. With marks of violence upon her person she was found dead in a well by Llwyngwenno farmhouse, then in the occupation of Thomas Thomas on the morning of Sunday, December 9th 1832. Although the savage murderer may escape for a season the detection of man, yet doubtless God hath left his mark upon him forever.
VENGEANCE IS MINE SAYETH THE LORD.
I WILL REPAY.

*Memorial to Eleanor Williams, 1832. (Author's collection)*

**1870** Miners at the Brithdin Colliery at Llansamlet were preparing to reach coal vein by blasting the roof of one of the underground passages. They drilled a hole and filled it with gunpowder before shouting the customary warning to stand clear.

While most of the miners retreated to a place of safety, John Bond made a split-second decision to rush past the charge to his workplace. As he reached the place where the shot was about to fire, it exploded, bringing down a large section of the roof and burying him under tons of rubble. It took several hours to extricate him, by which time he was dead.

**1875** The Wenvoe Castle estate was plagued by poachers and, in the early hours of the morning, shots were heard coming from a wood. Wenvoe policeman David Butler and a colleague concealed themselves near the entrance, along with an estate gamekeeper.

They waited for whoever was shooting to leave and before long, two men walked out of the wood, carrying several dead pheasants. Unfortunately, the poachers spotted the constables and immediately ran back the way they had come. The policemen and gamekeeper set off in pursuit but Butler was fastest and soon caught one the poachers.

As Butler grappled with him, the poacher called out to his companion 'Dan, fire' and got to his feet, pulling Butler with him and turning him, so that Butler was between him and the gun. The shot entered the back of Butler's neck, forcing him to release his grip on his captive. At that point, the gamekeeper and constable arrived and, mistaking Butler for one of the poachers, hit him hard on the head.

Although the shooter disappeared into the night, his companion was arrested and identified as John Elliott, a well known poacher. Descriptions of his accomplice led the police to arrest David 'Dan' Davies.

A recently fired gun was found in Davies's home, along with some poaching nets and he was known to have been at Elliott's house on the night of 10 December and to have left with him at midnight. Nevertheless, when the two men appeared at the Cardiff Assizes, charged with 'feloniously shooting at David Butler with intent, wilfully and with malice aforethought to kill and murder him', their defence counsel maintained that there was insufficient evidence to identify Davies as the gunman.

The jury found both men guilty of the lesser offence of 'unlawful wounding with intent to resist lawful apprehension' and Elliott was sentenced to two years' imprisonment with hard labour, Davies to five.

**1884** As five miners were lowered in a bucket into Treharris Colliery near Pontypridd, the rope suddenly snapped, sending the bucket freefalling almost 100 yards to the pit bottom.

Evan James, Evan Hughes, Thomas Sheen and Frank Wright fell into a drainage sump and were drowned in 8ft of water. The fifth man, Thomas Dodd, managed to cling to a guide rope for seven hours before being rescued, exhausted but uninjured.

The tragedy was inexplicable, since the rope had a breaking strain of fifty-five tons and the combined weight of the men was less than thirty hundredweight.

**13 DECEMBER**

**1887** John and Margaret Francis and their eight children were asleep over their tailor's shop in Planet Street, Cardiff, when a fire broke out. It took hold very quickly and, with the front of the house blazing, the family retreated to the workshop at the rear. With all other escape routes blocked, the only way out was through a trap door, which opened into a washhouse below.

John lowered the children down one by one. Sixteen-year-old Mary Ann, fourteen-year-old Alfred John, thirteen-year-old Elizabeth, and six-year-old Adeline were in the washhouse when, as John bent to lower two-year-old William, he tumbled through the hole, knocking himself unconscious. He and the five children were dragged to safety by neighbours.

By then, the police had arrived and were fighting the fire but tragically they were told that everyone had escaped, thus no attempt was made to rescue Margaret, six-year-old Margaret Eugene, ten-week-old Thomas Arthur or John Evan, who died on his eleventh birthday.

It proved impossible to establish the cause of the fire. Coroner Mr E.B. Reece noticed a strong smell, like furniture polish or naphtha. He sent several samples to the borough analyst, who found no trace of chemicals and suggested that the odour was due to the effect of heat on cloth. It was revealed at the inquest that, on the night of 10/11 June, someone broke into the shop and piled up several bundles of cloth, as though intending to steal them. The intruder(s) then turned on the gas taps and set fire to the premises but the children woke and alerted their father to the fire, which was put out before it could take hold. The incident was reported to the police, who could find no evidence that any of the doors or windows had been tampered with and no footprints in the garden.

The inquest jury returned a verdict that Margaret and the three children died from suffocation and that the origin and cause of the fire could not be ascertained.

**14 DECEMBER**

**1937** Soon after the installation of a new turbine at the Ely Paper Mills, Cardiff, it was discovered that steam was leaking into it from a nearby pipe. A stopper plate was fashioned to plug the leak but, on 14 December, the electric lights at the mill suddenly went out and the power house rapidly filled with steam. William Samuel Hawkins managed to crawl out before collapsing, saying, 'My mates are inside. Save them.'

Rescuers pulled Richard Barry, Frank Comer and Robert Brodie out of the steam-filled room. Barry, who had seven children, was scalded to death but his friends were still alive, although both later died in hospital.

Investigations revealed that the stopper plate had blown out, causing a blast of steam into the power house. Although the fitter who made the plate described it as 'a rush job', the inquest jury returned verdicts of 'accidental death' on all three men. While they believed that there was 'a want of care' in the selection of the material for the stopper plate and an error of judgement regarding its strength, in the jury's opinion it did not amount to criminal negligence.

**15 DECEMBER**

**1889** As Edward (or Henry) Rees and his wife lay dozing in bed in Gower Terrace, Penclawdd, their two children screamed from the kitchen.

Both parents raced downstairs, finding five-year-old Margaret Ann and three-year-old James Henry enveloped in flames. As she tore off the children's burning nightclothes, Mrs Rees's own nightdress caught fire and she was forced to roll on the floor to extinguish the flames.

Leaving his wife to deal with Margaret, Edward rushed Henry outside, placing him in a water butt. However, the little boy was so badly burned that both he and his sister died from their injuries.

Coroner Mr T.N.T. Strick held an inquest on 17 December, at which time Mrs Rees was critically ill in hospital. The inquest supposed that the two children had decided to light the fire as a surprise for their parents and poured paraffin onto the smouldering sticks and paper, resulting in a belch of flame that set light to their nightclothes.

The inquest jury returned verdicts of 'accidental death' on both children.

**1889** As prison surgeon Dr D.F. Boulton did his rounds at Usk Prison, he was attacked by Benjamin Williams, who was serving time for burglary. Williams waited quietly in his cell until the doctor entered, before striking him on the head with the roller used to roll up the inmates' hammocks. Fortunately for Boulton, although he was knocked unconscious, his hat protected him from more serious injury.

Williams, who believed that the doctor had not treated him properly for a disease, was tried at the prison by visiting justices, who ordered him to receive thirty-six strokes with the cat-o'-nine tails.

16 DECEMBER

**1870** Having been woken by the sound of groaning, Blaina resident George Sainsbury found twenty-nine-year-old John Devine almost comatose on the bank of the river Ystruth.

Sainsbury fetched a policeman and Devine was carried to the police station and placed in front of the fire. A doctor was called but Devine died within fifteen minutes. A post-mortem examination showed that his stomach and intestines were shrunken and completely empty. Although he had been drinking shortly before being found, Devine had starved to death, his demise accelerated by exposure to cold.

At an inquest held by coroner Mr Brewer, the jury censured Sainsbury for '...acting in a very dilatory manner in running about for policemen and leaving the man where he did instead of taking him into his own home, which was only twenty yards distant.'

17 DECEMBER

**1911** Torrential rain brought destructive flooding to much of Glamorganshire, where between four and five inches of rain fell in less than a week.

At Aberdare, two boys were killed as they watched the river in spate. John Morgan Jones, aged thirteen, and fifteen-year-old Emmanuel Shott drowned when the raging water swept a bridge from beneath their feet.

18 DECEMBER

Entire houses were washed away and many more homes and business were flooded. Collieries and factories were inundated and the transport network almost paralysed as railway lines and roads were blocked by flood water or landslides, or disrupted by fallen bridges.

19 DECEMBER     **1890** Seaman David Harsent appeared at the Swansea Assizes, charged with the wilful murder of his landlady.

Whenever he was not at sea, Harsent lodged with Mr and Mrs Roderick in Christina Street, Cardiff but, in 1890, he inherited some money and stayed ashore for several months.

Harsent went out drinking on 20 October, returning to his lodgings at about 11.30 p.m. He immediately started arguing with Ann Roderick, who he believed was spreading rumours that he had committed acts of bestiality with the family's dog and cat. Antonio Roderick took exception to Harsent's 'filthy language' and told him to find alternative lodgings, at which Harsent pulled out a revolver and shot both Ann and Antonio.

Ann staggered outside, collapsing on the pavement, while Antonio made his way to a neighbour's house. Meanwhile, having heard the shots, Ann's daughter roused another lodger, Henry Jones, and the couple came downstairs to see what was happening. They were confronted by Harsent waving a revolver and threatening to 'serve them the same'.

Police Constable Benjamin Davies was patrolling nearby when he heard of the shooting. He went to Christina Street but Harsent ran off. Davies eventually cornered him in an alley and grappled for possession of the revolver, which Harsent had reloaded after shooting the Rodericks.

Ann died within minutes, leaving six children motherless, the youngest only two months old. Although Antonio's life was despaired of, he recovered to see Harsent tried for his wife's murder.

Harsent was almost certainly insane at the time of the shootings, suffering from delusions and wrongly believing that he was being persecuted and accused of a loathsome crime by Ann Roderick. Known to become excitable and aggressive after drinking, Harsent had a family history of insanity and some of his close relatives were said to possess 'homicidal tendencies.'

The jury found Harsent guilty but insane and he was sent to Broadmoor Criminal Lunatic Asylum, where he is believed to have died in 1909.

20 DECEMBER     **1870** Nine-year-old Henry Williams and his twelve-year-old brother Benjamin were hailed by a farm labourer as they walked to school at Llandilo Talybont. When the boys went to see what the youth wanted, he pointed a gun at Henry, telling him, 'Mind, my boy, I'll shoot you now.'

The gun misfired but Henry collapsed, having been shot in the hip. Benjamin rushed to fetch his father, who carried Henry home and sent for a doctor. The doctor found a deep wound in Henry's hip and a lesser wound in his right hand and treated the boy for five weeks before he recovered.

Sixteen-year-old William Mainwaring was arrested and tried at the Glamorganshire Assizes charged with maliciously wounding Henry, with intent to do him grievous bodily harm. The prosecution were unable to prove intent and Mainwaring was therefore found guilty only of unlawful wounding and sentenced to four weeks' imprisonment, in solitary confinement.

**1863** Sarah Lancastell appeared before Mr Justice Crompton at the Cardiff Assizes, charged with the wilful murder of her infant daughter at Llandaff.

After a long and difficult confinement, in a state described by doctors as 'post-puerperal mania', Sarah killed her baby by thrusting her hand down the infant's throat. The baby died almost immediately and, when questioned, Sarah explained that there was a fire burning inside the child, which had to be to put out.

At her trial, doctors revealed that Sarah's temporary insanity had endured and she was not fit to plead. Crompton ordered her to be detained in an asylum.

**21 DECEMBER**

**1892** Thirty-year-old Thomas Edwards was executed at Usk for the murder of prostitute Mary Connolly. Mary was found at Abergavenny on 16 September, her throat cut and a shilling clutched in one hand. She had been released from Usk Gaol only that morning and was seen with a man shortly before her body was found.

Edwards handed himself in to the police and, tried at the Monmouth Assizes, alleged that Mary had stolen £2 from him some months earlier and had also given him venereal disease. After one of his army colleagues was murdered by a prostitute six years ago, Edwards harboured a pathological hatred of such women and vowed to avenge the man's death.

Although there was a family history of insanity, the medical witnesses believed that Edwards was of sound mind.

**22 DECEMBER**

**1893** George Thomas Bellyse Cooper was orphaned at the age of thirteen months, when his parents drowned, and, had George's nanny not had an aversion to water, he might well have suffered the same fate.

On his twenty-first birthday, George inherited a considerable fortune, part of which he used to buy a yacht. George also loved shooting, acquiring a large collection of guns. A popular young man, he settled in Tenby and was due to marry in January 1894.

On 23 December, George placed the muzzle of one of his pistols in his mouth and pulled the trigger. His horrified fiancée, Georgina, screamed for his landlady to send for a doctor but, although one arrived within minutes, he was too late to save George.

There was nothing to suggest that Cooper was suicidal. He was devoted to Georgina, had no money worries and was eagerly looking forward to Christmas and to his forthcoming wedding. At the inquest, it was supposed that he intended only to tease his fiancée, who had a pathological fear of guns. Although George was a skilled shot, he was often careless when handling firearms and, returning a verdict of 'accidental death', the inquest jury concluded that he had simply forgotten that his revolver was loaded.

**23 DECEMBER**

**1884** A devastating fire broke out at the premises of pawnbroker Mr Goldstone at Swansea, trapping the occupants in the burning building. Mr and Mrs

**24 DECEMBER**

*Aerial view of Tenby.
(Author's collection)*

Goldstone and their servant were rescued using a portable fire escape, which was permanently located about 30 yards away. Even though Mr Goldstone's assistant, Philip Freeman, knew of the existence of the fire escape, he chose to jump from an upper-storey window rather than wait for it to be brought the short distance to the shop. He fell more than 40ft and died almost instantly.

**25 DECEMBER** **1891** Police Constable Rees Davies found Moses Lewis dead in the River Taff at Pontypridd. A post-mortem examination revealed multiple bruises and scratches and a Y-shaped wound on his right temple, beneath which the skull was fractured. There was no water in his lungs, indicating that Lewis had not drowned but was either thrown into the river dead or had accidentally fallen in and died from exhaustion or his head injury.

Lewis was last seen alive at around midnight on Christmas Eve by his cousin, Thomas Lewis and a friend, William Merchant. His head was bleeding and he was so drunk that he couldn't walk. His cousin tried to carry him home on his back but Moses was so intoxicated that he couldn't clasp his cousin's neck and, according to Thomas, 'it seemed as if there wasn't a bone in his body.'

Thomas propped Moses against a wall, taking his money for safekeeping, then went to try and get a cab. In the early hours of Christmas morning, there were none to be had and Moses eventually told his cousin to go home, saying that he would follow shortly.

Although nobody saw anything suspicious, a witness told the inquest that a group of men were arguing near where Moses was found and she distinctly heard someone say, 'Now, Moses, you bastard, speak the truth.' Thomas Lewis and William Merchant claimed that Moses was having 'cross words' in Welsh with a man named Henry Williams, who admitted to speaking to Moses but denied any argument between them.

*Municipal Offices, Pontypridd, 1919. (Author's collection)*

In the absence of any concrete evidence, the jury returned an open verdict, that the deceased was found dead in the River Taff but that there was nothing to show how he got there.

**1923** After locking the Cwmcarn Working Men's Club, steward Lewis Richards **26 DECEMBER**
went to his home adjoining the club, where he was holding a private birthday party, but, in the midst of the celebrations, the club caught fire. Richards and his guests ran next door to see if they could put the fire out, getting into the bar before being beaten back by heat and smoke.

The wooden building burned to the ground and, when the ruins were searched, two charred bodies were found in the debris. Identifiable only by their boots and by fragments of their clothing, James Nicholson and Archibald Davies perished in the conflagration.

A rumour circulated that Nicholson and Davies had concealed themselves in the club after closing time, starting the fire in a drunken state. However, at the inquest on their deaths, numerous people testified to seeing them at the party and it was surmised that they went into the club to try and save what they could and were overcome by smoke. Calling the rumourmongers 'evilly-disposed people', the coroner stated that it gave him great pleasure to exonerate both men, saying that no imputation or aspersion of any kind could be cast against them. The inquest jury returned verdicts of 'accidental death'.

**1919** A rowing boat left Pembroke Dock at 11 p.m., ferrying seven men to the **27 DECEMBER**
ships *Wisteria* and *Francol*. Although all of them were sober, an argument broke out between two of the sailors, one of whom climbed to his feet and made a rush at the other.

The boat capsized and, although it was only about 100 yards from shore at Milford Haven, only one of the sailors could swim. Mr Trudgeon seized one of his fellow passengers and tried to keep him afloat but the sailor struggled so much that Trudgeon was forced to let him go to save himself.

Patrick Ronayne clung to the upturned boat and his cries for help were heard by two brothers, who swam to his rescue. Sadly, he died within an hour of being dragged from the water, becoming the sixth victim of the tragedy.

**28 DECEMBER** 1916 Nineteen-year-old Winifred Ellen Fortt died from blood poisoning, having been repeatedly stabbed by her ex-boyfriend on Christmas Day.

Winifred's father ran a lodging house for Greek sailors in Cardiff and she began a relationship with lodger Alex Bakerlis. Twenty-four-year-old Bakerlis was insanely jealous, becoming enraged every time his girlfriend spoke to any of the other residents. So irrational was his behaviour that Winifred's father gave him notice to quit and Bakerlis moved to alternative lodgings.

Winifred broke off the relationship and asked a friend to return a ring and some letters to Bakerlis. However, he refused to accept them, saying that he would only take them if Winifred gave them to him personally.

On Christmas night, Bakerlis approached Winifred and her friend as they stood in Bute Road. He asked Winifred for the ring and letters and, taking the ring from her finger, Winifred handed it back to him, saying that she would slip inside and collect the letters. Before she could do so, Bakerlis knocked her over and stabbed her frenziedly.

Police Constable Arthur Moss saw Bakerlis running towards him, still holding a bloody knife. Moss apprehended Bakerlis, who readily admitted to stabbing Winifred moments earlier.

When Winifred died, Bakerlis was charged with wilful murder, appearing at the Assizes in Cardiff on 6 March 1917. He was found guilty and executed at Cardiff on 10 April by John Ellis.

**29 DECEMBER** 1891 Coroner Mr E.B. Reece held an inquest on the deaths of Elizabeth Smith and her son William Charles Smith of Union Street, Cardiff, who died on 27 December.

Elizabeth's husband, a night worker, returned home at 6.30 a.m. and, opening the front door, found the house full of smoke. He roused his neighbour, Thomas Griffiths, and sent him for help, before breaking into the back of the house.

By that time, much of the smoke had cleared and when Griffiths arrived with PC Green, they saw that a sofa and chairs in the kitchen and part of the staircase were on fire. Twenty-eight-year-old Elizabeth lay on the kitchen floor, her body burned so badly that parts of it crumbled to ash when touched.

Police Constable Green extinguished the fire with a couple of buckets of water, enabling the men to get upstairs where three-year-old William lay in bed. He had been suffocated by the smoke and although Green made desperate efforts to revive him, he was beyond help.

Every morning, Elizabeth lit the fire and put the kettle on, so that her husband had a hot drink when he arrived home from work. The remains of a paraffin lamp were found on the stairs and the coroner theorised that Mrs Smith had tripped or spilled burning oil as she went downstairs, setting light to her clothing. (Although her body was badly burned, she died from suffocation.)

The inquest jury returned verdicts of 'accidental death' on mother and son.

**1872** Police Constables Perry and Phillips accompanied a lunatic to the Workhouse. Once he was safely there, Phillips returned to Cardiff in the cab, leaving Perry to handle the lunatic's admission.

Soon afterwards, Perry set off to walk back to Cardiff. He was seen in the company of butcher John Jones (aka Benjamin Swann), the two men apparently enjoying a friendly conversation.

As they neared the Westgate Hotel, Perry staggered a few steps before collapsing in the hotel doorway. Immediately afterwards, Jones rushed into the hotel brandishing a large knife.

'I have done for him and now I'll do for myself,' he proclaimed, deliberately thrusting the knife twice into his own chest. He then sat down, placing the knife on the table.

The police arrived to find Perry dead from a single stab wound in his heart and his assailant sitting quietly in the hotel, waiting to die. However, Jones was still very much alive and seemed perfectly sober and mentally sound. Initially, he was expected to recover from his self-inflicted injuries but infection set in and he died on 8 January 1873.

Inquests on Perry and Jones recorded verdicts of wilful murder and suicide, while of sound mind. It was suggested that Jones held a grudge against Perry, who had supposedly arrested him for creating a public nuisance and for assault. However, Mrs Perry denied the existence of any quarrel, pointing out that the Perrys purchased all their meat from Jones.

Perry's wife had an uncanny premonition of her husband's murder. Just two nights before his death, she dreamed that a large number of people followed him to the Westgate Hotel, where one of them plunged a knife into his chest.

Note: The date of Perry's murder is given as 31 December in some sources.

31 DECEMBER **1889** Thirty-year-old William Hussey, the head bailiff at Old Park Farm in Margam, was visited by William Henry Bissett and Thomas David. To celebrate the end of the old year, Hussey sent thirteen-year-old Philip Davies to the cellar for some beer and, when he arrived back with the jar, Hussey poured some into a jug, which he offered first to David.

The youth took a swig and pulled a face, saying that the beer tasted as if there were coal tar in it. Thinking he was joking, Hussey took a mouthful and immediately realised that the jar contained not beer, but carbolic acid used for dipping sheep.

David rushed into the yard to vomit, returning home after drinking a glass of milk. Thinking that he had not consumed enough acid to harm him, Hussey delayed seeking medical attention and, by the time the doctor was summoned, Hussey's condition was hopeless. Both he and fifteen-year-old David died within hours from carbolic acid poisoning.

Coroner Mr Howel Cuthbertson placed no blame for the tragedy on Philip Davies, who had picked up the jar without realising that it contained anything other than beer.

# BIBLIOGRAPHY

*Bristol Mercury*

*The Cambrian*

*The Guardian*

*Illustrated Police News*

*The Manchester Guardian*

*The Morning Chronicle*

*The Morning Post*

*The Star of Freedom*

*The Times*

*Western Mail*

# INDEX